Animal bones in Australian archaeology

Tom Austen Brown Studies in Australasian Archaeology

Peter Hiscock, Series Editor

Coming in 2016
Blood from the bones: a zooarchaeological and taphonomic study of the archaeology of the Queensland highlands
Brit Asmussen

Animal bones in Australian archaeology

A field guide to common native and introduced species

Melanie Fillios and Natalie Blake

SYDNEY UNIVERSITY PRESS

Sydney University Press
Fisher Library F03
University of Sydney NSW 2006
AUSTRALIA
Email: sup.info@sydney.edu.au
sydney.edu.au/sup

National Library of Australia Cataloguing-in-Publication Data

Title:	Animal bones in Australian archaeology: a field guide to common native and introduced species / Melanie Fillios and Natalie Blake.
ISBN:	9781743324332 (paperback)
	9781743324592 (wiro bound)
	9781743324349 (ebook: epub)
	9781743324356 (ebook: mobipocket)
Series:	Tom Austen Brown studies in Australasian archaeology.
Notes:	Includes bibliographical references and index.
Subjects:	Animal remains (Archaeology)--Australia--Identification.
	Animal remains (Archaeology)--Australia--Social aspects.
	Archaeology--Methodology.
	Bones--Identification.
Dewey Number:	930.10285

Cover image: Sheep skull, Flinders Ranges © iStock.com/CreativaImages
Cover design by Miguel Yamin

Contents

List of figures

2: Scapula

3: Humerus

4: Radius

5: Ulna

6: Pelvis

7: Femur

8: Tibia

9: Extremities

Foreword

Apart from being a faunal manual, *Animal bones in Australian archaeology* focuses on important issues in zooarchaeology. The first involves the examination of the foraging economies of people living in Australia. Both Aboriginal Australians and European settlers exploited native fauna for food, though in different ways. And both before and after the arrival of Europeans, animals were brought to different parts of the continent by humans; certainly at least the dingo in pre-historic times and a myriad of mammals, birds, and reptiles in historic times. Human predation and the introduction of exotic animals had demonstrable impacts on Australian ecosystems, and there were probably more impacts than have been demonstrated.

But the economic actions of early peoples not only transform environments, they also reveal the resources available to and selected by the people in those environments. Archaeologists are therefore able to study assemblages of animal bones to reconstruct the kinds of hunting or domestication that took place in the past. For decades scientists of many flavours, including archaeologists, have debated the history of hunting in Australia: pondering what contribution human hunting made to the extinction of the last giant marsupials, and hypothesising trends towards focused, almost single-species hunting systems during some periods, as well as trends towards a broad spectrum of hunting in other times and places. At least initially, such investigations demand a knowledge of the diversity of animals represented by the bones found in archaeological assemblages. This knowledge has traditionally been developed and utilised by archaeologists who had the skills to identify the species from which each bone had come and could thus compile a list of all animals represented by any collection of bones.

However, reconstructing ancient economic activities ultimately requires much more information than a list of species. Many powerful reconstructions of hunting activities have been based on the particular combinations of animal name (the taxon) and the body part (the element) found at a site, allowing archaeologists to study phenomena such as which animal species were carried back whole, and which were butchered immediately and portions (elements) carried away selectively. Additional analyses are needed to characterise more complex qualities of hunting strategies, such as the hunter's selection of prey age and sex or the season of their capture – but even those measurements are often specific to taxa and so must be built upon accurate identification of the animal species.

The capacity to identify animal remains not only offers insights into earlier economies but also reveals the extent to which an archaeological deposit preserves a reliable record of past events. Like all forensic researchers, archaeologists are aware of the effects of contaminants. For example, the identification of the bones of a species introduced in the historical period alerts archaeologists to one of two situations. Either the layer being excavated dates to recent centuries or the bones have intruded into prehistoric levels and reveal disturbance. Certainly the ability to recognise the bones of burrowing introduced animals, such as rabbits, enables archaeologists to identify the formational history of their site and diagnose the appropriate chronological scale for their economic interpretations.

Another issue raised in this book is the necessity for accuracy in archaeological data collection. In faunal analysis the correctness of identification of taxon and element is critical for the sorts of interpretations already mentioned. Of course there are research specialists who are highly trained in recognising bones and who can accurately identify animals from even small, damaged fragments of their skeletons. But such specialists are few and they cannot be with every team in the field or in every laboratory as bones are examined. *Animal bones in Australian archaeology* will guide non-specialists, including archaeology graduates, other professionals, and even the broader public, in interpreting unexpected bones. In the field, archaeologists, police and even farm and construction workers may have to make important interpretations about bones they encounter: whether it is human or non-human, native or introduced as part of the faunal suite from the historical period, and so on. Having systematic keys to guide the classificatory inference will enhance their ability to unlock information about past events. Specialists may still be employed to assess the interpretations, but by using *Animal bones in Australian archaeology* field researchers will have a clearer sense of their findings.

Beyond the practical uses of this manual, there is a larger question. How do archaeologists transmit information to the next generation? Specifically, how are future faunal specialists and field archaeologists trained? The answer is that students must learn, apprentice-like, from experts in the discipline: experienced practitioners in universities and in private enterprise. This answer, while true, omits any description of how the teaching can be effective. Traditionally, apprentice archaeologists sit for prolonged periods in laboratories filled with specimens, and academic teachers of archaeology understand that there is no substitute for handling the material objects. In many sub-specialities of archaeology that laboratory training is scaffolded and enhanced by texts that explain how practitioners make their decisions and illustrate what features are most significant for classifying and understanding the objects. Archaeology students learning how to identify different categories of ceramics or glass or stone artefacts have long had a variety of such texts to assist them.

This has not been the case for students learning how to identify Australian animals. While there have been a few published guides to identifying animals from specific sites or regions there has been no broadly applicable manual of the kind represented in this book, and while some academics have prepared handouts for their students they have not been broadly available and easily followed. This book will be used to train students in laboratories across the country, and those students will find it has continuing value when they graduate and practise archaeology. *Animal bones in Australian archaeology* will guide researchers, consultants, and a generation of university students in their quest to accurately identify the animals whose bones they study.

Peter Hiscock
November 2015

Acknowledgements

We would like to thank the following people and institutions for their generosity in providing access to skeletal material: Denise Donlon, Jennifer Menzies and the teaching collection at the Shellshear Museum, the University of Sydney; Marcus Robinson, Department of Anatomy and Histology, the University of Sydney; the Department of Archaeology, teaching collection, and the Department of Zoology, the University of Sydney; Sandy Ingleby, the Australian Museum; Mathew Lowe, the University Museum of Zoology, University of Cambridge; Kimberlee Newman and Mark Moore, University of New England; Jennifer Wells, and the Australian Research Council (DP0985375). Thank you also to Jillian Garvey, Jennifer Menzies and one anonymous reviewer for valuable comments on the manuscript. Finally, thank you to Professor Peter Hiscock for making this book a reality.

Glossary

This manual is an introductory guide and does not assume any prior knowledge of the mammalian skeleton. However, osteological identification often necessitates an unavoidable amount of specialist vocabulary, so correct anatomical terminology has been maintained throughout to avoid ambiguity. The following table provides a list of common terms used in this volume and in other faunal reference books. Labelled diagrams of a quadruped (sheep) and biped (kangaroo) are also included to illustrate the articulation of major bones in different species (Figures 0.1 and 0.2).

Anterior	Toward the front, analogous to ventral.
Appendicular	The part of the skeleton that contains the limbs.
Articulation	The place where two bones meet (often a joint).
Axial	The part of the skeleton that contains the trunk (and often head).
Biped	An animal that habitually walks on two legs.
Buccal	Facing the cheek.
Caudal	Toward the tail.
Cavity	An open area (analogous to a fossa).
Condyle	A rounded process at the point of articulation.
Cortical	The type of bone found in shafts of long bones and flat bones, also called lamellar bone.
Cranial	Toward the head.
Crest	A projecting ridge.

Deciduous teeth	Milk (baby) teeth.
Diaphysis	The shaft of a long bone (mid-section).
Diastema	A space between two teeth.
Distal	Away from the trunk of the body (along a limb).
Dorsal	Toward the back or of the back; analogous to posterior in humans.
Element	The type of bone (e.g. femur, scapula).
Epiphysis	The end of a long bone, attached to the diaphysis, which is unfused in juveniles.
Foramen	A hole or opening.
Fossa	A pit or depression (analogous to a cavity).
Inferior	Lower.
Lateral	To the side, away from the centre of an individual.
Lingual	Facing the tongue.
Longitudinal	Lengthwise.
Medial	Toward the middle or centre of an individual.
Occlusal	The biting or chewing surface of the teeth.
Posterior	Behind (analogous to dorsal in quadrupeds).
Post-cranial	Referring to all bones below the head.
Post-depositional	After burial.
Process	Any outgrowth or projection of bone.
Proximal	Toward the trunk of the body (along a limb).
Quadruped	An animal that habitually walks on four legs.
Superior	Above, top.
Taphonomy	Everything that happens to an individual between death and archaeological recovery (see in 'Bone identification 101', 'Post-depositional processes').
Tooth types	Most species have four major types of teeth: canines, incisors, molars and premolars.
Trabecular	Spongy bone, also called cancellous bone; found in the epiphysis of long bones, it acts as a cushion for joints.

Glossary

Tubercle   Small, knob-like projection.

Tuberosity   Large, rough projection.

Ventral   Toward the stomach or the front; analogous to anterior.

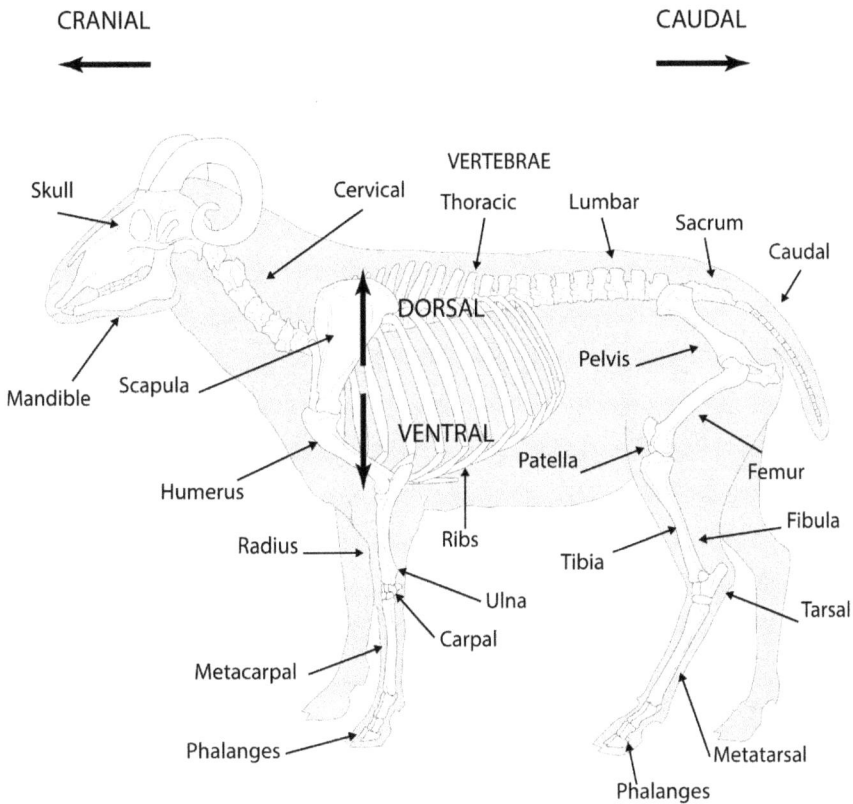

Figure 0.1: Articulated sheep skeleton, with bones and orientations labelled.

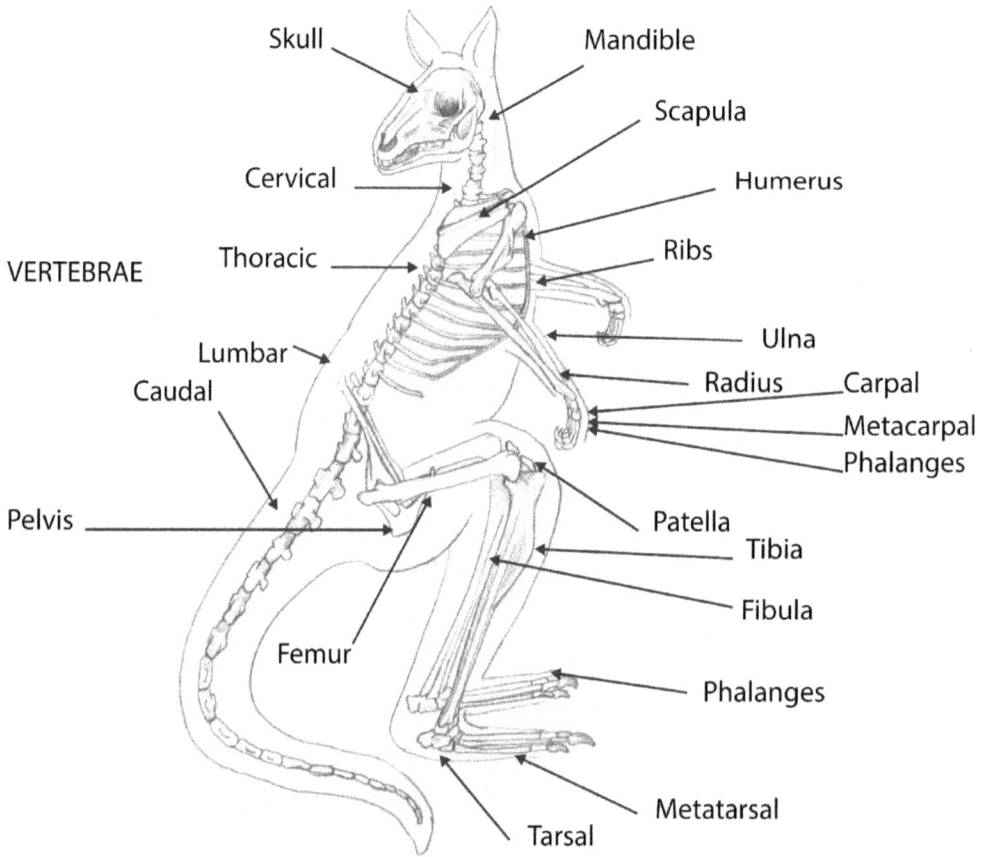

Figure 0.2: Articulated kangaroo skeleton, with bones labelled.

Introduction

This book was developed out of a need for a clear and concise field manual that could be used to make basic identifications of animal bones from archaeological sites in Australia. While there are many excellent manuals that cover the identification of European and North American fauna, and a few that address Australian fauna, there are none that combine common introduced animals with both Australian native species and humans.

This manual will be an asset to students of archaeology and faunal analysis, as well as law enforcement, forensic investigators, and the general public. It is an introductory field guide written primarily for Australian archaeologists working on both Indigenous and historic sites. It does not assume any prior knowledge of the mammalian skeleton and includes 16 species commonly encountered in most environments and archaeological contexts. Since it is impractical for a field manual to provide an exhaustive list of all the potential species that may appear, the aim is to provide basic knowledge needed to identify bones and species that are relevant to most Australian contexts. This manual is intended as a starting point for the non-specialist.

Identification of bone can be difficult, even for the most experienced faunal analyst, and especially when faced with smaller elements with less-obvious diagnostic features. For this reason, smaller bones, such as many of the small hand and foot bones, ribs and vertebrae, have been excluded from this manual. For those bones and for species not included, as well as additional information, we have added a suggested reading list. Given that bone from archaeological contexts is often fragmentary, making identification much more difficult, definitive identification is always best accomplished by a trained specialist and based on a good comparative collection back in the lab.

How to use this manual

This manual begins with an introductory chapter that provides a background to the range of factors that are important to consider before starting any zooarchaeological research. These include (but are not limited to) the importance of correct anatomical terminology and some tips about initial approaches to use during the early stages of the identification process (including morphological markers characteristic of species and the significant influence taphonomy has on assemblages). A suggested reading list at the end of this manual provides a number of sources that explore each of these issues in greater detail. Chapters dedicated to each of the major bones follow, and include correct anatomical terminology, diagnostic features, the way these diagnostic features differ by species, and notes about the way each bone can generally present when recovered in an archaeological assemblage. This information is then synthesised in the decision process flowchart and illustrated by photographs designed to help you make final identifications of the element, and species if possible.

For ease of standardisation, all elements depicted on the figures are from the left side of the individual's body. When practical, every effort was made to illustrate size differences between species. Elements of similar size are generally shown side by side, since determining the size of an individual is one of the first steps in identification. Scales accompany all images, although variation between individuals due to age and/or sex may translate into larger size differences than those shown in the examples.

Layout

The major bones of Australian native species (kangaroo, wallaby, wombat, possum, quoll, bandicoot and emu) are depicted alongside introduced species commonly found in archaeological contexts in Australia (cow, horse, sheep, pig, dingo [dog], cat, rabbit, and chicken). Major modern human bones are also included. Each of the major skeletal elements has its own chapter (e.g. mandible, femur) that includes the following sections:

- 'Diagnostic features' which provides information on the major landmarks on each bone that aid identification;
- 'Orientation and siding' which provides a summary explaining how to orient the bone for identification and side of the body (i.e. the individual's left or right);
- 'Species identification', which provides major morphological features useful for species identification.

Decision processes

After identifying a particular skeletal element, the next step is to identify the species from which it came. To help in this process, a flow chart called a decision process has been included with each skeletal element, for use alongside the individual species photographs (e.g. Figure 1.10 in Chapter 1). The decision process poses a series of questions to narrow down the list of potential species from which a bone likely came. In many cases, there is more than one species listed at the end of a branch. In this case, or even if you are confident that you have made a correct identification, it is necessary to go to the photographs and compare the bone to the list of possible species, as the more visual cues you use to identify an element to species, the better your decision. At this stage, you may also need to use relative size as a deciding factor.

Bone identification 101

The aim of this section is to demystify the process of identifying bones. It provides concrete methods that can be used to identify bone on Indigenous and historic sites across Australia. At the same time it explains the broad anatomical differences between marsupial and placental mammals. This section also briefly outlines the major components of bone, the effect of post-depositional processes on bone preservation, and some guidelines on cleaning and storing bone from archaeological contexts.

The major components of bone

Bone has both an organic (collagen and non-collagenous proteins) and inorganic (hydroxyapatite) component. The organic component (30%) is the first to disappear after the death of an organism. This explains why most archaeological bones have a lighter, brittle feeling in comparison with fresh bone. There are two main types of bone, cortical or lamellar bone and trabecular or cancellous bone. Cortical bone is found in the shafts (diaphyses) of long bones, as well as in many flat bones, like the pelvis, scapula and skull. Trabecular bone (sometimes called spongy bone) is found in the ends (epiphyses) of long bones, and functions as a cushion of sorts for the body's joints. Morphological differences between the two types of bone have direct bearing on their preservation in archaeological contexts. For example, trabecular bone is very porous, and generally less dense than cortical bone. For this reason, when carnivores, like a dingo, chew a bone, they tend to destroy the ends. Similarly, the cortical bone, in the form of bone shafts, is generally left behind because it is denser and hardier than the epiphyses. These shafts are frequently splintered – a result of marrow extraction by carnivores (and humans), or an effect of weathering. Understanding this relationship may help identify some of the processes affecting the site and its assemblage, leading to more accurate final site interpretations.

First steps in the identification process

Identification of an unknown bone can seem to be a daunting task. When starting this process it is helpful to consider that form is a reflection of function. For example, an animal that walks on four legs (quadruped) uses each limb to support a heavy head and body. Therefore, arms and legs will be similarly sized, as both fore limbs and hind limbs are used to support the animal's weight. However, in a biped (in this book, humans and macropods), the arms or fore limbs are used mainly for carrying and fine manipulation, and, while these may also be used for support, it is to a lesser extent than in dedicated quadrupeds. This translates into fore limb/arm bones that are generally smaller than the hind limb/leg bones. Similarly, bones of the cranium (head), pelvis (hips) and scapula (shoulder blade) are often referred to as flat bones; again, this reflects their function as more than strictly weight bearing. Vertebrae, carpals and tarsals are all classed as irregular bones, and have varying functions in the spine, wrist and ankle, respectively. Lastly, the relative thickness and/or robustness of all bones can be a further useful indicator of general species size and skeletal element. The general size and shape of a bone can be a first step in the identification of both elements and species, and is a good basic way to narrow down a potentially large number of elements into a manageable list.

While size can be a useful way in which to make sense of what can initially seem to be an impossibly large task, we must also ascertain whether the bones in question are from an adult or a juvenile. The study of juvenile and neonatal skeletal elements is a large and complicated subject, therefore this manual will touch on just some of the main issues surrounding their identification.

Juvenile skeletal elements are difficult to identify for a variety of reasons. First, the morphology of juvenile bones may differ from adult bones because these bones may not be fully fused. For example, in juveniles the tibia is initially comprised of three bones – proximal epiphysis, shaft, and distal epiphysis – that eventually fuse together to form one bone as it grows (Figures 0.3a and b). The majority of bones in the body undergo a similar process, and the rate of fusion for each bone is unique and varies by species. While this can be very helpful in determining an age at death for a particular individual, juvenile bones can make identification difficult because unfused portions of a bone may be missing in archaeological assemblages, leaving just the shaft or other fragmentary portions. When this occurs, juvenile shafts may be mistaken for other skeletal elements, and mistakenly compared with an adult bone.

The second issue in the identification of juvenile bones is the likelihood that they will not survive as well as adult bones due to their lower bone density. This means that they may be either fragmentary, or disappear altogether, in contexts where adult bone survives. Given the difficulties, juvenile bone identification should be made by a specialist and with the help of a skeletal reference collection that includes bones from immature individuals.

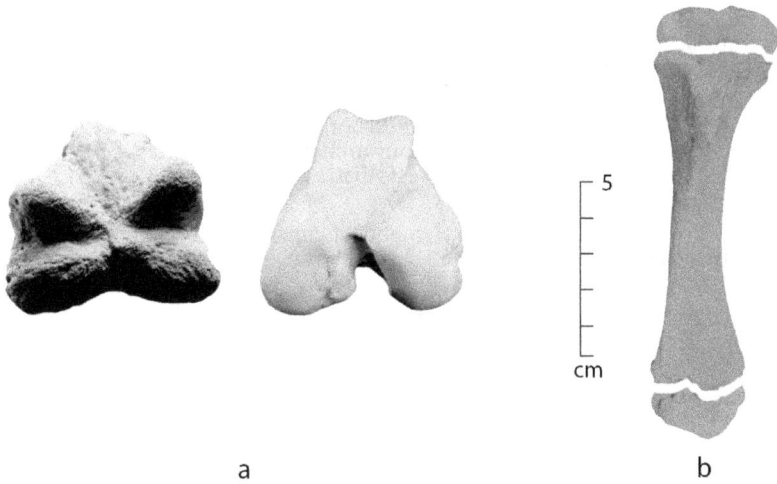

Figure 0.3: (a) A distal left pig femur with an unfused epiphysis on the left, compared to the distal end of an adult pig on the right, (b) an unfused juvenile pig tibia.

Species included

Generally, the first and arguably most important question accompanying the discovery of bone on many archaeological sites, is whether it is human or animal. This is followed by whether the bone is from an introduced or native species. Given these basic divisions, the following 16 species have been included with a view to encompassing the human–animal and the native–introduced species distinctions, as well as the historic–Indigenous site distinction.

Native species

Kangaroo (*Macropus giganteus*)	Elements from an eastern grey kangaroo will permit broad identification of a bone as belonging to a large macropod. Finer distinctions between sub-species are often difficult to make on the basis of post-cranial (from the neck down) elements alone. Kangaroos occur in both historic and Indigenous contexts, although they are generally more common in the latter.
Wallaby (*Macropus rufogriseus*)	Red-necked wallabies may be found in both historic and Indigenous contexts. As with kangaroos, finer distinction between sub-species must rest with a specialist.
Wombat (*Vombatus ursinus*)	The common wombat is similar morphologically to the southern hairy-nosed wombat. Wombats are more common in Indigenous contexts.
Possum (*Trichosurus vulpecula*)	A brushtail possum is similar morphologically to a ringtail possum. Possums may occur in a variety of contexts.

Quoll
(*Dasyurus maculatus*)

A tiger quoll (often referred to as a native cat) is included in this manual as an example of one of Australia's few native carnivorous marsupials.

Bandicoot
(*Perameles* sp)

A long-nosed bandicoot (*Perameles nausuta*) is included due to its ubiquity in many archaeological sites, especially Indigenous sites in north-west Australia.

Emu
(*Dromaius novaehollandiae*)

Post-cranial elements of emus may be found in Indigenous contexts. Smaller wing bones are rarely recovered in archaeological contexts.

Introduced species

Human
(*Homo sapiens*)

In most cases, the most significant question asked when bone is found is whether it is human or animal. For this reason, human elements have been included for comparison.

Dingo/dog
(*Canis dingo/Canis familiaris*)

While often viewed as a native species, the dingo was introduced to Australia during the Holocene. Morphologically, domestic dogs and dingoes are nearly indistinguishable, with the latter having slightly more robust cranial features and teeth. Distinction between the two necessitates examination by a specialist. In prehistoric contexts, dingoes may also be mistaken for thylacines (the extinct marsupial wolf) due to their morphological similarity.

Sheep
(*Ovis aries*)

As sheep are more common than goats on most Australian historical sites, sheep bones have been depicted throughout this manual. While these elements can also be used to identify goat, the distinction between the two can be difficult. A specialist and a comparative collection should be consulted for distinction.

Cow (*Bos taurus*),
Pig (*Sus scrofa*) and
Rabbit (*Oryctolagus* sp)

Each of these species is a common food animal in Australian historic assemblages.

Chicken (domestic fowl)
(*Gallus* sp)

In general, bird bones are relatively easy to identify due to their distinctive morphology and comparatively lighter bone weight. Chickens and domestic fowl are relatively common in urban historical assemblages.

Horse/donkey
(*Equus caballus/asinus*)

Horses generally appear in rather low frequencies in historical assemblages. They are morphologically similar to donkeys and, due to their size, may be mistaken for cow. Cattle and horse are depicted side by side in this manual to illustrate their morphological differences.

Cat
(*Felis domesticus*)

Cats may have entered the archaeological record due to post-depositional commensal activity and are frequently encountered as intentional burials, in foundation deposits and in wells.

The species recovered from most archaeological contexts in Australia can be quite variable, and this variability is greatly dependent on the geographic region and environment in which the assemblage is located. This manual therefore contains those native and intro-duced species most commonly found in both historic and prehistoric assemblages. Birds, with the exception of emus and chickens, as well as rodents and fish, have been excluded. There are several good references that cover these species, and a 'field' manual quickly be-comes a large reference book if every species of animal were to be included.

With respect to size, the species used in this manual are grouped under the general umbrella terms 'small' 'medium' and 'large' to help with the identification process. These are relative terms, so a guide has been included to avoid ambiguity (Figure 0.4). Nev-ertheless, it is important to consider individual variability on size. For example in this framework, an adult human can range from medium to large, as can a kangaroo and emu. Do not use this framework if juvenile bones from any species are suspected.

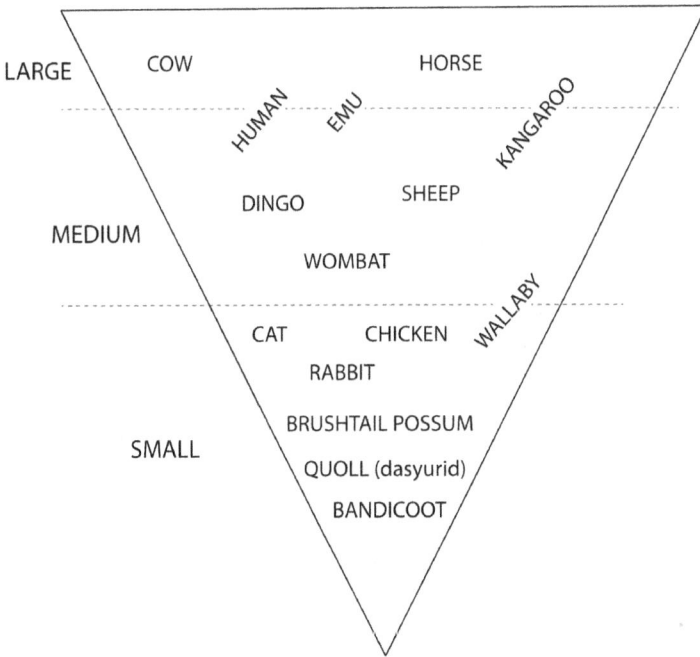

Figure 0.4: Overview of the small, medium and large animal groupings used in this manual.

Skeletal elements included

For ease of use and practicality, only selected elements are depicted in this manual. Em-phasis is placed on bones that are both found in archaeological assemblages in Australia with some frequency and can be identified to species by a non-specialist, especially if in-complete.

This manual emphasises the post-cranial skeleton (neck down). However, mandibles have been included because they are commonly recovered. Teeth have also been given brief attention as part of the mandible, because they are frequently well preserved and can provide a definitive species determination, complete with age and sometimes sex. Given the specialised nature of teeth, they are a topic unto themselves, and for this reason have not been addressed in greater detail by this manual (for more information, see Hillson 2005). Crania (skulls) have also been omitted, as often they are too fragmented to be identified in the field. Mandibles often survive much better than other parts of the crania. The mandibular hinge, coupled with any in situ teeth, renders mandibles highly diagnostic elements for species identification.

The post-cranial skeleton can be sub-divided into axial (trunk), appendicular (limb) and manus/pes (hand/foot) elements. This sub-division is a useful distinction when addressing economic and subsistence-based questions, such as butchery and consumption.

The axial skeleton is comprised of vertebrae, ribs, pelvis and scapula (sometimes included in the appendicular skeleton). Due to the difficult nature of identifying ribs and vertebrae to species, this manual has omitted these elements. Their identification necessitates the use of a specialist and a good comparative collection. However, the pelvis and scapula are both elements that are highly identifiable to species, and in the case of the pelvis, sex designation may also be possible. For these reasons both the scapula and pelvis have been included.

The appendicular skeleton is comprised of the bones of the fore limb/arm (humerus, radius, ulna) and hind limb/leg (femur, tibia, fibula). With the exception of the fibula, these bones are frequently identifiable, even when fragmentary. The fibula has been excluded from this manual because although often present in archaeological assemblages, its fragmentary nature makes identification to species difficult.

The post-cranial skeleton is also comprised of manus (hand) and pes (foot) bones. As with most of the axial skeleton, these bones are more difficult to identify without the aid of a comparative collection. For this reason, the foot is treated as a distinct entity, and is depicted articulated. Several elements are highlighted in greater detail, namely the calcaneus and astragalus, because they are frequently encountered, often complete, and easily diagnostic to species.

As is evident by those bones included and omitted, this manual is not intended to provide all the answers, nor can it replace the experience of a professional zooarchaeologist or forensic osteologist. Rather it is intended as an introductory guide that will facilitate initial distinctions between human and animal, and introduced and native species. Nearly every bone can be identified at some level, especially given recent advances in molecular biology (DNA). That said, the preciseness of identification is often a result of a need to balance time, money and research questions, and this is where specialist expertise may be necessary.

Anatomical differences between marsupial and placental mammals

An important component of this manual is the depiction of both native (often marsupials) and introduced (placental) species commonly found in Australian archaeological sites. Distinguishing between these two broad groups is a lot easier with a cursory understanding of some fundamental morphological differences. The most visible difference between marsupial (metatherian) and placental (eutherian) mammals is the presence of a pouch in the former, in which immature young remain while they mature. Moreover, there are a number of morphological differences between the two that are often visible on the skeleton. The following are some general morphological variations that may be useful in distinguishing between marsupials and placentals, and thus native and introduced animals. Further specific differences are discussed in the relevant identification chapters.

Mandible

Typically the rear portion of the mandible is turned inward in marsupials (inflected jaw angle), as opposed to outward in placentals. This 'angular process' forms a pronounced shelf that projects medially from the posterior mandible (Figure 0.5).

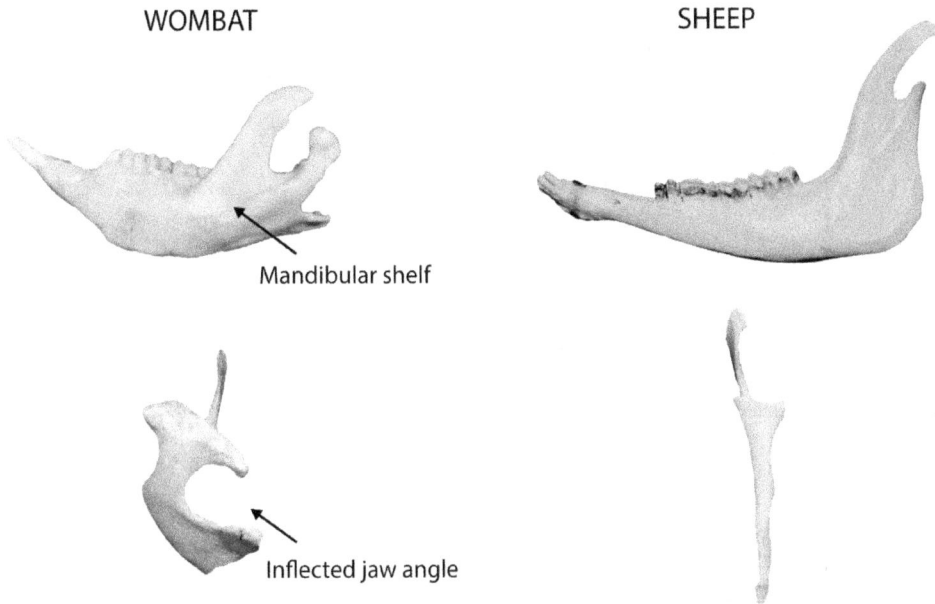

WOMBAT   SHEEP

Mandibular shelf

Inflected jaw angle

Figure 0.5: Comparison of a wombat and sheep left mandible showing the characteristic mandibular shelf and inflected jaw angle of a marsupial.

Dentition

In general, marsupials have different dental patterns than placental mammals, often having three premolars and four molars on each side in both the upper and lower jaw (P3/3; M4/4). In placental mammals, the general dental formula is four premolars and three molars on either side in both the upper and lower jaw (PM 4/4; M 3/3). The third premolar is the only deciduous tooth in marsupials, leading to what is often termed 'molar progression', whereby it is eventually lost later in life. The presence or absence of the third premolar may be used in age estimates.

Pelvis

Nearly all marsupials have two epipubic bones, which extend outward from the front of the pelvis (anterior pelvic symphysis) (Figure 0.6). Although some have argued that their function is unresolved, it is commonly thought they act either as support for the pouch and/or the stomach muscles. These bones generally disarticulate from the rest of the pelvis after deposition and may not be recovered.

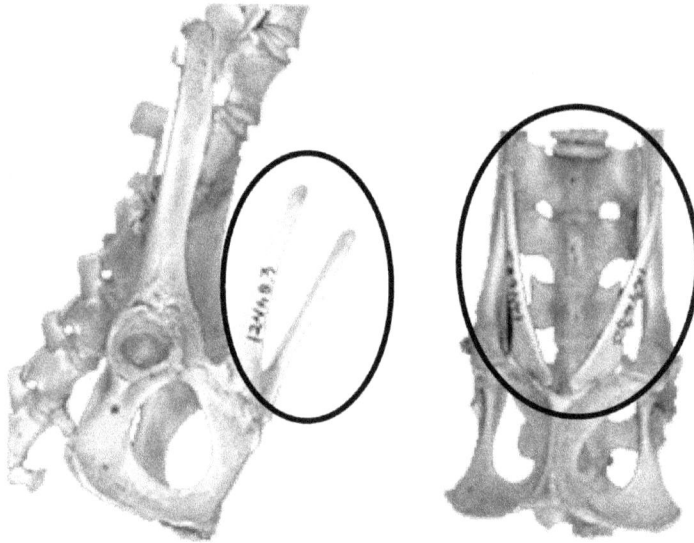

Figure 0.6: An articulated possum pelvis showing the epipubic bone (circled).

Flared humerus

The medio-distal humerus of most marsupials is characterised by marked flaring, often culminating in a sharp crest found on the lateral side, which 'points' up to the proximal end. This crest is balanced by an epicondylar foramen on the medial side (Figure 0.7).

Epiphyseal fusion

In marsupials, the proximal tibia and proximal humerus often fail to fully fuse.

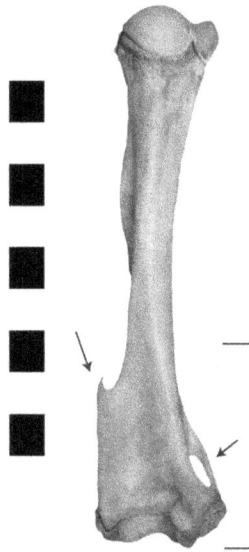

Figure 0.7: A kangaroo humerus showing the flared medio-distal portion, and the lateral crest and epicondylar foramen (arrows).

In general, consideration of the environment in which the species are found can be an important aid in the initial differentiation between marsupial and placental (or native and introduced) species, providing valuable clues about the types of animals you can expect to recover. For example, the species found in an urban domestic rubbish pit would vary greatly from those you might encounter during a survey in the Pilbara. While there are exceptions to this generalisation, any information that can help to narrow down the potential list of species is useful.

Post-depositional processes (taphonomy)

Taphonomy is the study of everything that happens to an individual after death. Understanding the range of factors that could have affected bones after they were deposited is necessary to provide a full interpretation of an archaeological site. There are many taphonomic factors that could exert an influence on bones in an assemblage, and this manual will prioritise those that are easily identifiable for a non-specialist, and most relative to Australian contexts (for a detailed discussion of taphonomy, see Lyman 1994).

Factors that can affect bone after an organism's death can be loosely grouped into two categories: natural and anthropogenic. Modifications resulting from natural causes include scavenging by other species (Figures 0.8a and b), as well as extremes of heat and cold (Figure 0.8c), floods, drought and soil chemistry. As with any once living thing, environmental changes, such as fluctuations in temperature and moisture, are enemies of long-term preservation. Other natural factors affecting preservation include movement by wind or water, or trampling by animals. These types of movement can scatter assemblages and leave tell-tale abrasions on bone surfaces that may be visible under a microscope (and occasionally by the naked eye). Animals such as feral pigs and dingoes also scavenge carcasses, and in addition to leaving tooth marks on bones (Figures 0.8a and b), may destroy and scatter elements.

a

b

c

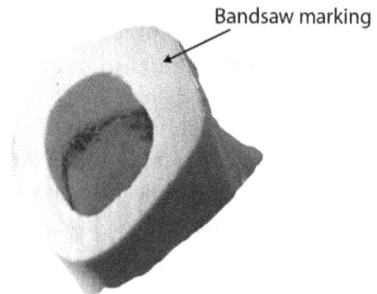

Bandsaw marking

d

Figure 0.8: Bone modifications from natural and anthropogenic causes: (a) the distal end of a gnawed rib, (b) a bone heavily gnawed by a rat, (c) a bone showing characteristic cracking and flaking from exposure, and (d) a bone sawing through the shaft, illustrating the distinctive marking that results from a band saw.

Anthropogenic factors affecting preservation can include cut marks resulting from butchery. These may be quite subtle, or in the case of historic period abattoirs, quite obvious, such as the distinctive striations left by butcher's band saws (Figure 0.8d). Human agency is also a key factor in skeletal element patterning in archaeological assemblages. For example, an assemblage dominated by limb bones may suggest the remains of dietary refuse (as these elements typically contain a lot of meat). If this same assemblage does not contain cranial or foot bones, we could further suggest that initial butchery took place elsewhere, with the limb bones subsequently transported for sale and consumption. Conversely, if relatively complete skeletons are recovered, on-site butchery or death may have occurred. Humans may also cook bone, and so elements can bear traces of burning and/or boiling. Industrial activities are also a possibility, and these include glue and tallow manufacturing, along with tanneries and craft workshops. Recent advances in DNA have now made it possible to potentially identify the species from which worked bone objects, such as buttons and beads, originally came.

Post-excavation cleaning and storage

Fluctuations in temperature and/or humidity, and insect activity are major issues in bone preservation following excavation. Therefore, the best way to store bone is in a dry, cool environment that is free from insects and rodents (who like to gnaw on dry bone). Bone should be cleaned after excavation with a soft, dry brush. A little water may be used if necessary. Harsh chemicals and detergents should be avoided, as well as stiff brushes, as these may mar and destroy some of the bone surface and obliterate any traces of bone surface modifications such as cut and/or tooth marks. If water is used, bone should be dried slowly on a clean sheet of absorbent material out of direct heat or sunlight.

Never put wet bones in a plastic bag or any airtight container, as this can lead to mould and their eventual destruction. Bone should be stored in a dry place, in a clean, dry polyethylene bag into which small holes are made so that the bone does not 'sweat' in case any temperature fluctuations do occur. An acid-free tag containing any identifying information should be placed inside the bag with the bone. Writing on the outside of the bag is generally not recommended, as this can rub off and leave an unprovenanced bag of bone that is worthless.

1
Mandible

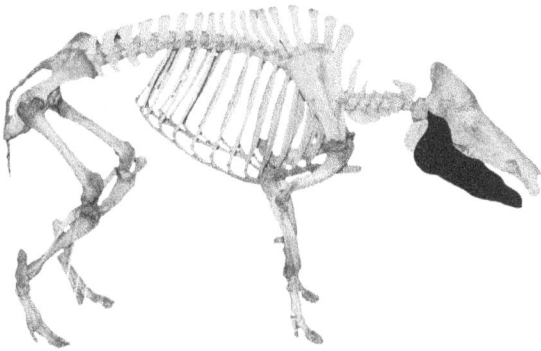
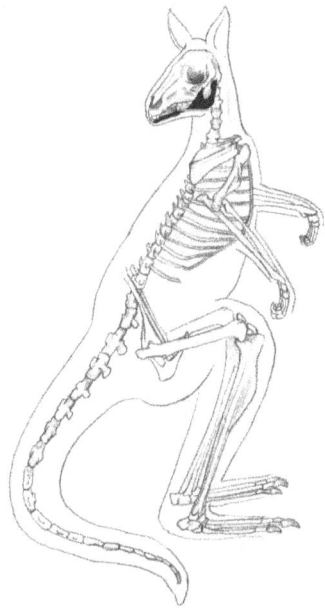

The mandible, or jaw bone, is one of the most useful elements in species identification, especially when teeth remain in situ. Just as most major bones in an animal's body reflect the way in which that individual moves, a species' dentition and chewing muscles reflect an individual's diet. As the mandible provides the surface for the attachment of the chewing muscles, as well as the anchor point for the teeth, its morphology can facilitate species identifications at both broad and fine levels. Since there are numerous publications on the identification of teeth (see Hillson 2005), we will devote more attention to the mandible itself, and will conclude with some basic features of dentition that can be used to distinguish between species at a broad level (e.g. herbivore from carnivore, marsupial from placental).

There are morphological differences between the mandibles of marsupial and placental mammals, which means that it is possible to broadly differentiate between these two groups by examining a few specific traits. In particular, the rear portion of the mandible is typically turned inward (inflected jaw angle) in marsupials, as opposed to outward in placental mammals (refer to Figures 0.5 and 1.1). In marsupials, the angular process forms a pronounced shelf that projects medially (lingually) from the posterior mandible (especially notable in wombats). And lastly, the mandibular foramen is an opening that can be viewed from both the buccal and lingual sides in marsupials, as opposed to just the lingual side in placentals (Figure 1.2).

Diagnostic features

Diagnostic features of the mandible are shown in Figure 1.1. The mandible is comprised of two halves (bodies), which join and fuse together anteriorly at the **mandibular symphysis** (1). **Mental foramina** (2), small openings in the bone for the insertion of nerves and blood vessels, are present anteriorly on either side of the mandibular symphysis. The mandibular symphysis of many animal species remains cartilaginous throughout life, and therefore in many archaeological assemblages, it becomes 'unfused' over time, resulting in just one side or body being recovered. The largest portion of the mandibular body is the **ascending ramus** (3), a broad, 'flattened' area of the distal mandible. Typically, animals engaged in heavy chewing have a larger ramus. Extending upward from the ascending ramus is a smooth, rounded (either concave or convex) articular surface, called the **mandibular condyle** (4), which forms the temporomandibular joint with the cranium. The **coronoid process** (5) also extends upward from the ramus, opposing the mandibular condyle, and serves as the point of attachment for the temporalis muscle. The coronoid process and mandibular condyle are separated by the **mandibular notch** (6). The **masseteric fossa** (7) on the buccal (cheek) side of the ramus, is an indentation in which sits the masseter muscle. On the lower distal portion of the mandible, the **angular process** (8) is an outward projection found in many species, including some marsupials and carnivores, and serves as another attachment point for the masseter muscle. Also on the buccal side, the morphology of the **mandibular shelf** (9) and location of the **mandibular foramen** (10) can be used to distinguish between species. The length and location of the **diastema** (11), a space commonly found before the cheek tooth row on most mammals, is also diagnostic of species.

(1) Mandibular symphysis   (5) Coronoid process   (9) Mandibular shelf
(2) Mental foramina   (6) Mandibular notch   (10) Mandibular foramen
(3) Ascending ramus   (7) Masseteric fossa   (11) Diastema
(4) Mandibular condyle   (8) Angular process

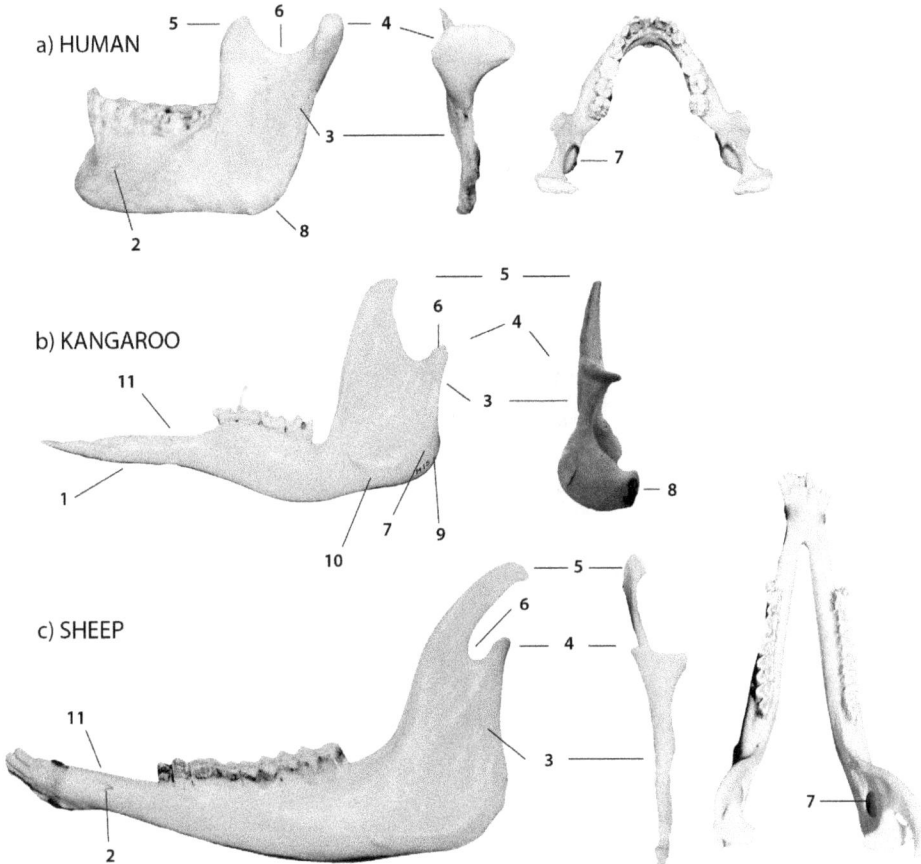

Figure 1.1: Mandibles labelled with diagnostic features; (a) human, (b) kangaroo and (c) sheep; the buccal, posterior and superior (occlusal) views are shown for the human and sheep (L to R).

Orientation and siding

To orient one side (body) of the mandible, the roughened area at the mandibular symphysis indicates the anterior portion of the bone, with the alveoli or in situ teeth facing up (cranially). Any mental foramina are generally anterior and lateral (buccal). The ascending ramus, coronoid process and mandibular condyle are posterior (toward the back).

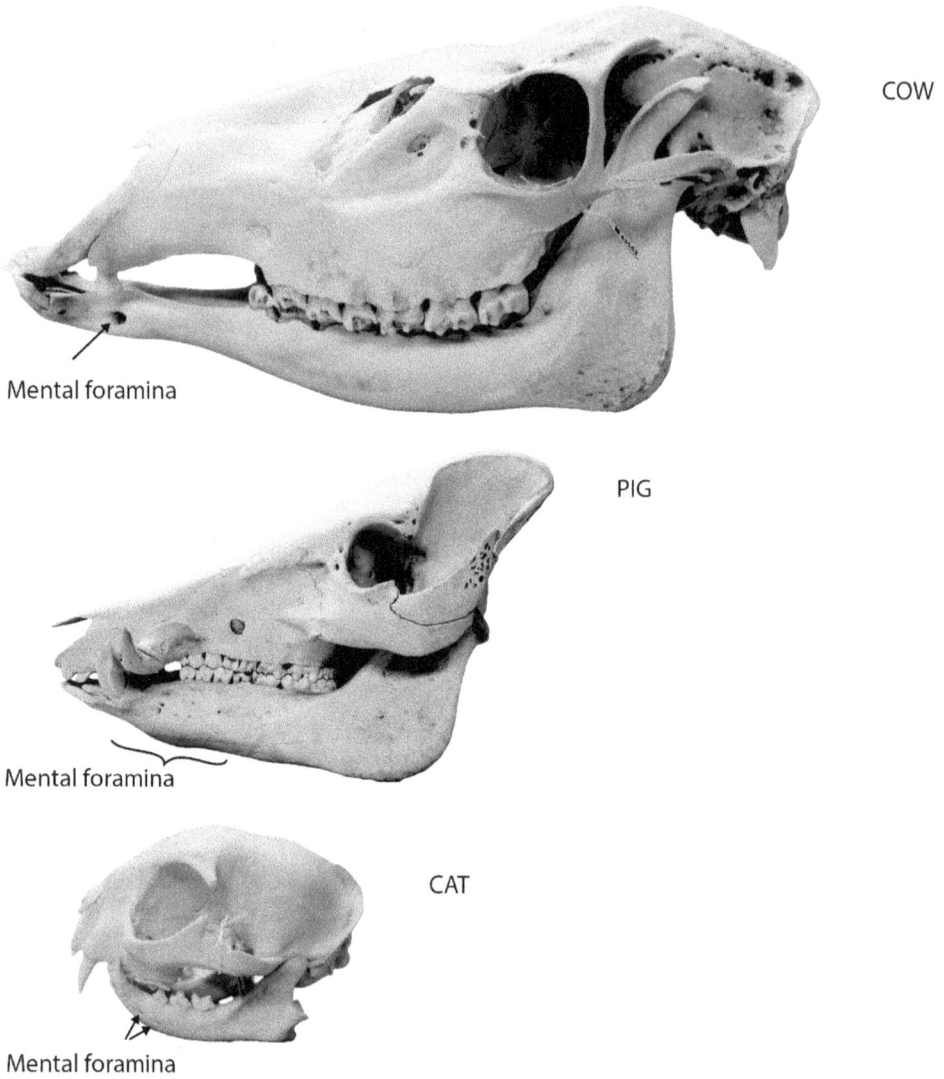

Figure 1.2: Comparison of the mental foramina of a cow, pig and cat.

Species identification

Refer to Figures 1.3–1.8 for species identification using the mandible. If a mandible has teeth in situ, identification to species is much easier. In the absence of dentition, and assuming the mandible is fragmented, the following traits can be used for identification.

Distinguishing between humans and animals

- Humans have a chin; the mandibular symphysis remains cartilaginous, and therefore unfused in most animals, but is replaced with bone (and therefore fused) early on in humans.
- Humans have a U-shaped dental arcade (when viewed from above), visible in intact mandibles (Figure 1.1a).

The size, shape and angle of the ascending ramus

- Dingoes and cats both have a distinct angular process posteriorly (toward the back).
- Marsupials (kangaroos, wallabies, wombats, possums) all have a distinct mandibular shelf lingually (tongue side).
- Pigs and horses have a curved distal ramus that is roughed in appearance, with strong ridge marks.

Morphology of the mandibular condyles

- Dingoes, cats, horses, pigs and humans all have rounded condyles with a 'rolled' or convex appearance.
- Wombats have rounded condyles that slope inward (lingually).
- Rabbits have small, ball-like condyles.
- Possums have rounded condyles that are oblong bucco-lingually (cheek to tongue side).
- Cattle, sheep, kangaroos and wallabies all have flattened, saddle-shaped (concave) condyles.

Morphology of the coronoid process (when viewed from the side)

- Dingoes and cats both have a substantial, wide coronoid process.
- Pigs have a low, pointed process that curves posteriorly.
- Humans have a process that is intermediate in height and almost triangular in shape with a very wide mandibular notch.
- Horses have a long, high, almost rectangular-shaped process with a rounded proximal edge that is angled posteriorly (but not curved).
- Cattle also have a long, high process, but one that curves proximally posteriorly.
- Sheep have a prominent, arched process that curves posteriorly.
- Kangaroos and wallabies have a process that is intermediate in height, and curved posteriorly with a shark fin-like appearance.
- Wombats have a process that is tall, curved slightly posteriorly, and culminates in a sharp point.
- Rabbits and possums are similar in size, but the rabbit does not have a process, while the possum has a triangular process with a straight posterior border.

Location of mental foramina

- Most species have one foramen on the buccal anterior surface of each mandibular body.
- Cats and dingoes have two foramina.
- Pigs and rabbits have numerous foramina (Figure 1.2).

Morphology of the mandibular notch

- Humans have a notch that is very wide and open, whereas in most other species, the notch is pronounced (compare Figures 1.3b and c).
- Rabbits have no notch.
- Possums have an L-shaped notch.
- Kangaroos have a notch that appears like a curved L shape that is slightly slanted anteriorly.
- Wallabies have a semilunar shaped notch.
- Wombats have a notch that is a rounded V shape.
- Pigs, dingoes and cats have a very shallow notch.
- Cattle, horses and sheep all have a deep, rounded notch.

The pattern of alveoli (tooth sockets) can be used for species identification (see Hillson 1992), especially the position and length of the diastema (space) between the canines and premolars (or between the incisors and premolars).

The masseteric fossa is very deep and pouch-like in large marsupials (wombats, kangaroos, wallabies).

Distinguishing between kangaroos and wallabies

- In complete mandibular bodies, the curvature of the diastema (the space between the incisors and premolars) can be used to differentiate between macropods.
- Kangaroos have a diastema that curves upward, toward the tooth row, giving the teeth the appearance of sitting higher than the anterior portion of the mandible (Figure 1.4b).
- Wallabies have little to no curvature of the diastema, giving the tooth row the appearance of sitting on the same level (Figure 1.4c).

Common state in archaeological assemblages

The mandible of most animal species is commonly recovered unfused in most archaeological assemblages. Therefore, the morphology of the ascending ramus, mandibular condyles and, if intact, the coronoid process, can be used for species identification. If the mandible is fragmentary, it may be possible to use the location, number and size of the mental foramina and the mandibular symphysis for identification. The mandible is sometimes confused with an innominate when fragmented, as both elements are irregularly shaped. Cut marks are often found on the mandibular condyle, resulting from disarticulation from the skull, and may also be found on the buccal surface resulting from tongue removal.

Teeth tend to preserve well in most environments, with the teeth of smaller individuals often faring the best. Large premolars and molars from horses, cattle and even sheep or goats and marsupials commonly break, with the enamel often shearing off. When this occurs, it may be difficult to distinguish between horse and cattle, and even between cattle and sheep. Isolated teeth belonging to either kangaroos or wallabies are also frequently difficult to distinguish, as the shape of the mandible is the best indicator to distinguish between several species of macropods (Figures 1.4b and c).

a) PIG

5
cm

Narrow mandibular notch

b) WOMBAT

5
cm

Wide mandibular notch

c) HUMAN

5
cm

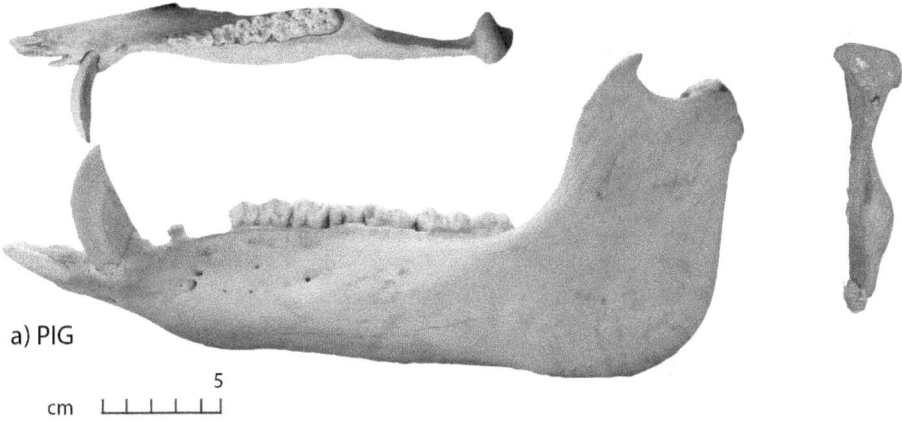

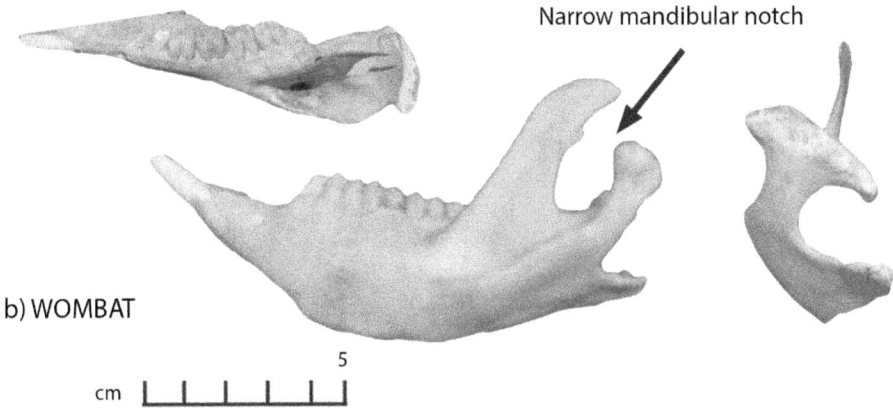

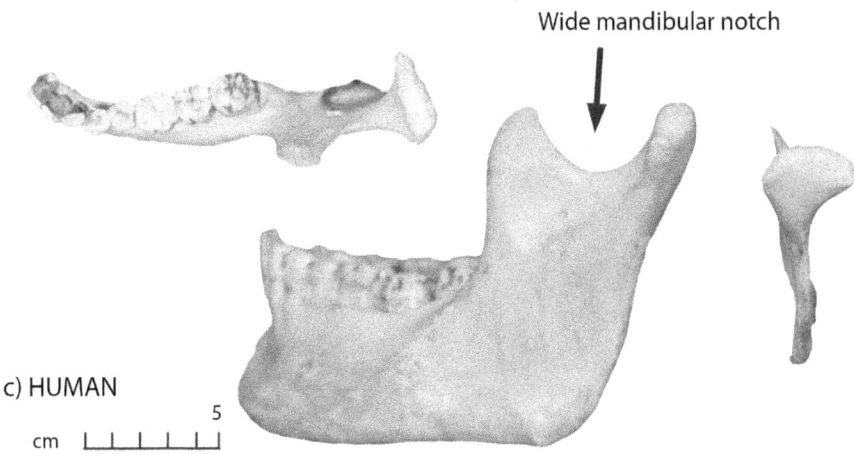

Figure 1.3: Mandibles in buccal and posterior views; (a) pig, (b) wombat and (c) human.

a) SHEEP

b) KANGAROO

c) WALLABY

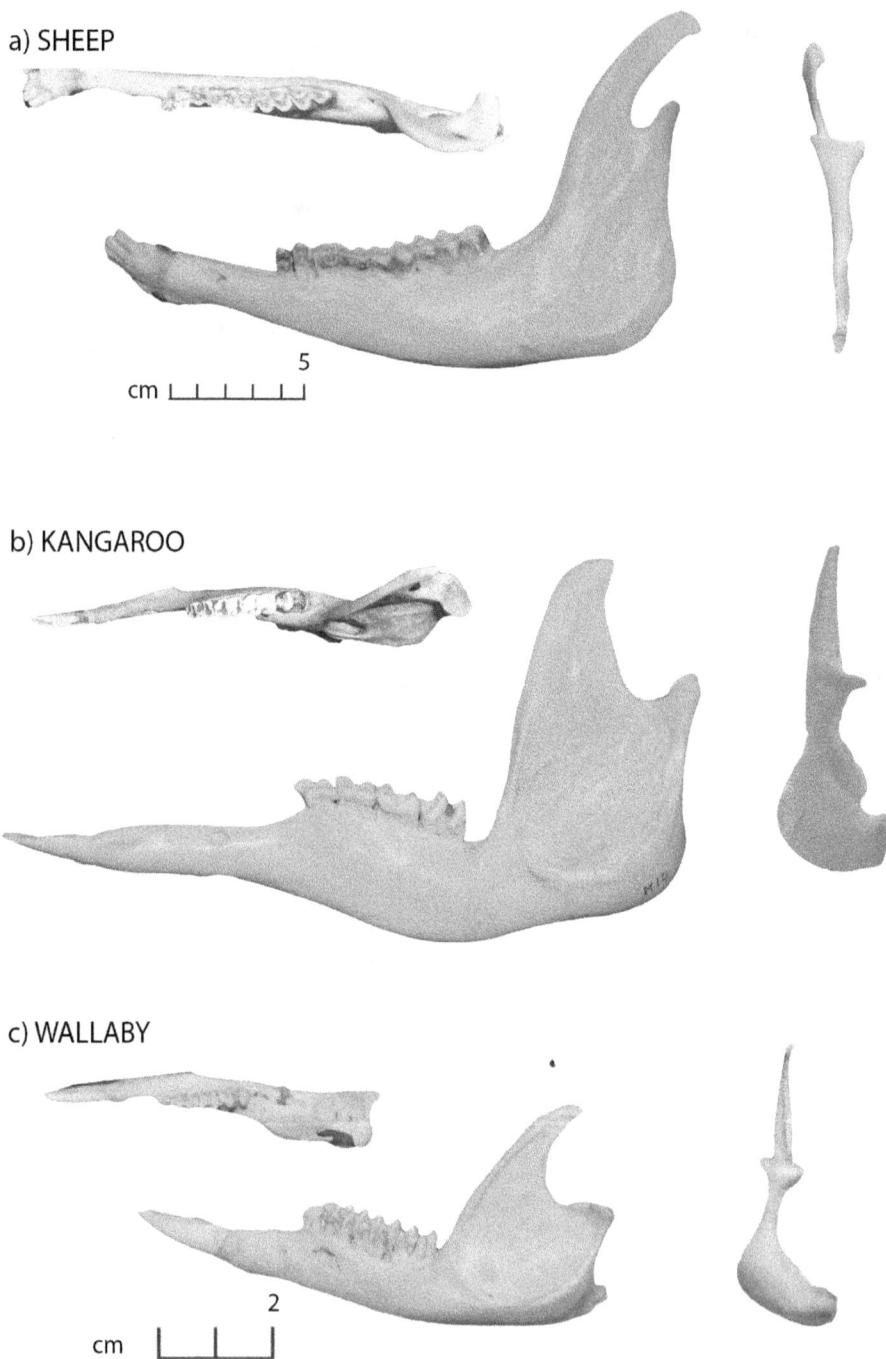

Figure 1.4: Mandibles in buccal and posterior views; (a) sheep, (b) kangaroo and (c) wallaby.

HORSE

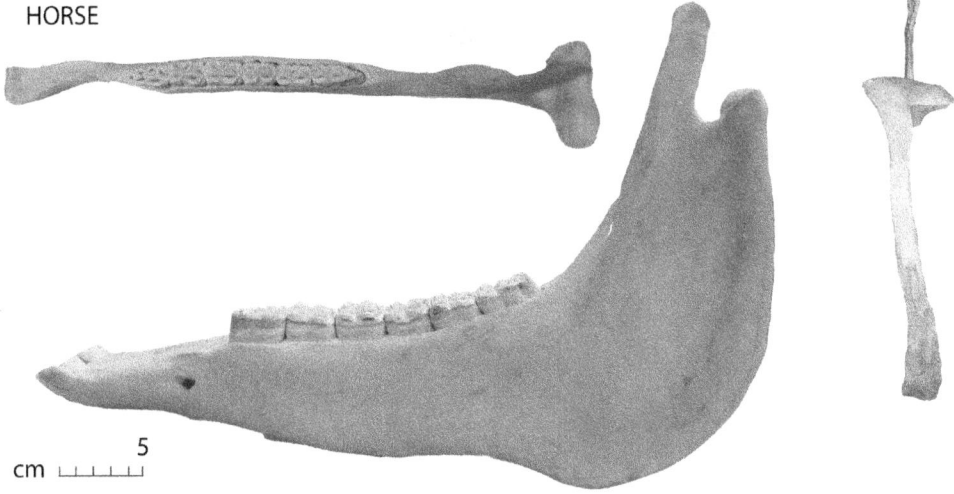

5
cm

Figure 1.5: Horse mandible in buccal and posterior view.

COW

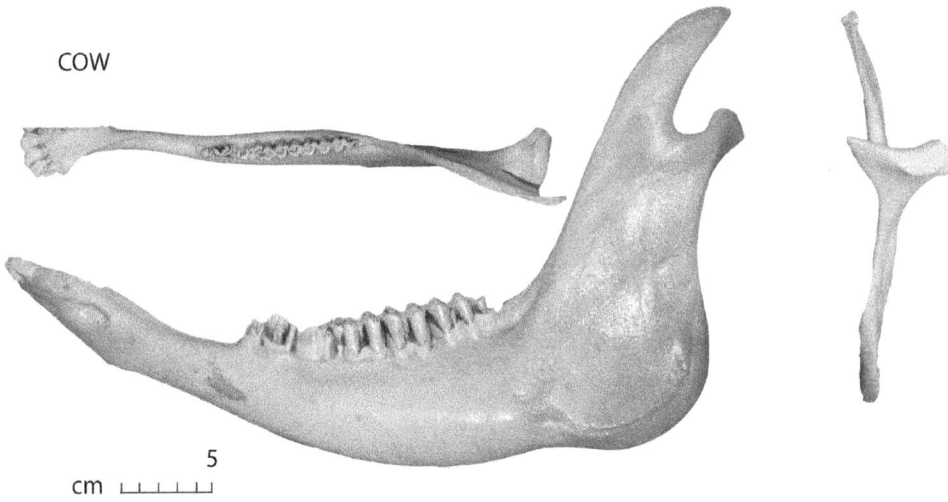

5
cm

Figure 1.6: Cow mandible in buccal and posterior view.

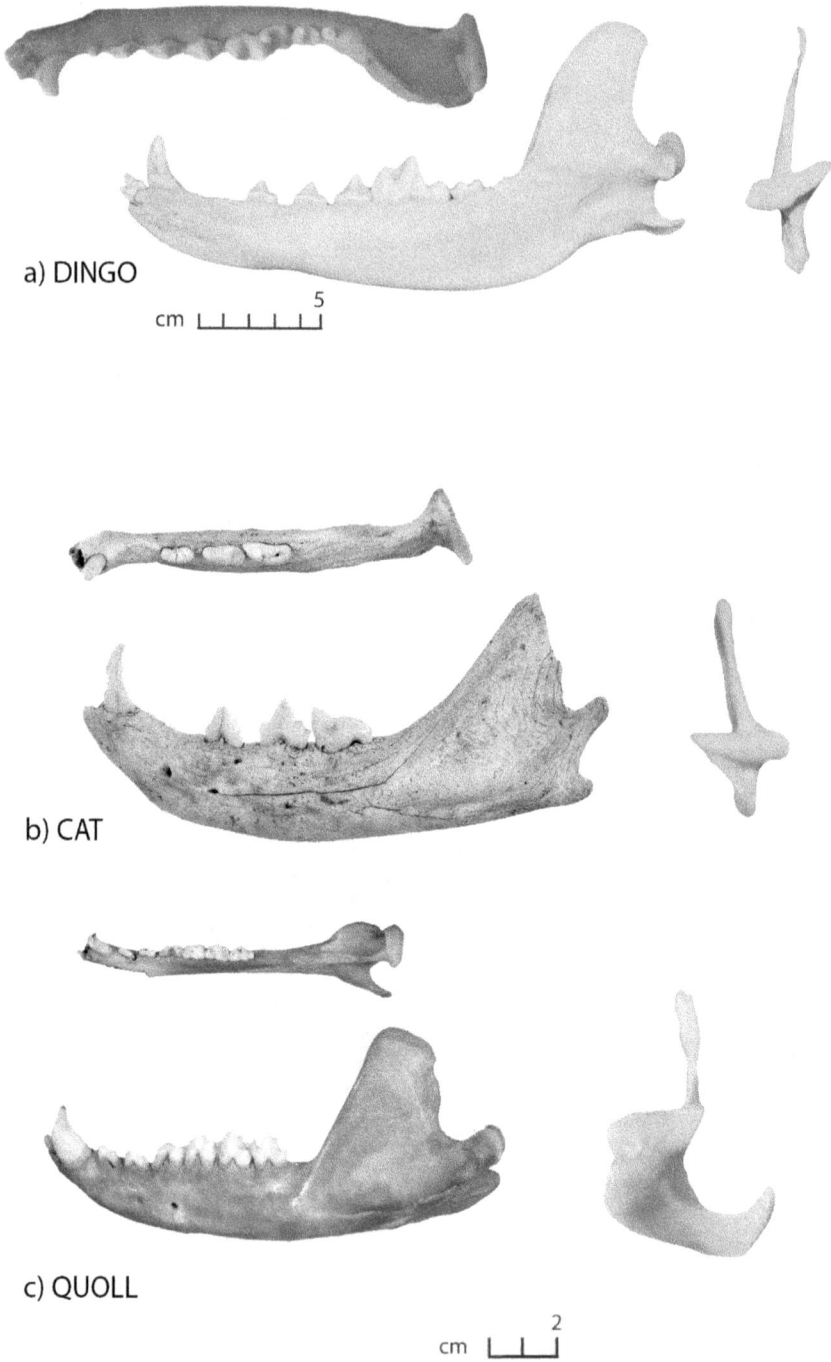

a) DINGO

b) CAT

c) QUOLL

Figure 1.7: Mandibles in buccal and posterior views; (a) dingo, (b) cat and (c) quoll (buccal image right side of animal).

a) RABBIT

cm ⊔⊔⊔ 2

b) POSSUM

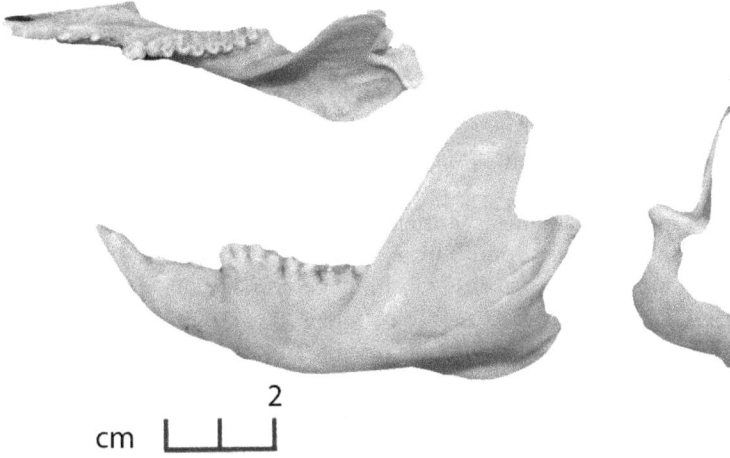

cm ⊔⊔⊔ 2

c) BANDICOOT

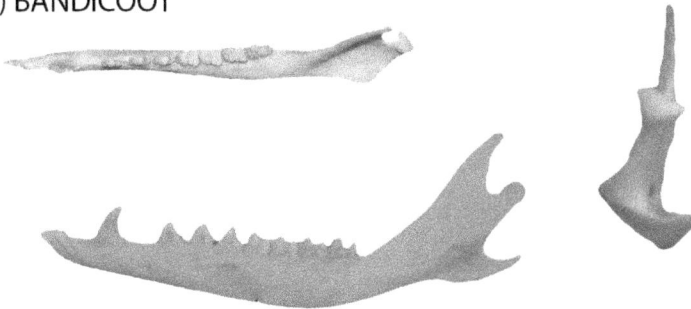

Figure 1.8: Mandibles in buccal and posterior views; (a) rabbit, (b) brushtail possum and (c) bandicoot.

Dentition

The teeth of all species have distinct morphological traits that are extremely useful in identification. All mammals have the same basic types of teeth – incisors, canines, premolars and molars, the shape of which varies between species largely due to dietary differences. All animals (including humans) can be classified according to one of several broad dietary preferences: herbivore, folivore, omnivore, carnivore and insectivore. Horses, cattle, sheep, rabbits, kangaroos, wallabies and wombats are grazing herbivores, subsisting largely on grasses, while goats are browsing herbivores, eating a variety of grasses, leaves, bark and shrubs. Possums are largely folivores, eating mainly leaves, while dingoes, quolls and cats are carnivores, subsisting largely on meat. Humans, pigs and bandicoots are omnivores – eating most things that come their way. Dietary differences are generally best reflected in the premolars and molars (cheek teeth), as these teeth tend to do the majority of the grinding, tearing and shearing needed to process different food sources. In the images found on the following pages, the occlusal (biting) surface of the teeth is illustrated, as this surface contains the clearest morphological differences useful in distinguishing between species. For detailed discussions and information on the dentition of various species, see Hillson (2005, 1992).

Along with morphological differences, every species has a unique dental formula – that is, a specific number of each of the major types of teeth (incisors, canines, premolars and molars) – that is useful in identification (see Figure 1.9). Dental formulas are expressed by taking into consideration one half of the entire mouth and counting the number of each type of tooth. For example, the original mammal dentition formula has the same number of teeth on the top and bottom, and is written 3.1.4.3 / 3.1.4.3. Starting from the midline, this translates into three incisors, one canine, four premolars and three molars on each half of the upper and lower jaws. An easier example to visualise may be the human dental pattern – 2.1.2.3 / 2.1.2.3. This translates into two incisors, one canine, two premolars and three molars in each quadrant of the human mouth. However, some species have different numbers of upper and lower teeth. For example, both bovids (sheep, goat, cattle) and cervids (deer, antelope) do not have upper incisors; bovids also lack upper canines. The following are the dental formulas for the species covered by this manual, followed by some general dental morphological differences between species that may be useful as a starting point in identification. Please note, however, that tooth morphology rapidly changes over an individual's lifetime due to age or wear, and whether the tooth in question is deciduous (milk tooth) or permanent. Given this large morphological variability in teeth, comparative reference materials should be consulted for accurate identification.

Human	**Horse***	**Cow and sheep**
2.1.2.3 / 2.1.2.3	3.1.3-4.3 / 3.1.3-4.3	0.0.3.3 / 3.1.3.3

Pig	**Dingo and cat**	**Kangaroo and wallaby^**
3.1.4.3 / 3.1.4.3	3.1.4.2 / 3.1.4.2	1.0.3.4 / 1.0.3.4

Wombat	**Possum**	**Rabbit**
1.0.1.4 / 1.0.1.4	3.1.1.5 / 2.0.1-2.4	2.0.1-3.3 / 1.0.1-3.3

Figure 1.9: Dental formulas (incisors, canines, premolars and molars) for some of the species in this manual. *Some horses have vestigial first premolars called wolf teeth. ^The third premolar is the only deciduous tooth in marsupials, leading to what is often termed 'molar progression', whereby it is eventually lost later in life. In many marsupials, molar progression makes distinguishing between premolars and molars a less than clear-cut task. Incidentally, the presence or absence of the third premolar may be used in age estimates.

Marsupials differ from placentals in their dentition. In general, marsupials have more teeth than placental mammals, often having three premolars (PM) and four molars (M) on each side in both the upper and lower jaw (PM 3/3; M 4/4). In placental mammals, the general dental formula is four premolars and three molars on either side in both the upper and lower jaw (PM 4/4; M 3/3).

Species identification

Refer to Figures 1.3–1.8 for species identification using dentition.

Horse	Cheek teeth (molars and premolars) are rectangular in outline (as opposed to tapered), blocky, tall, and all similar to one another in form; upper and lower incisors are conical in form (Figure 1.5).
Cow, sheep and goat	Cheek teeth are high-crowned, with deep infoldings (crescent moon appearance); lower incisors and canines are spatulate in form (Figure 1.6).
Kangaroo and wallaby	Cheek teeth are characterised by an H pattern on the occlusal surface; lower incisors are large, pointed, and projecting with small, spatulate upper incisors (Figure 1.4).
Wombat	Cheek teeth are blocky with an M-shaped outline; incisors are large and projecting (almost tusk-like). Their rootless teeth grow continuously (Figure 1.3b).
Cat, dingo and quoll	Cheek teeth are sharp, and blade-like with several points; incisors are spatulate and pointed; canines are sharp and pointed (Figure 1.7).

Human and pig Cheek teeth are rounded and broad in profile with several cusps; incisors are spatulate, while canines are pointed (male pig canines are tusks). Pig and human teeth are commonly mistaken for each other, but can be easily differentiated by their cusp patterns (Figures 1.3a and c).

Rabbit Cheek teeth are ridged and blocky, all of similar size; incisors are large and projecting (Figure 1.8a).

Possum Cheek teeth are pointed, comprised of two parallel crests, separated by a trough; lower incisors are large and projecting (growing throughout life), while upper incisors are small and spatulate (Figure 1.8b).

Bandicoot Cheek teeth are distinctly 'pointed' on the buccal side; premolars are sharp and pointed (Figure 1.8c).

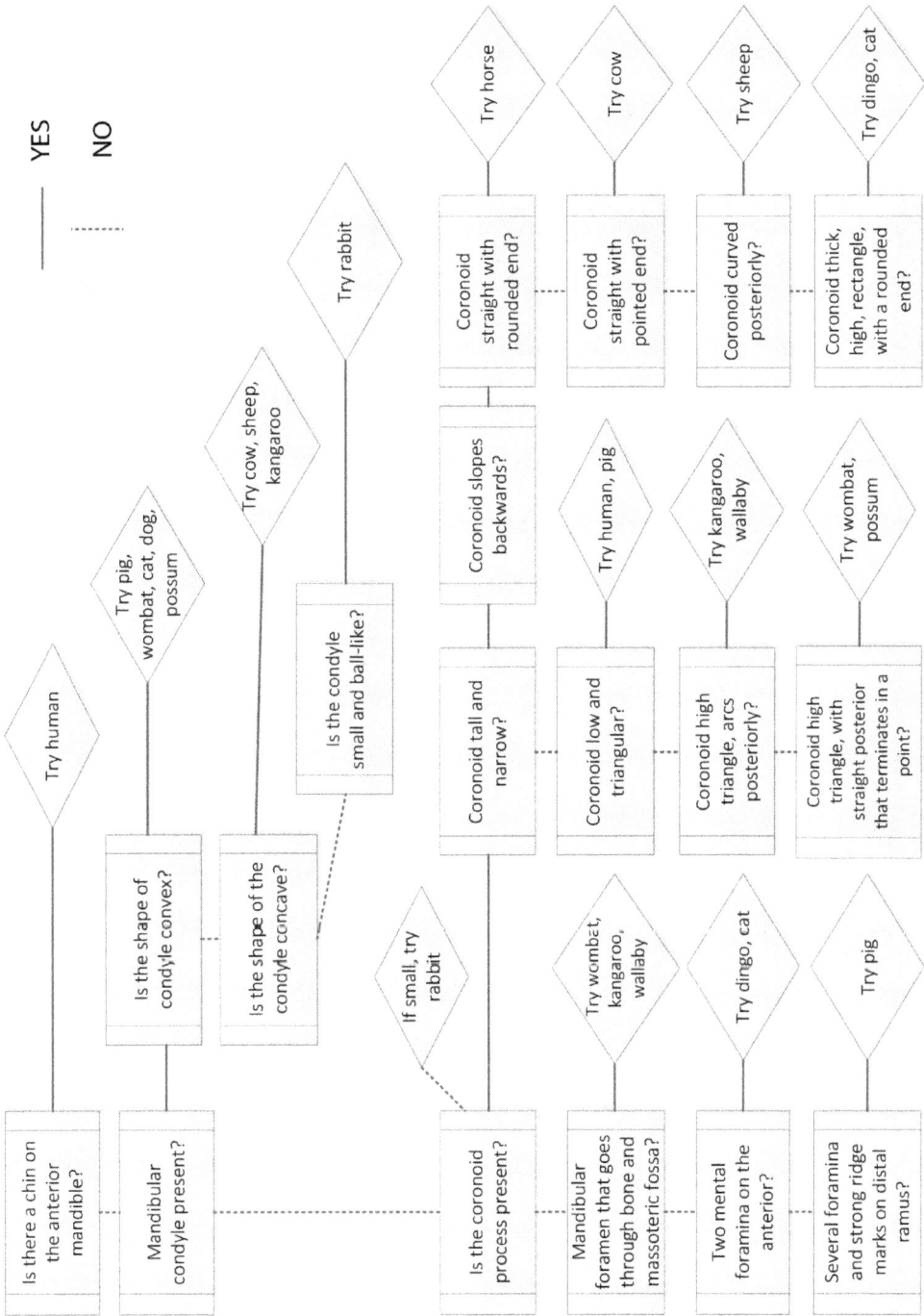

Figure 1.10: Mandible decision process.

2
Scapula

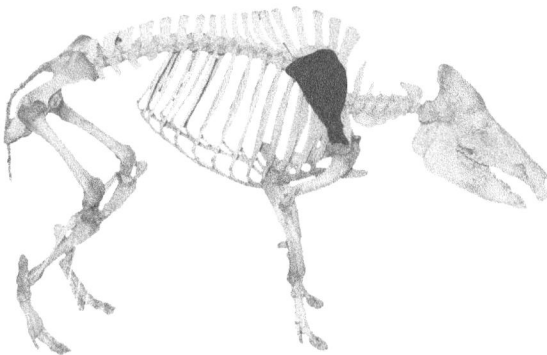

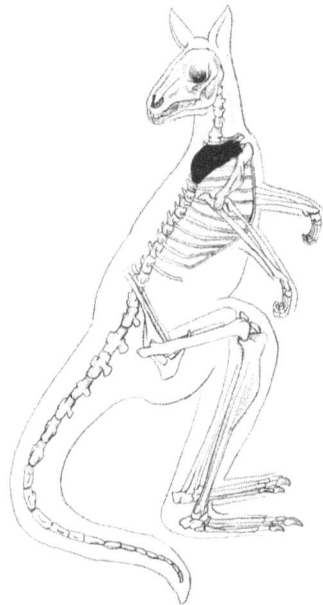

The scapula, or shoulder blade, is a flat bone with a raised ridge, readily identifiable when complete. When fragmented, the distal portion (neck and glenoid fossa) is commonly recovered from archaeological contexts, and is one of the easier bones to use in the identification of species.

Diagnostic features

Diagnostic features of the scapula are shown in Figure 2.1. The scapula is distinguished by its triangular shape (1), which is often fragmented in archaeological assemblages. The distal articulation or **glenoid fossa** (2), articulates with the humerus to form the shoulder joint, and its morphology is diagnostic of species. The **spine** (3), which rises off the blade on the dorsal surface, is also a diagnostic feature of the scapula, as is the swollen process at its end, the **acromion** (4), which articulates with the clavicle. The **coracoid process** (5) extends out from the cranial side of the **neck** (6) on the dorsal side. The distal scapula is one of the most diagnostic bones for species identification.

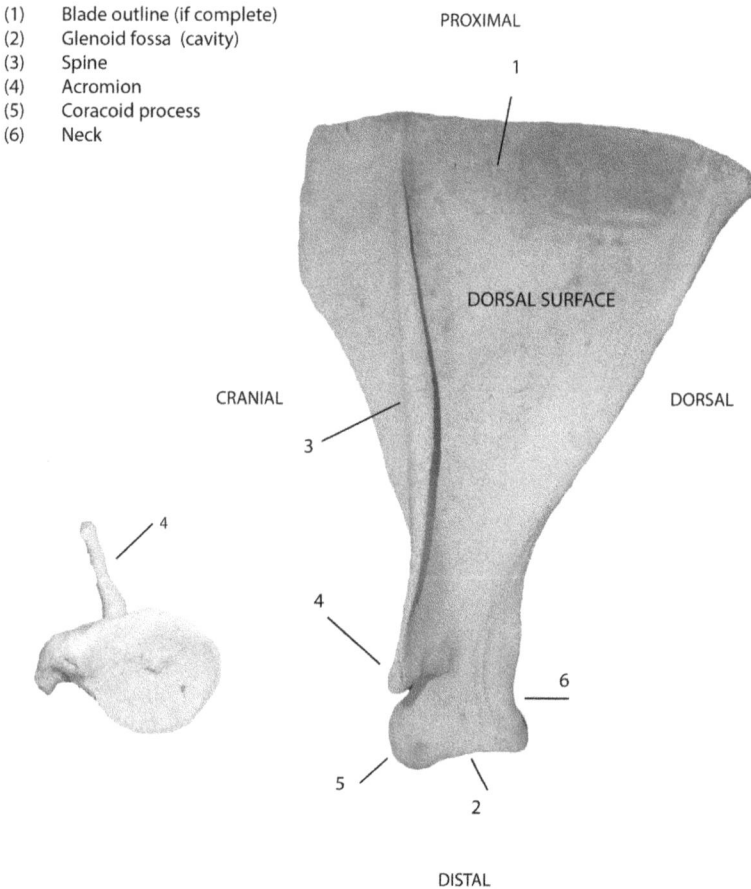

(1)   Blade outline (if complete)
(2)   Glenoid fossa (cavity)
(3)   Spine
(4)   Acromion
(5)   Coracoid process
(6)   Neck

Figure 2.1: Sheep scapula with orientations and diagnostic features labelled.

Orientation and siding

In both humans and animals, the spine points to the glenoid fossa. In quadrupeds, the scapula rests on the dorso-lateral surface of the trunk, and the spine and glenoid fossa point down when in anatomical position (see Figure 2.2). In humans and macropods (kangaroos and wallaby), however, the scapula rests on the upper back, and the spine appears horizontal when in anatomical position. To side the scapula in quadrupeds (Figure 2.2), orient the bone so the spine is lateral (to the side), the glenoid fossa points downward, the coracoid process is anterior (forward), and the more 'rounded' side of the blade is nearer the individual's head. In bipeds, orient the bone so the glenoid fossa is lateral and the spine is horizontal.

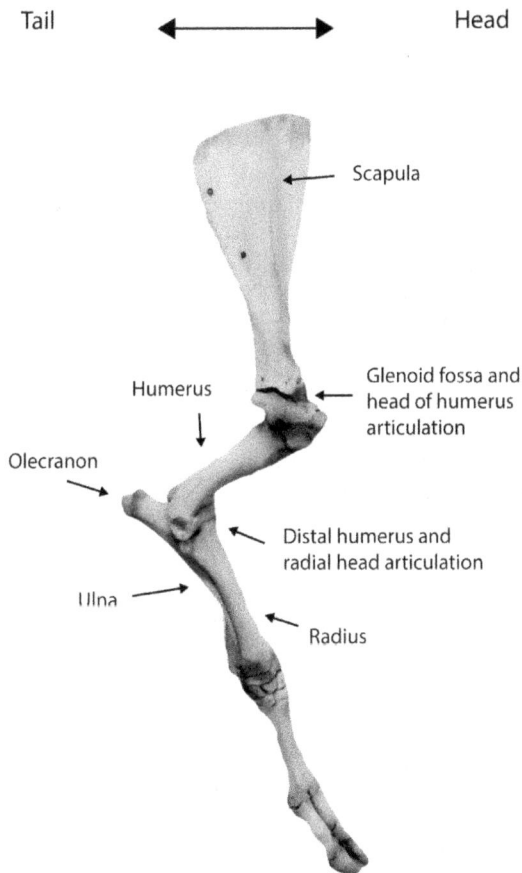

Figure 2.2: Articulated cow fore leg (right) illustrating the articulation of the scapula and humerus.

Species identification

Refer to Figures 2.3–2.8 for species identification using the scapula.

Distinguishing between humans and animals

- The shape of the scapula is elongated in most non-human animals.
- The shape is triangular in humans (Figure 2.4b).

Blade outline

- If the scapula is complete, use the blade outline and the length of the spine and acromion for species identification.
- The blade outline is an elongated triangle in cattle (Figure 2.3b), sheep (Figure 2.4a), and pigs (Figure 2.4c).
- The blade outline is tall and narrow in horses (Figure 2.3a).
- The blade is almost rectangular in shape in dingoes (Figure 2.5d).
- The blade outline is a rounded triangle in macropods (Figures 2.5b and c).

Acromion

- The acromion extends beyond the glenoid fossa in kangaroos, wallabies, possums, wombats, and humans.
- It is nearly even with the glenoid fossa in dingoes, cats and quolls.
- It flares posteriorly in rabbits.
- The distal acromion is flared and triangular in shape in humans.
- There is no acromion in horses or pigs.

Neck

- If only the medio-distal portion of the scapula is extant, with a missing and/or broken spine, use the neck for species identification.
- The neck is long and flattened in horses.
- The neck is long but less flattened in cattle.
- Sheep and pigs have a distinct, short neck.
- Macropods, dingoes and cats have a short neck which is barely visible.
- Rabbits have a very slender, narrow and distinct neck.
- Humans have a neck barely recognisable as a distinct feature. It is very broad, and flattened dorso-ventrally.

Glenoid fossa/coracoid process

- If the distal portion of the scapula is extant, but the neck is missing, use the shape of the glenoid fossa and/or coracoid process for species identification (Figure 2.8).
- The glenoid fossa is rounded in cattle, sheep, horses, pigs and cats.
- The glenoid fossa is teardrop-shaped in kangaroos, wallabies, humans and possums.
- The glenoid fossa is oval-shaped in wombats.
- The glenoid fossa is almost rectangular in dingoes.
- The coracoid process is curved and projecting in rabbits, dingoes and humans.
- The coracoid process is strongly developed in horses, and visible in cattle, sheep and pigs.

As in all elements, general size is a good way in which to differentiate between species. When following the decision processes, always use size as both an initial and final determining factor in species identification.

Common state in archaeological assemblages

The distal end of the scapula (neck and glenoid fossa) is commonly intact, but the blade is often missing and/or broken; the spine and acromion are commonly broken, especially in humans, cats, dingoes, kangaroos, wallabies, possums and rabbits. Cut marks are commonly found around the neck and glenoid fossa, resulting from disarticulation of the joint, and may also be found on the blade as a result of skinning.

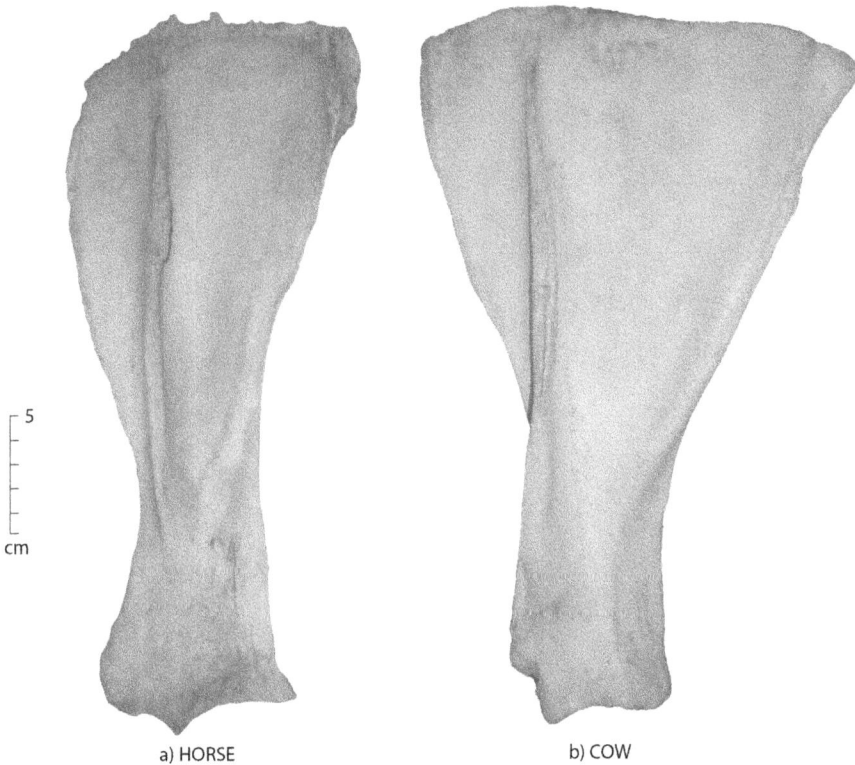

a) HORSE   b) COW

Figure 2.3: Scapula in dorsal view; (a) horse and (b) cow.

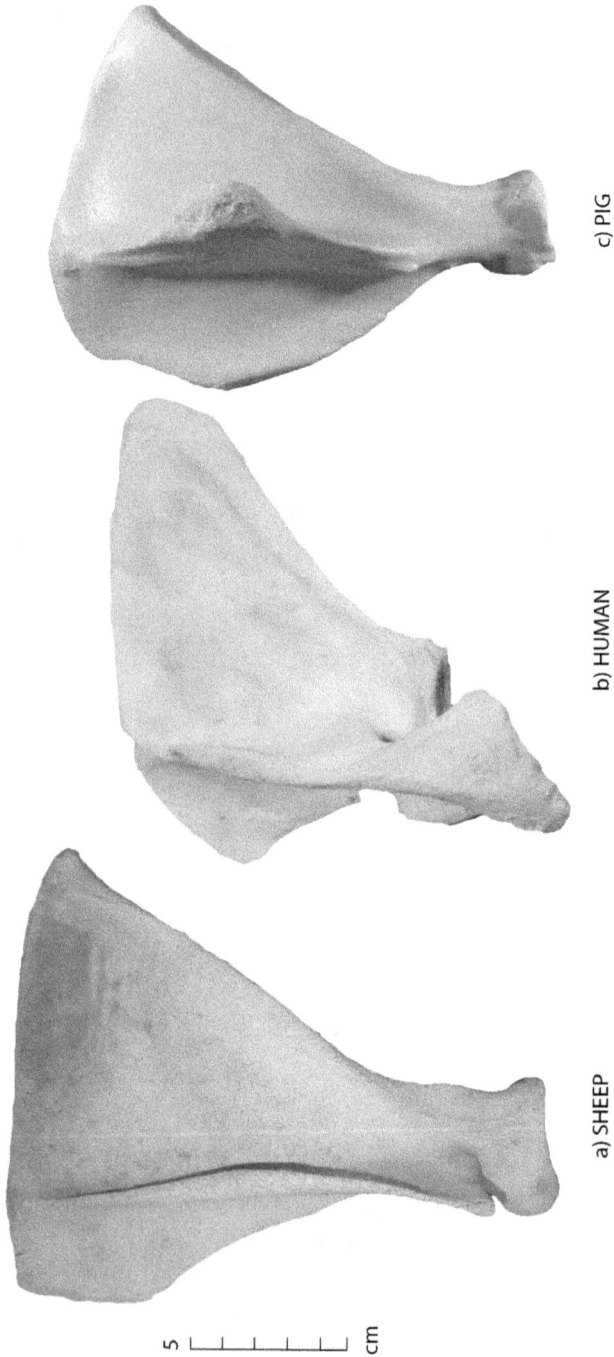

Figure 2.4: Scapula in dorsal view; (a) sheep, (b) human and (c) pig.

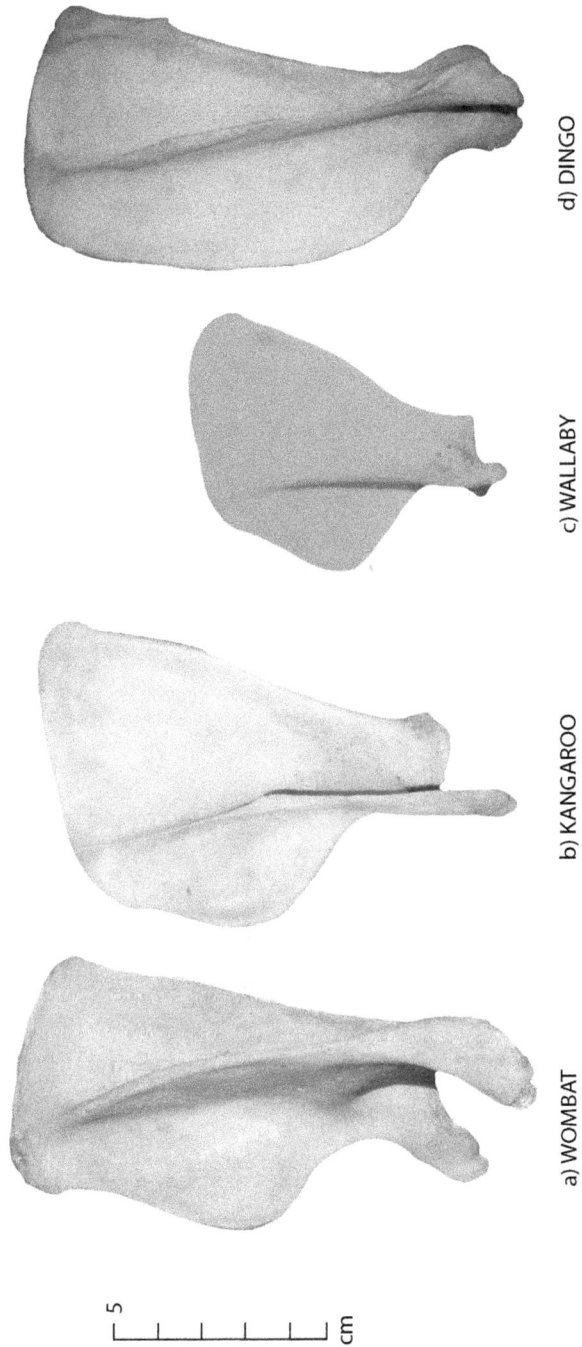

Figure 2.5: Scapula in dorsal view; (a) wombat, (b) kangaroo, (c) wallaby and (d) dingo.

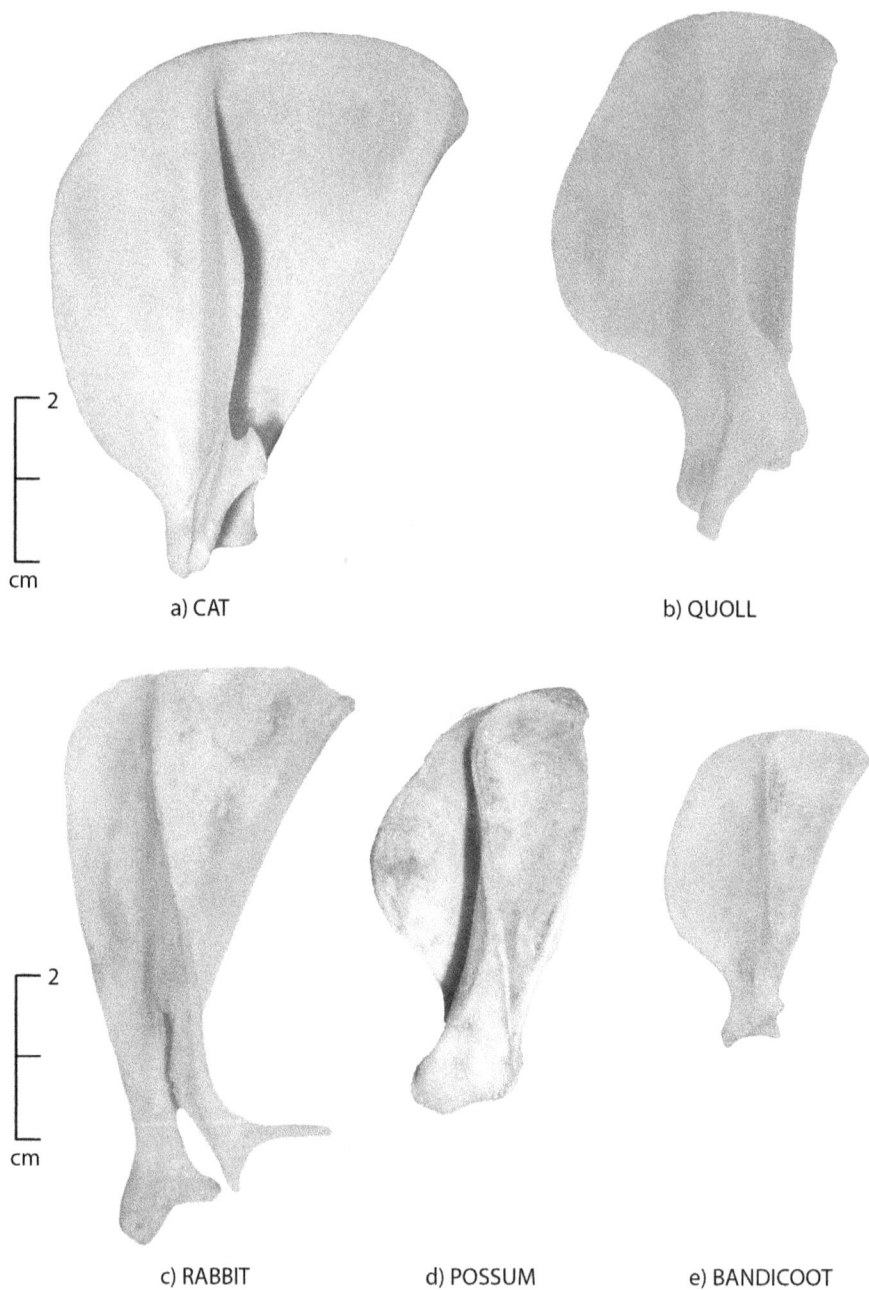

Figure 2.6: Scapula in dorsal view; (a) cat, (b) quoll, (c) rabbit, (d) brushtail possum and (e) bandicoot.

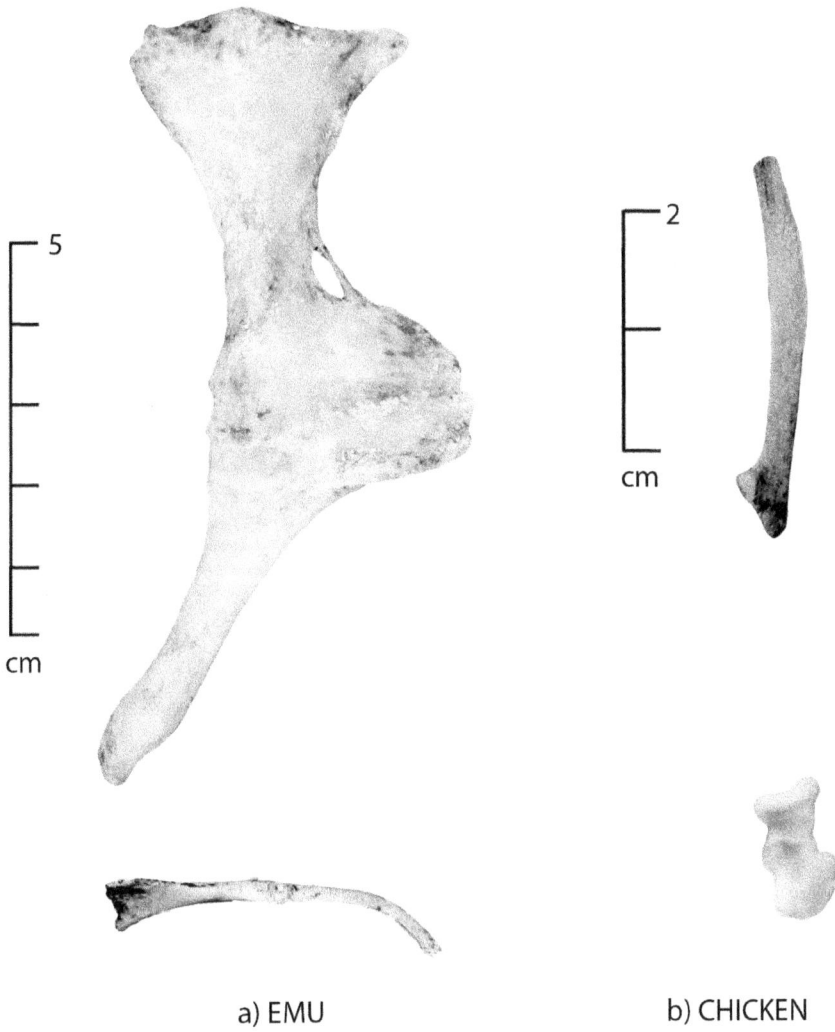

Figure 2.7: Scapula in dorsal view and detail of glenoid fossa; (a) emu and (b) chicken.

GLENOID FOSSA

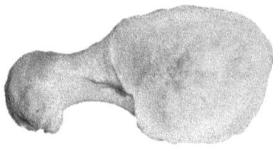

HORSE

COW

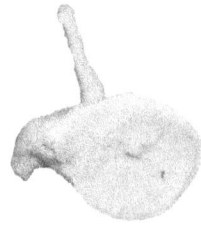

SHEEP

HUMAN

PIG

WOMBAT

KANGAROO

WALLABY

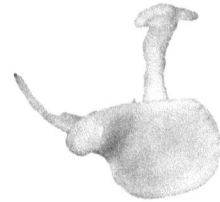

DINGO

CAT

QUOLL

RABBIT

BRUSHTAIL
POSSUM

BANDICOOT

Figure 2.8: Distal views of the glenoid fossa of all species. Those of smaller species are shown at an exaggerated size to show detail.

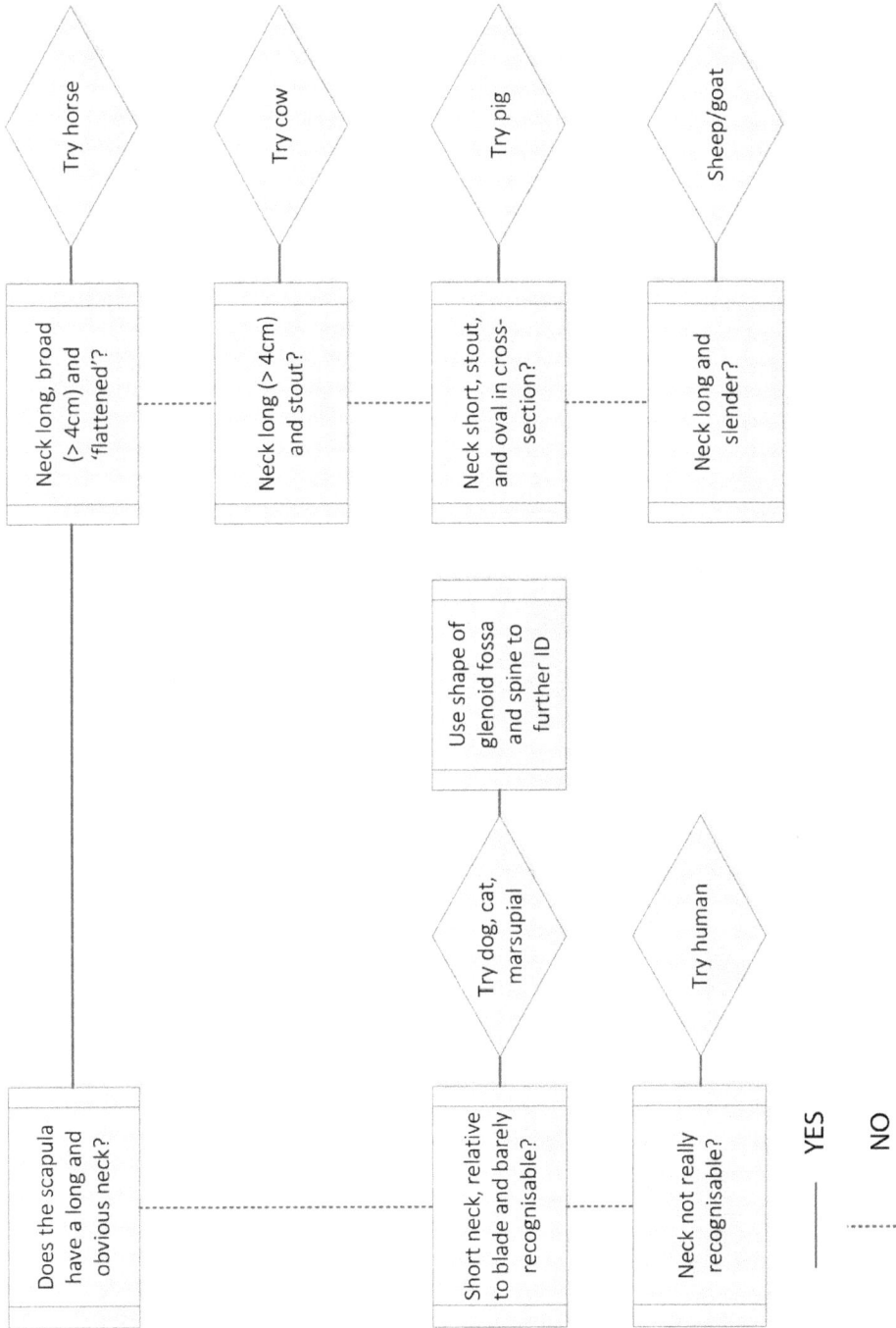

Figure 2.9: Scapula decision process 1. Use this decision process if the scapula is complete or if the medio-distal end is extant (using the neck, glenoid fossa, acromion and/or coracoid process).

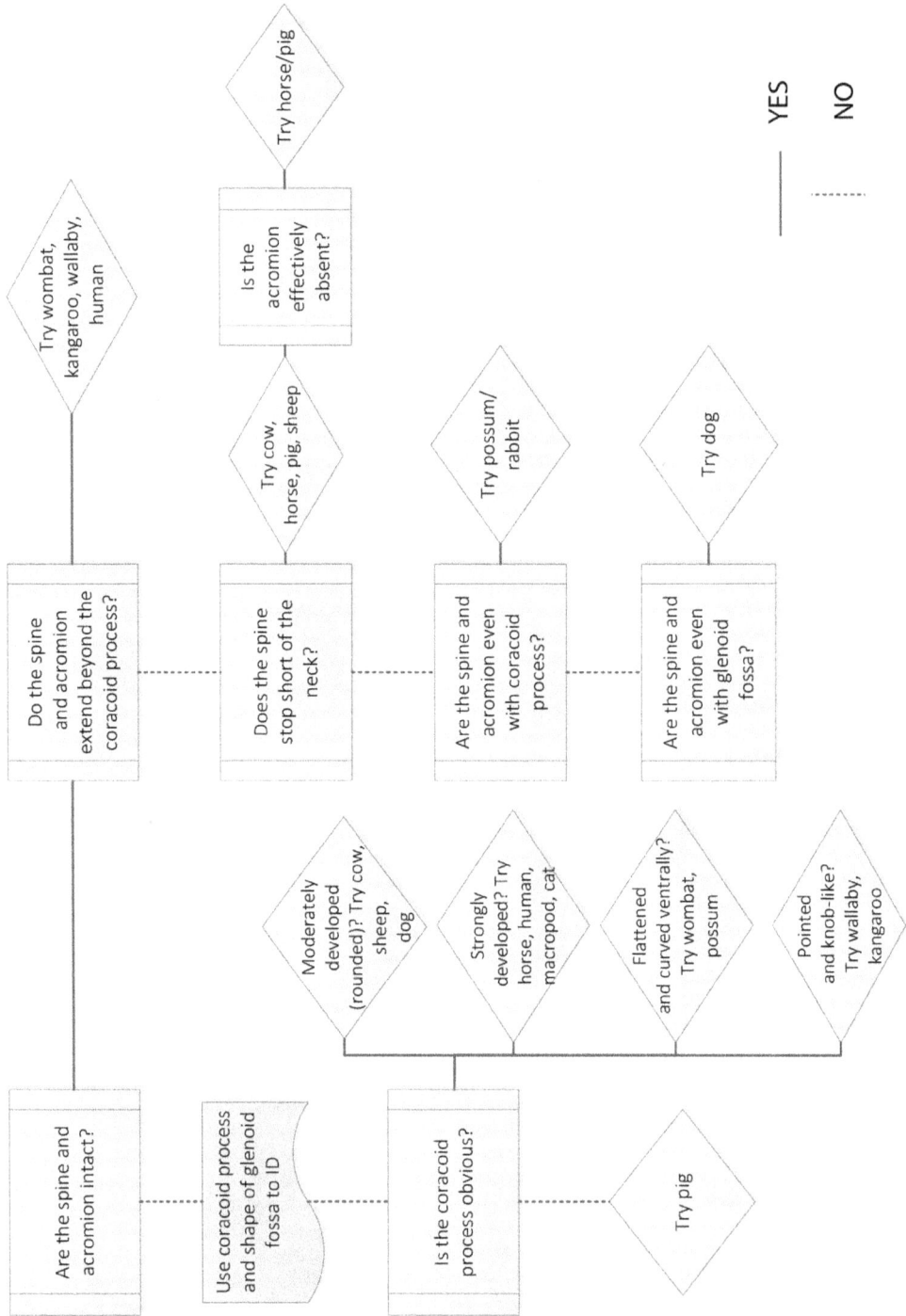

Figure 2.10: Scapula decision process 2. Use this decision process if you only have the acromion and coracoid process

3
Humerus

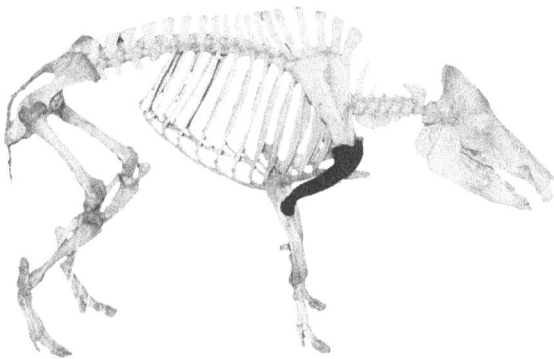 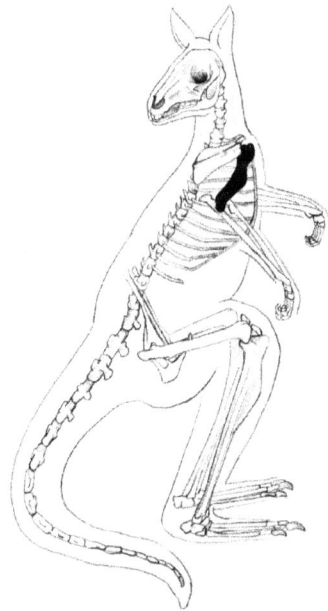

The humerus, or upper arm/fore leg bone, is commonly recovered in archaeological contexts. While it is often fragmented, the distal end which forms the elbow joint often remains intact, and is very useful in making positive species identifications.

Diagnostic features

Diagnostic features of the humerus are shown in Figure 3.1. The humerus is the largest bone in the upper arm. It is a long bone distinguished by a rounded proximal end, the **head** (1), which articulates with the glenoid fossa of the scapula to form the shoulder joint. While all species have a rounded humeral head, the diagnostic features around the head vary considerably, largely due to differences in locomotion. For example, the **greater tubercle** (2), to which are attached the supra- and infra-spinatus muscles, is very large and pronounced in most quadrupeds. The **lesser tubercle**/deltoid tuberosity (3), which lies on the lateral upper humeral **shaft** (4) and is an attachment point for the subscapularis muscle, is also more pronounced in quadrupeds, as is the bicipital/**intertubercular groove** (5), which lies between the two and serves as an attachment point for the biceps muscle. The spool-shaped distal end, the **trochlea** (6), is an articular surface that has a pronounced notch on its posterior side, the **olecranon fossa** (7), for articulation with the ulna. The olecranon fossa divides the distal humerus into **medial** (8) and **lateral** (9) **epicondylar** areas. The **capitulum** (10) is a further articular surface on the distal end, located on the lateral side, where the radius joins the humerus.

Macropods have two additional features that can often be used to help distinguish their bones. On the medial distal end, there is an **epicondylar foramen** (11), which is also found in felines, while on the distal lateral shaft, there is a pointed projection, called the **lateral supracondylar** or supinator crest (12). Several species also have a hole just above the trochlea, called a **supratrochlear foramen** (13). The humerus, radius and ulna form the elbow joint. The humerus is a highly diagnostic bone for species identification. If fragmentary, the humerus can still be distinguished from the femur, the element for which it is most commonly mistaken, by the following morphological characteristics:

- The head of the humerus is smooth and does not have a small hole in it (fovea capitum), unlike the head of the femur.
- The shaft of the humerus is 'twisted' as opposed to straight in nearly all animals (except humans).
- There is a nutrient foramen (small hole) on the shaft of the humerus, which points downward; it can be useful in distinguishing the humerus from other long bones.

Orientation and siding

In all species, the rounded head points cranially (toward the head), and the spool-shaped distal articulation points toward the feet. To side the humerus, hold it in anatomical position and orient the head so that it is medial/slightly posterior and the greater trochanter is anterior/slightly lateral – the olecranon fossa should be posterior. The lesser tubercle/deltoid tuberosity (if visible) will be lateral.

3 Humerus

(1) Head
(2) Greater tubercle
(3) Lesser tubercle/deltoid tuberosity
(4) Shaft
(5) Intertubercular groove
(6) Trochlea
(7) Olecranon fossa
(8) Medial epicondyle
(9) Lateral epicondyle
(10) Capitulum
(11) Epicondylar foramen
(12) Lateral surpracondylar crest
(13) Supratrochlear foramen

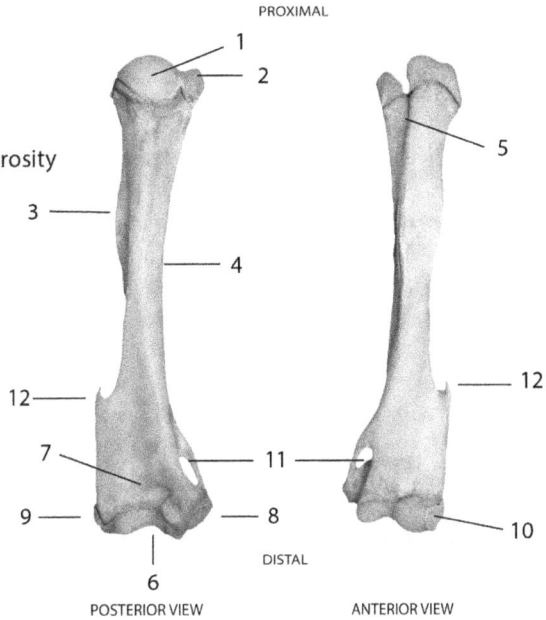

a) KANGAROO

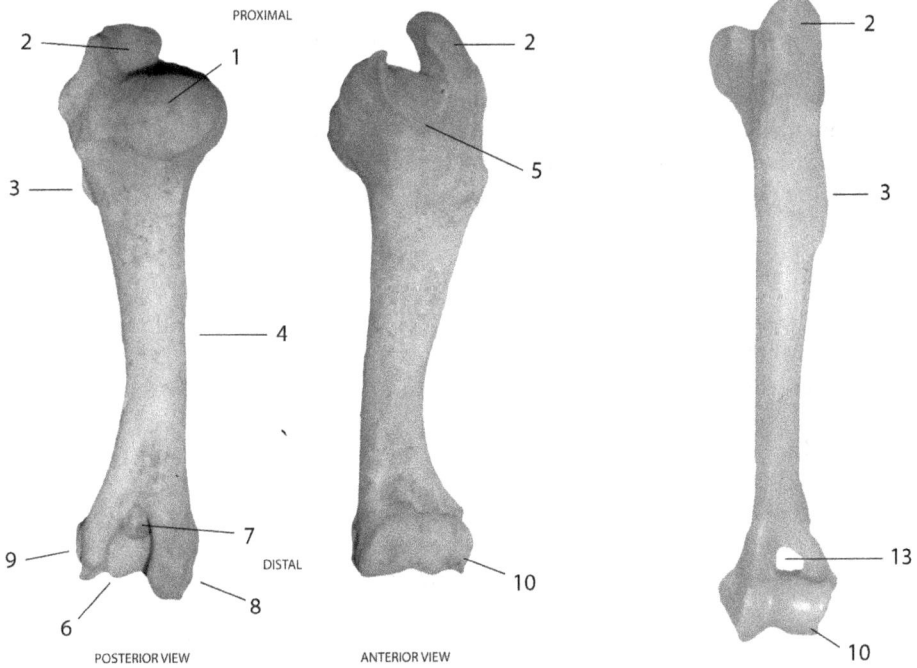

b) SHEEP

c) DINGO

Figure 3.1: Humeri with diagnostic features labelled; a) kangaroo, b) sheep and c) dingo.

Species identification

Refer to Figures 3.2–3.8 for species identification using the humerus.

If the humerus is **complete**, use the head and size of the greater tubercle on the proximal end, and the presence/absence of any of the following distinctive features on the distal end: supratrochlear foramen, supinator crest, epicondylar foramen, size of the lateral/medial epicondyles.

If just the **proximal** end of the humerus is extant, use the head and size of the greater tubercle for identification (see Figures 3.1 and 3.9).

If just the **distal** end of the humerus is extant, use the presence/absence of any of the distinctive features on the distal end: supratrochlear foramen, supinator crest, epicondylar foramen, size of the lateral/medial epicondyles (see Figures 3.1 and 3.11).

If all that survives of the humerus is the **medial shaft**, it is likely that identification of the element will be difficult enough. If you are able to identify the shaft fragment as a humerus, then the morphology of the humeral shaft may be used to narrow down the range of possible animals, as it varies by species. The following generalisations use a combination of the cross-sectional morphology and location/size of the deltoid tuberosity as clues to identification, and are divided by size of species (i.e. large, medium and small). However, species identification must be finalised by comparison with a physical reference collection.

Large animals

- Cows and horses have a round- to oval-shaped humerus shaft cross-section that is variable along the length of the shaft.
- Horses have a very prominent deltoid tuberosity that is located on the upper third of the proximal shaft (Figure 3.2a).
- Cows have a deltoid tuberosity that is moderately prominent and located on the upper third of the proximal shaft (Figure 3.2b).

Medium animals

- Humans have a square-shaped humerus shaft cross-section that is uniform in size along the length of the shaft.
- Large dogs, sheep, pigs and kangaroos have an oval cross-section that varies along the length of the shaft.
- Wombats have a cross-section that is twisted and irregularly shaped, with a very prominent deltoid tuberosity located on the mid-shaft (Figure 3.3c).
- In humans the deltoid tuberosity is only visible as a slight roughening or swelling on the proximal half of the shaft.
- Dingoes and kangaroos have a deltoid tuberosity marked by a slight ridge on the upper shaft.

Small animals

- In cats and rabbits the humerus shaft cross-section is very round in shape and fairly uniform along the length of shaft.

- In possums and chickens, the cross-section shape is oval and varies in size along the length of shaft.
- Both rabbits and chickens have no marked deltoid tuberosities (Figures 3.6a and 3.4d).
- Wallabies have deltoid tuberosities that are small and slightly raised.
- Possums have a prominent, pointed deltoid tuberosity just above the mid-shaft.

As in all elements, general size and robustness of the humerus are good measures to differentiate between species. Of the species included in this manual, horse and cow are the largest and most robust, while emu, kangaroo and wallaby are the slightest; smallest are cat, possum, rabbit, chicken and emu. When following the decision processes, always use size as a final determining factor in species identification.

Distinguishing between humans and animals

- In humans, the humerus is long, slender and fairly uniform in shape and size along its shaft.
- In quadrupeds, the humerus is robust, stout and has a variable shaft cross-section morphology (narrowest at the mid-shaft and becoming slightly wider at both ends).
- In quadrupeds, the greater tubercle is generally well developed, while in humans it is less developed and difficult to see.
- In humans and marsupials, the medial epicondyle is pronounced, while in introduced quadrupeds it is generally larger.

Macropods can be identified by the presence of both a supracondylar/supinator crest on the lateral side of the medio-distal humerus and an epicondylar foramen on the medial side. Most carnivores (dogs, pigs), and often rabbits, have a supratrochlear foramen.

Distinguishing between dogs and cats

- Cats have a epicondylar foramen and no supratrochlear foramen (Figure 3.4a).
- Dogs have a supratrochlear foramen and no epicondylar foramen (Figure 3.5d).

Distinguishing between marsupials

- Kangaroos, wallabies, (Figures 3.5b and c) and possums (Figure 3.6b) all have nutrient foramina on the anterior surface of the medio-distal shaft, while in wombats the nutrient foramen is located proximal-medially on the posterior surface of the shaft.
- Kangaroos, wallabies and possums all have very similar humerus morphology, so use size as an initial criterion to differentiate between them (Figures 3.7 and 3.8).
- To differentiate kangaroos from wallabies: the proximal epiphysis is the same shape in both; the only difference is size (e.g. in an average grey kangaroo, the proximal epiphysis is twice the size than that of a Bennet's wallaby).
- To differentiate wallabies from possums (both similar in size): the wallaby has a well-developed, larger trochanter than the possum. The possum has a well-developed deltoid tuberosity, while in the wallaby it is not well developed.
- The wombat humerus has a rather broad proximal end with a deep bicipital groove anteriorly and poorly developed greater and lesser trochanters.

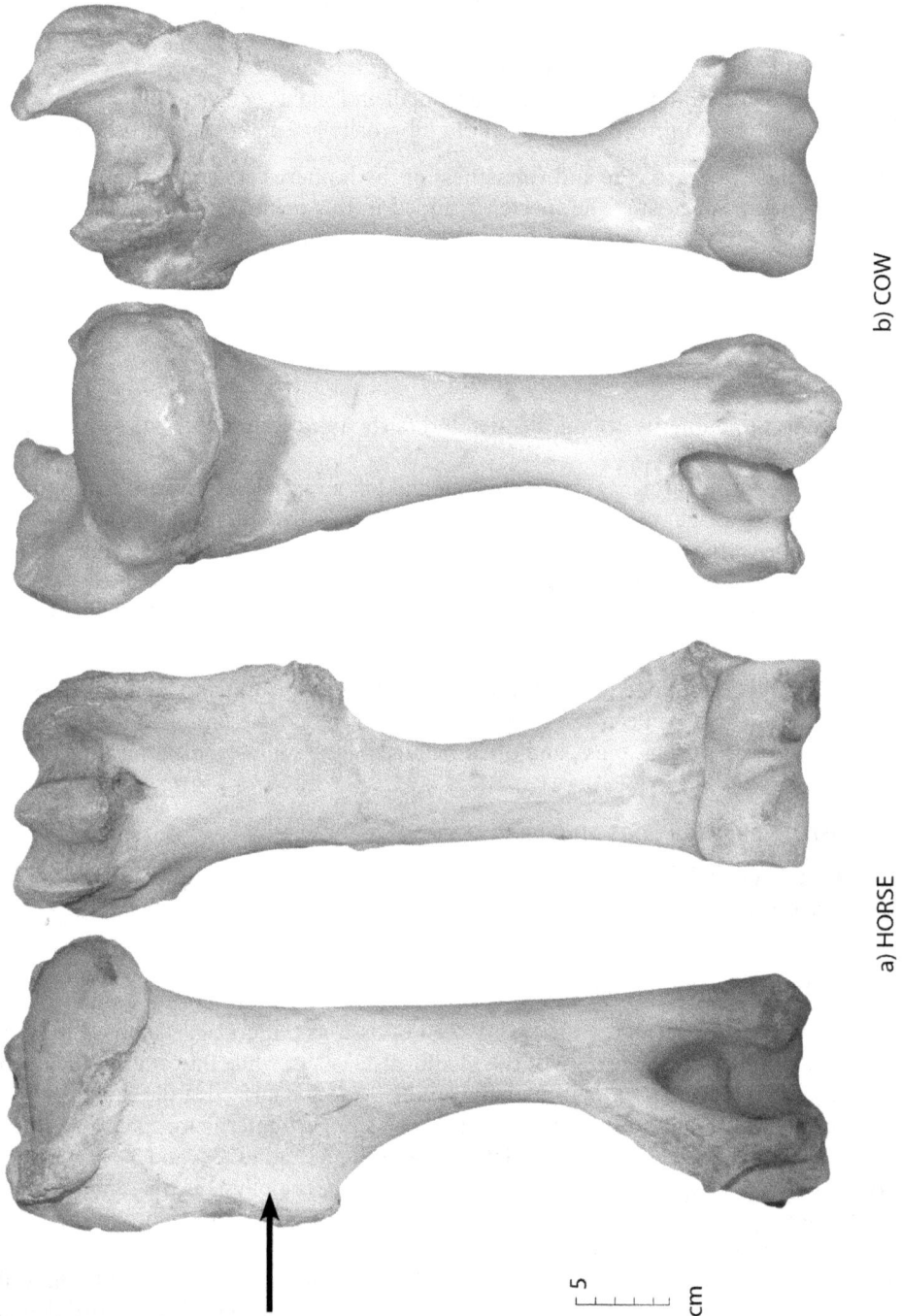

Figure 3.2: Posterior and anterior views of the humerus; (a) horse and (b) cow. The deltoid tuberosity is most prominent on the horse (arrowed), and is also present on the cow, though not as prominent and located on the upper third of the proximal shaft.

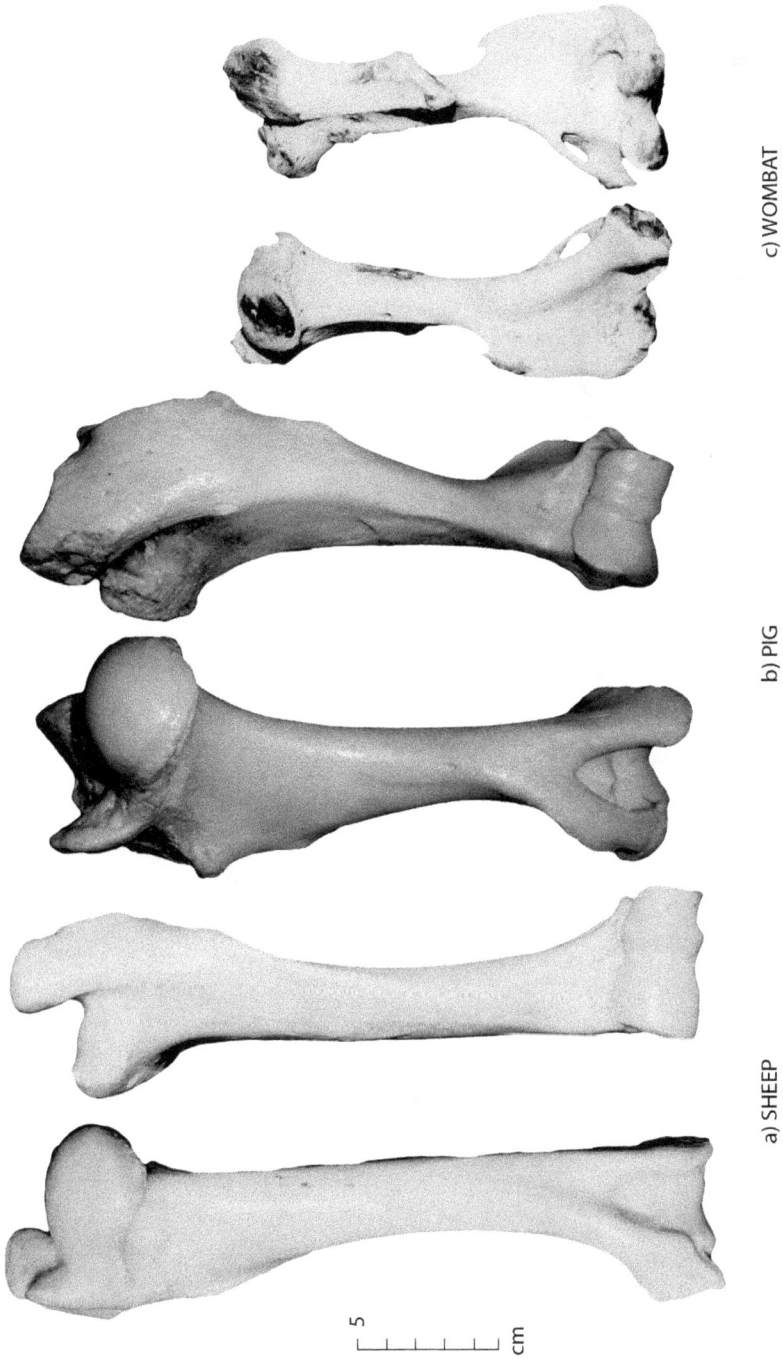

Figure 3.3: Posterior and anterior views of the humerus; (a) sheep, (b) pig and (c) wombat.

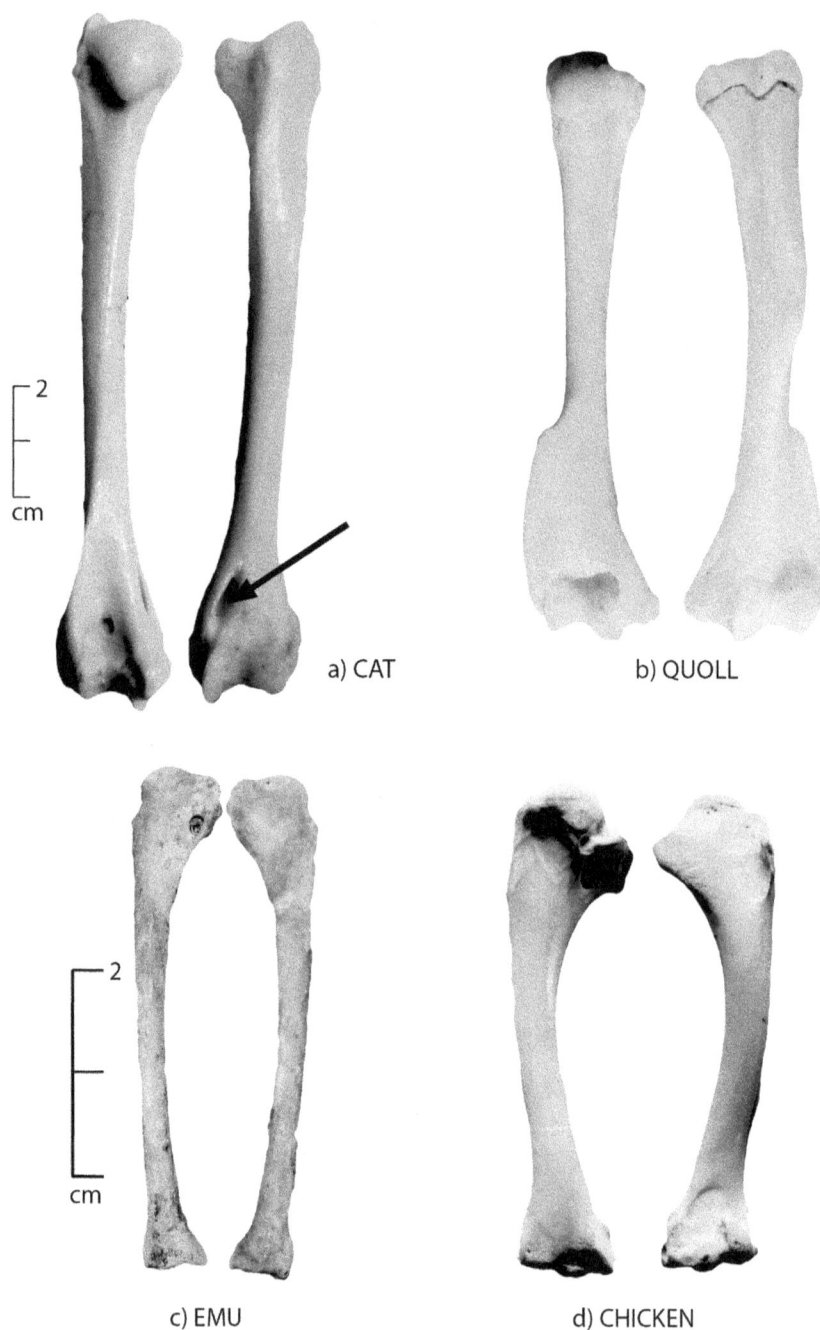

Figure 3.4: Posterior and anterior views of the humerus; (a) cat, (b) quoll, (c) emu and (d) chicken. The chicken and emu have no marked deltoid tuberosity, while cats have an epicondylar foramen (arrowed).

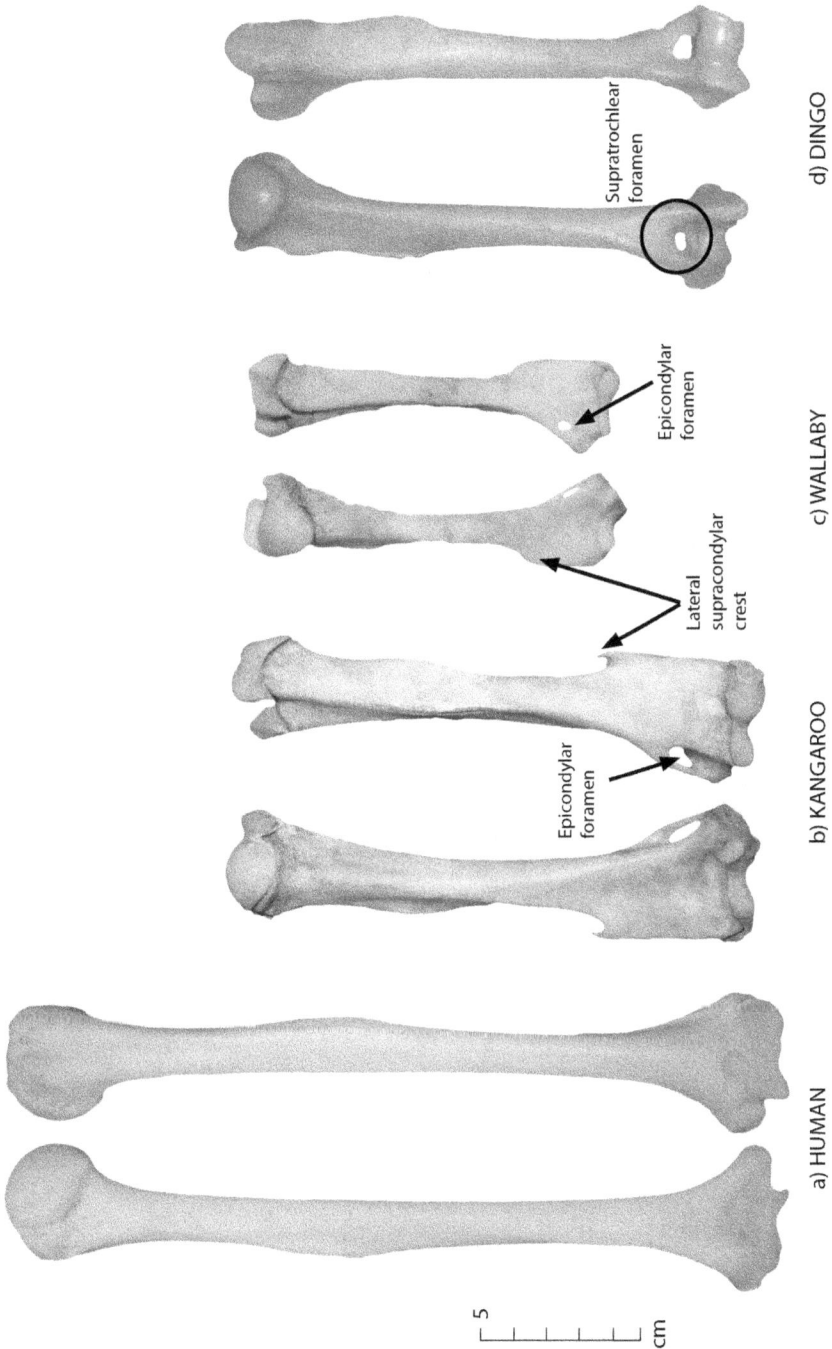

Figure 3.5: Posterior and anterior views of the humerus; (a) human, (b) kangaroo, (c) wallaby and (d) dingo. Dingoes have a supratrochlear foramen (circled). These views have been angled slightly to illustrate the lateral supracondylar crest and the epicondylar foramen.

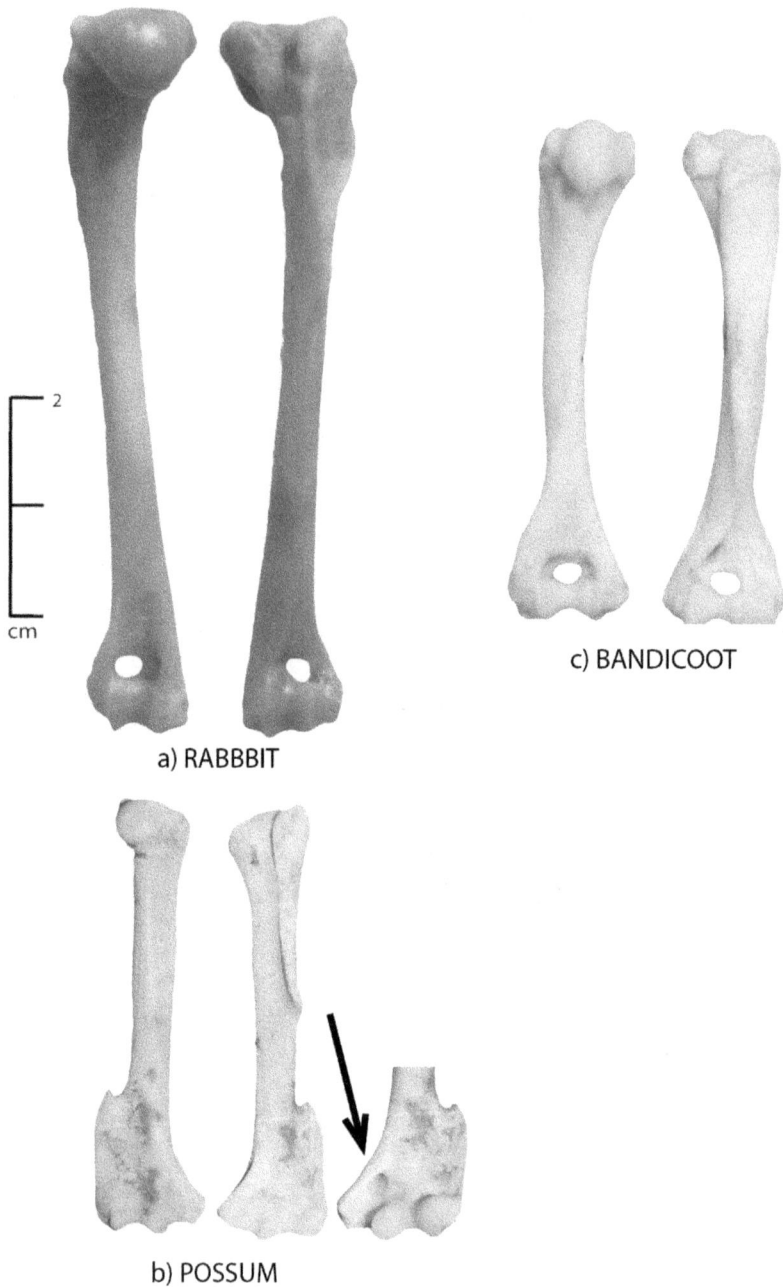

Figure 3.6: Posterior and anterior views of the humerus; (a) rabbit, (b) brushtail possum and (c) bandicoot. Note the nutrient foramen on the brushtail possum; an extra view is provided to show its location (arrow).

PROXIMAL HUMERUS

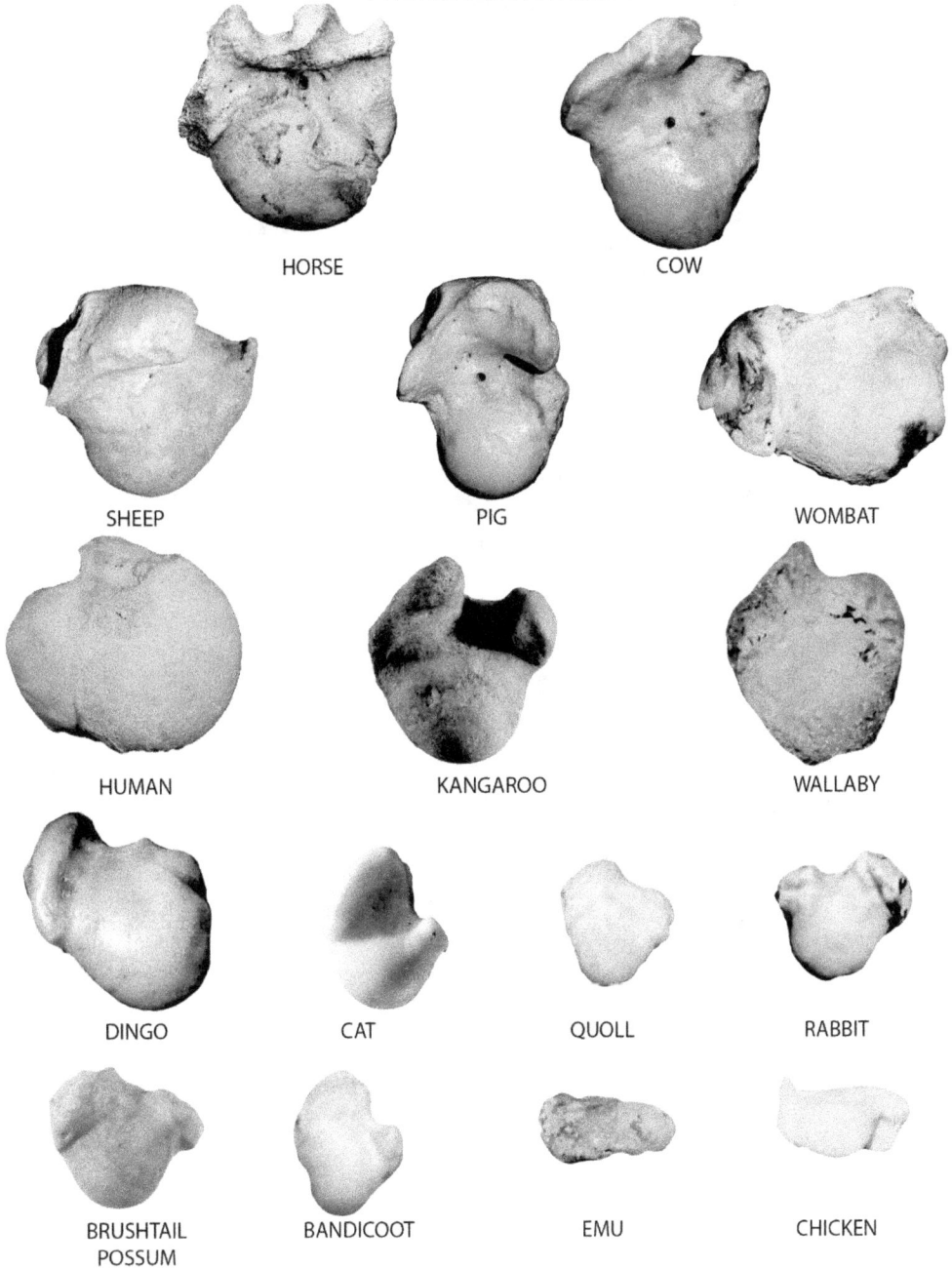

HORSE COW

SHEEP PIG WOMBAT

HUMAN KANGAROO WALLABY

DINGO CAT QUOLL RABBIT

BRUSHTAIL BANDICOOT EMU CHICKEN
POSSUM

Figure 3.7: Proximal humerus of all species (in order of decreasing size). Those of smaller species are shown at an exaggerated size to show details.

DISTAL HUMERUS

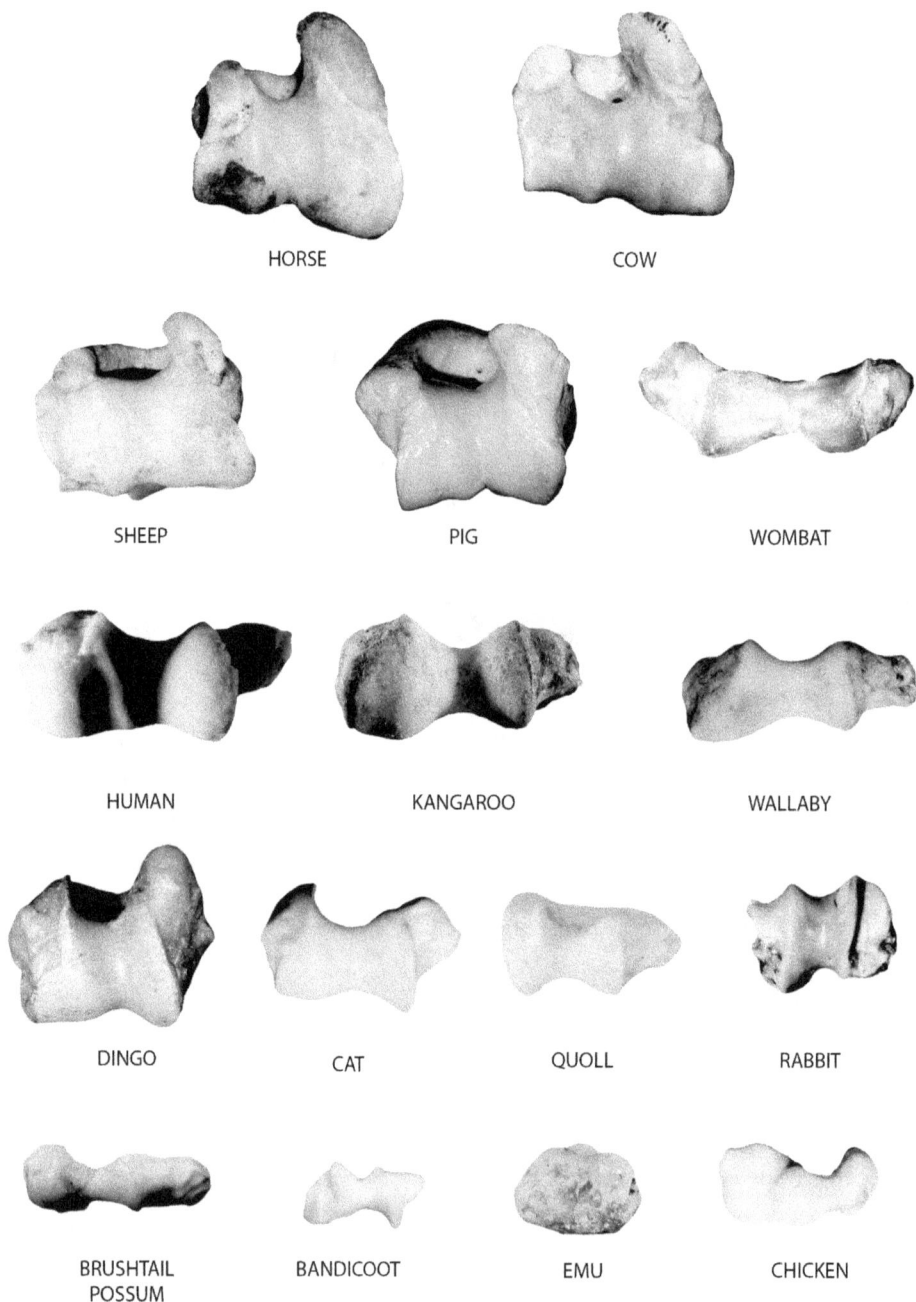

HORSE   COW

SHEEP   PIG   WOMBAT

HUMAN   KANGAROO   WALLABY

DINGO   CAT   QUOLL   RABBIT

BRUSHTAIL   BANDICOOT   EMU   CHICKEN
POSSUM

Figure 3.8: Distal humerus of all species (in order of decreasing size). Those of smaller species are shown at an exaggerated size to show details.

Common state in archaeological assemblages

The distal humerus of many quadrupeds is a delicacy for carnivores who love to chew, and is therefore commonly missing from many historic assemblages. The proximal and medial humerus often fare better, and are frequently intact in older animals. However, many species (especially sheep, goats, pigs and cattle) are slaughtered at an age before the proximal and distal epiphyses fuse, and these are therefore commonly missing in assemblages where these animals were slaughtered at a younger age. The humeri of macropods and emus are rather small, compared to the other skeletal elements, and are also frequently absent from archaeological assemblages. The humerus is a bone that frequently bears traces of butchery on quadrupedal animals, especially in assemblages that date after the introduction of the band saw. Marks from butchery are commonly found just above the distal articulation with the radius/ulna to form a shoulder/forequarter meat cut. The humeral mid-shaft is also commonly found in many archaeological assemblages and its cross-sectional morphology can be used as an indicator of species.

Figure 3.9: Humerus decision process 1. Use this decision process to identify species when the proximal end of the humerus is extant and large.

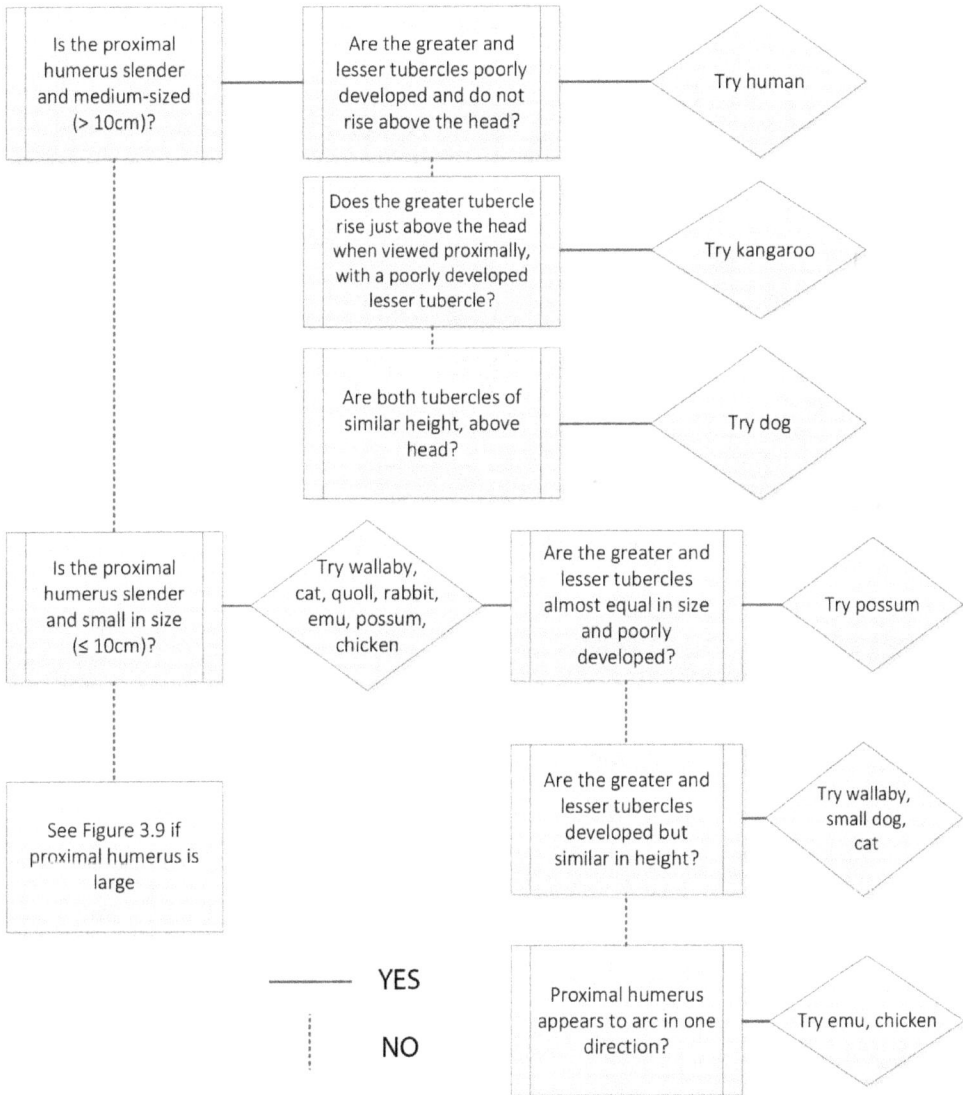

Figure 3.10: Humerus decision process 2. Use this decision process to identify species when the proximal end of the humerus is extant and medium or small.

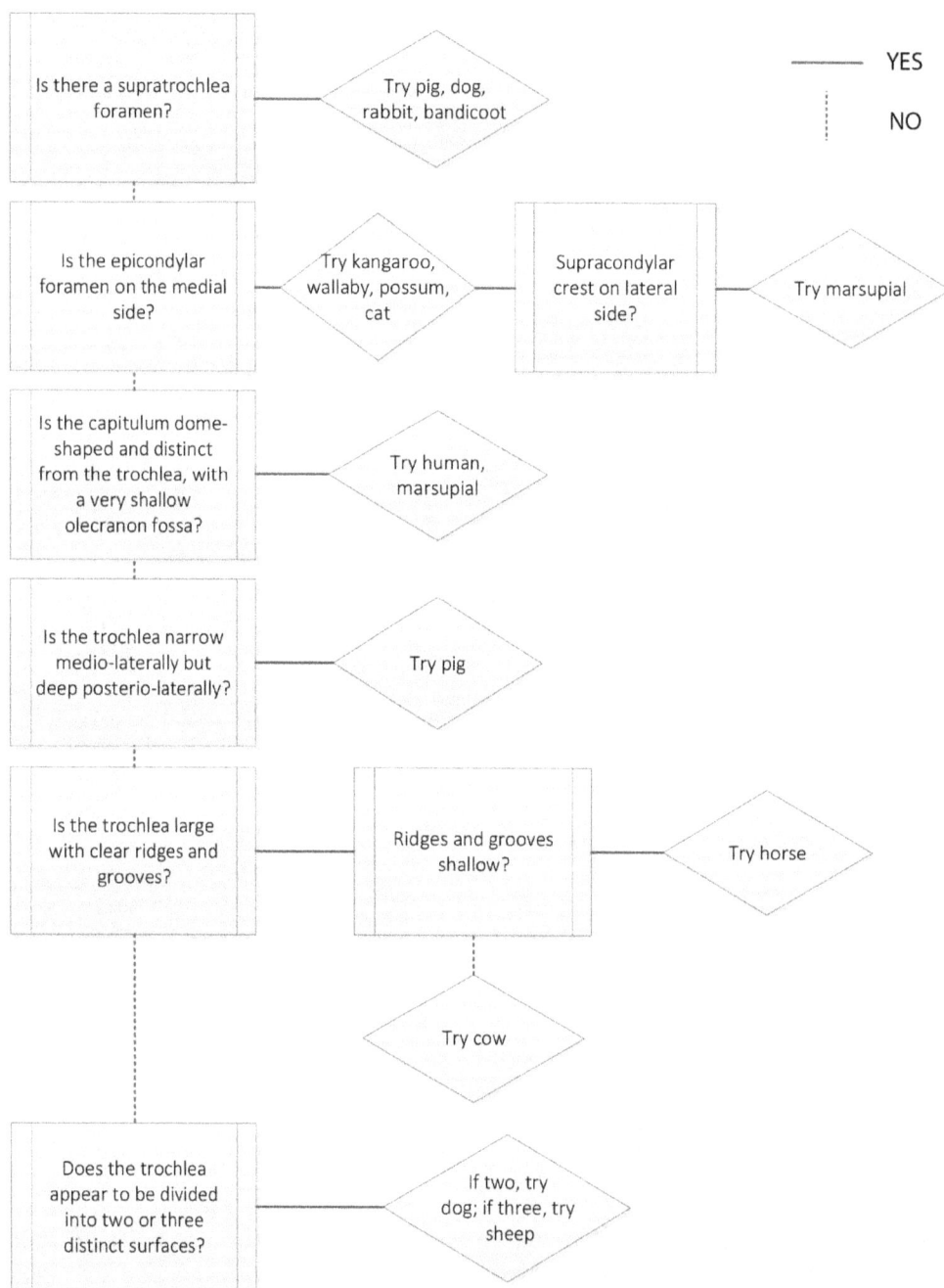

Figure 3.11: Humerus decision process 3. Use this decision process to identify species when the distal end of the humerus is extant.

4
Radius

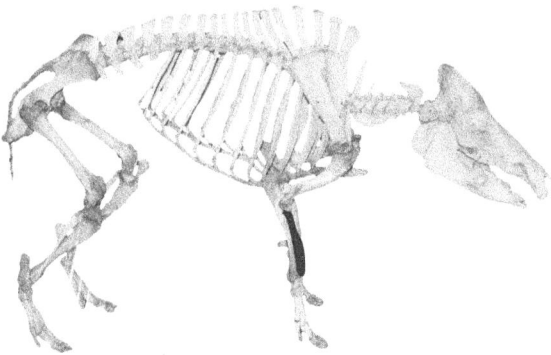

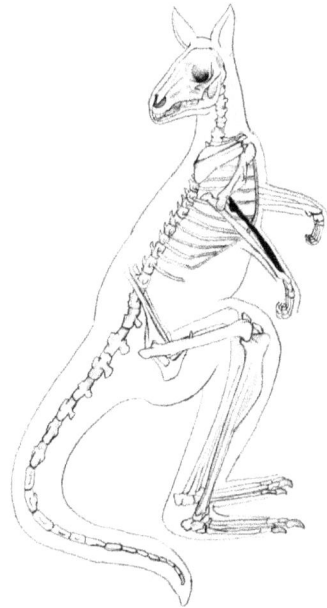

The radius is the larger of two paired bones that make up the fore limb (the other being the ulna). In bipeds (humans and many macropods), the radius moves over the ulna. This motion is reflected in the rounded proximal head that is generally characteristic of bipeds. Other species, particularly large ungulates (hoofed animals) like cows, horses, sheep and deer do not have a rotating radius, which often fuses with the ulna in adulthood. This results in a large 'oversized' radius, and an ulna that is greatly reduced in size. For this reason, some images found on the following pages will depict a fused radius/ulna. It is also important to note that in species with a fused radius/ulna, the two bones are generally separate in immature animals. In all of the other species presented in this manual, the two bones remain separate throughout life.

Diagnostic features

Diagnostic features of the radius are shown in Figure 4.1. The **radial head** (1) varies morphologically by species. In humans, macropods and carnivores, it is a 'swollen' articular area that articulates proximally with the capitulum of the distal humerus and trochlear notch of the ulna. In species with a separate radius and ulna, there is an articular facet on the radial head for articulation with the ulna. In species in which the radius and ulna are fused, the bone tends to be 'flattened' anterio-posteriorly (front to back) and convex anteriorly, with a wide proximal end onto which fits the ulna. Distally, the radius articulates with the ulna and carpals (depending on the species), and is distinguished by a **styloid process** (2) on the lateral side and an **ulnar notch** (3) on the medial side (in most species, except horse). The radius can be further distinguished by the **radial tuberosity** (4), located on the medial proximal shaft just below the head. The **radial shaft** (5) may also have a sharp **interosseous crest** (6) on its medial side.

Orientation and siding

Refer to Figure 4.1 for orientation and siding, and for species identification use the Radius decision process (Figure 4.9). To side the radius, place the head proximally (up), with the radial tuberosity anterior (front) and medial. The shaft is generally concave on the anterior side. The styloid process should be on the lateral side of the distal end, while the ulnar notch will be on the medial side of the distal end (in species with unfused radii). In some species, the medial edge of the radius (interosseous crest) is sharp. If siding a human, remember to side the radius, when in anatomical position, with palms facing up (imagine Da Vinci's famous man).

(1) Head   (3) Ulnar notch   (5) Shaft   (7) Ulna
(2) Styloid process (4) Radial tuberosity (6) Interosseous crest

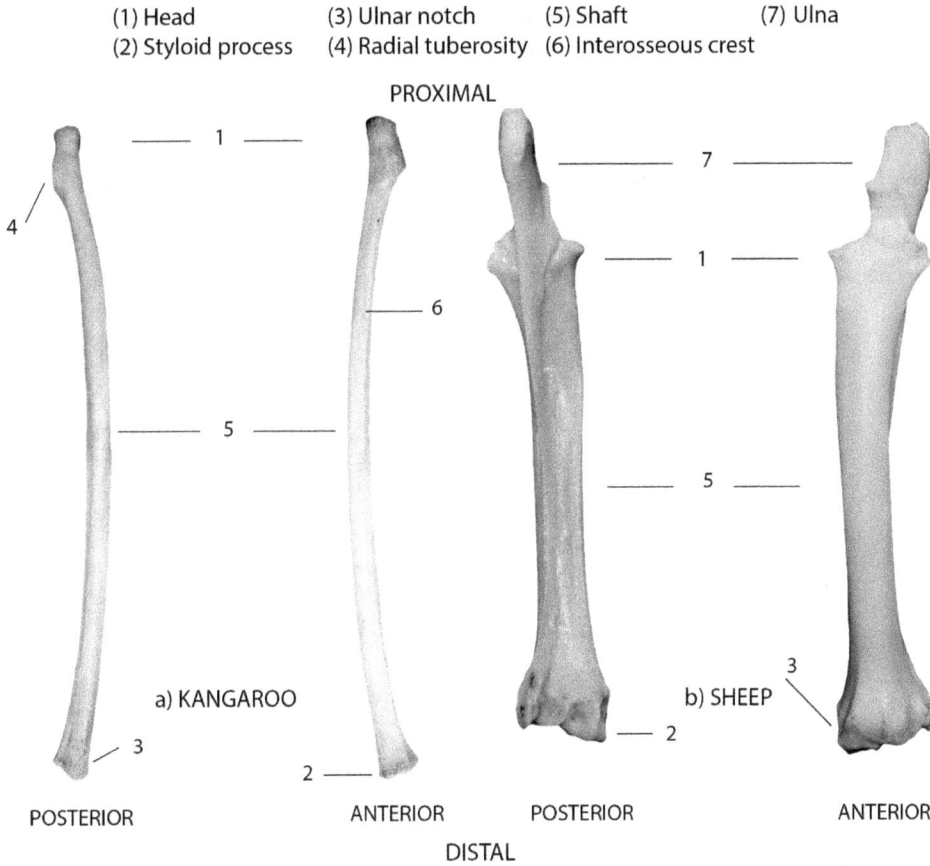

Figure 4.1: Radii with diagnostic features labelled; (a) kangaroo radius and (b) sheep fused radius/ulna.

Species identification

Refer to Figures 4.2–4.8 for species identification using the radius.

Humans, kangaroos, wallabies, cats, rabbits and possums have a long and slender radius with a rounded proximal end, and a round to oval cross-section. The radii of dingoes and cats are also long and slender, but have a D-shaped cross-section.

Distinguishing between human and kangaroo

To an inexperienced eye, human and kangaroo radii can appear quite similar. To differentiate between the two, consider the following (see Figure 4.2):

- Human radial shafts bear a sharp interosseous crest along their length, while in macropods this crest is very subtle and is only present on the upper third of the shaft (near the proximal end).

- Proximally, human radial heads are very round, while in macropods these are oval in shape. An unfused kangaroo radius may be easily confused with an unfused human radius. The head of the macropod radius is flush with the shaft, while the head of a human radius protrudes outward at the epiphyseal line. It is especially important that an expert be consulted if there is a possibility the bone could be human (see also the comparison of the proximal human and macropod radii given in Figure 4.8).
- The distal human radius is flared and curves medially, with the appearance of an askew triangle, while a straighter shaft and a sharp, distinct styloid process characterise the distal macropod radius.

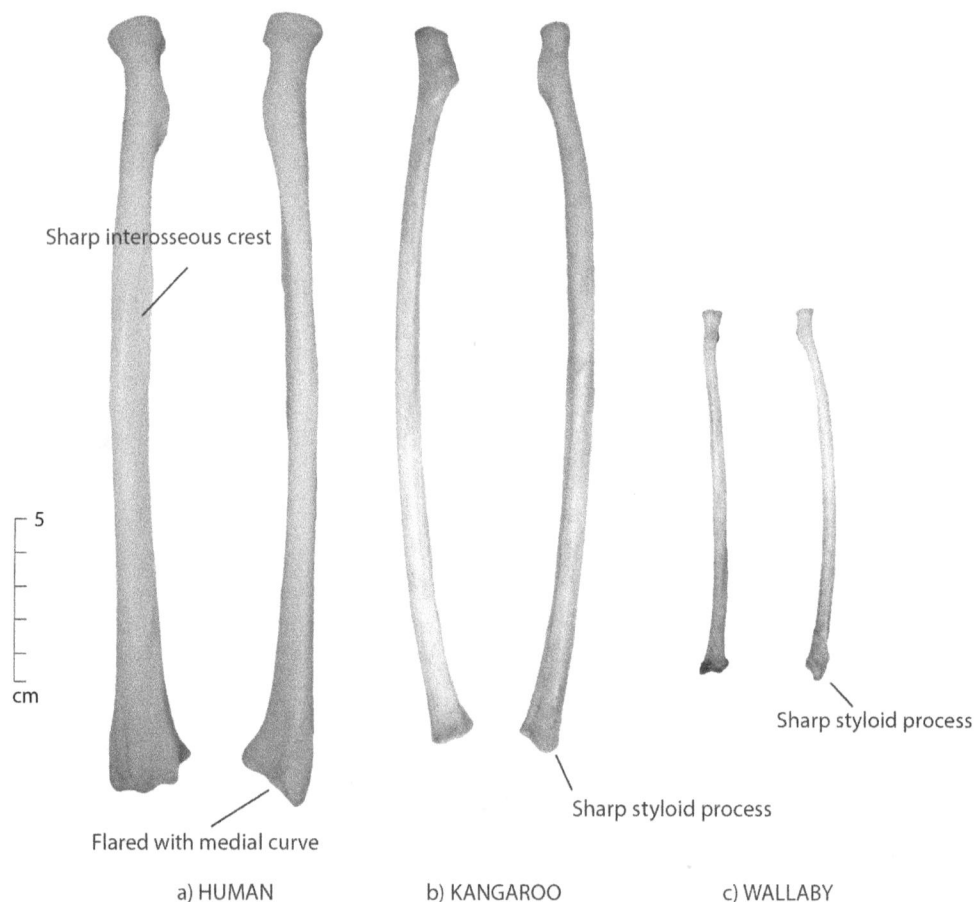

Figure 4.2: Human and macropod radius compared; (a) human, (b) kangaroo and (c) wallaby.

Distinguishing between humans and others

- A human radius has a very prominent, sharp crest along its shaft.
- A human radius can be differentiated from that of a carnivore by the kidney bean-shaped proximal articulation of the latter.

Other comparisons

- The radius and ulna are fused in adult horses, cattle and sheep (Figures 4.3 and 4.4a).
- Ungulate (hoofed animals) radial shaft fragments are characterised by a long appearance that is 'flattened' anterio-posteriorly, often with traces of an ulna shaft remnant on the posterior surface.
- When fragmentary, the proximal and distal portions of the radius of large ungulates are commonly mistaken for the distal tibia.
- The distal radius of quadrupeds is characterised by a set of 'ridges' (which may be canted) for articulation with the carpals.
- A dingo's radius (Figure 4.5d) is flatter than a cat's radius.
- The radius of a wombat is curved with a sharp interosseous crest that begins half-way down the shaft and creates a flattened distal half (Figure 4.4c).
- The radius of small macropods (e.g. wallabies, Figure 4.5c) is nearly indistinguishable from the radius of possums (Figure 4.6f). Use a comparative collection for differentiation.

Common state in archaeological assemblages

The radius of many quadrupeds, especially cows, horses, sheep and pigs, is one of the few long bones that is frequently found intact in archaeological contexts. Since the radius is commonly a robust bone for its size in these species, it tends to preserve quite well. In large species utilised for meat (e.g. cattle), primary butchery of a carcass tends to make an initial cut just above, or at, the articulation of the radius and humerus to disarticulate the upper from the lower leg. In smaller European 'food' animals (e.g. sheep or pigs), the radius and ulna are often left articulated with the humerus to form a leg cut (e.g. ham or lamb) that may be cooked with the bone intact. Rabbit radii are commonly intact, as rabbits were commonly cooked whole. These European cultural patterns of meat consumption generally result in relatively complete radii in good state of preservation in historical archaeological contexts. The radii of other species are subject to different preservation. For example, emu radii are rarely found intact, as the wing is either one of the first body parts to be scavenged or is left behind by hunters who take the meatier leg and torso back for consumption. In kangaroos, wallabies, and wombats there is little meat on this element, and it may also be left behind by hunters interested in higher meat-bearing elements. In naturally accumulated assemblages, macropod radii are commonly found articulated with the entire hand or wrist (ulna, radius, carpals, metacarpals and phalanges), as even scavengers tend to ignore this element. The same pattern is commonly encountered in dingoes, cats, rabbits, wombats, possums and similar small species.

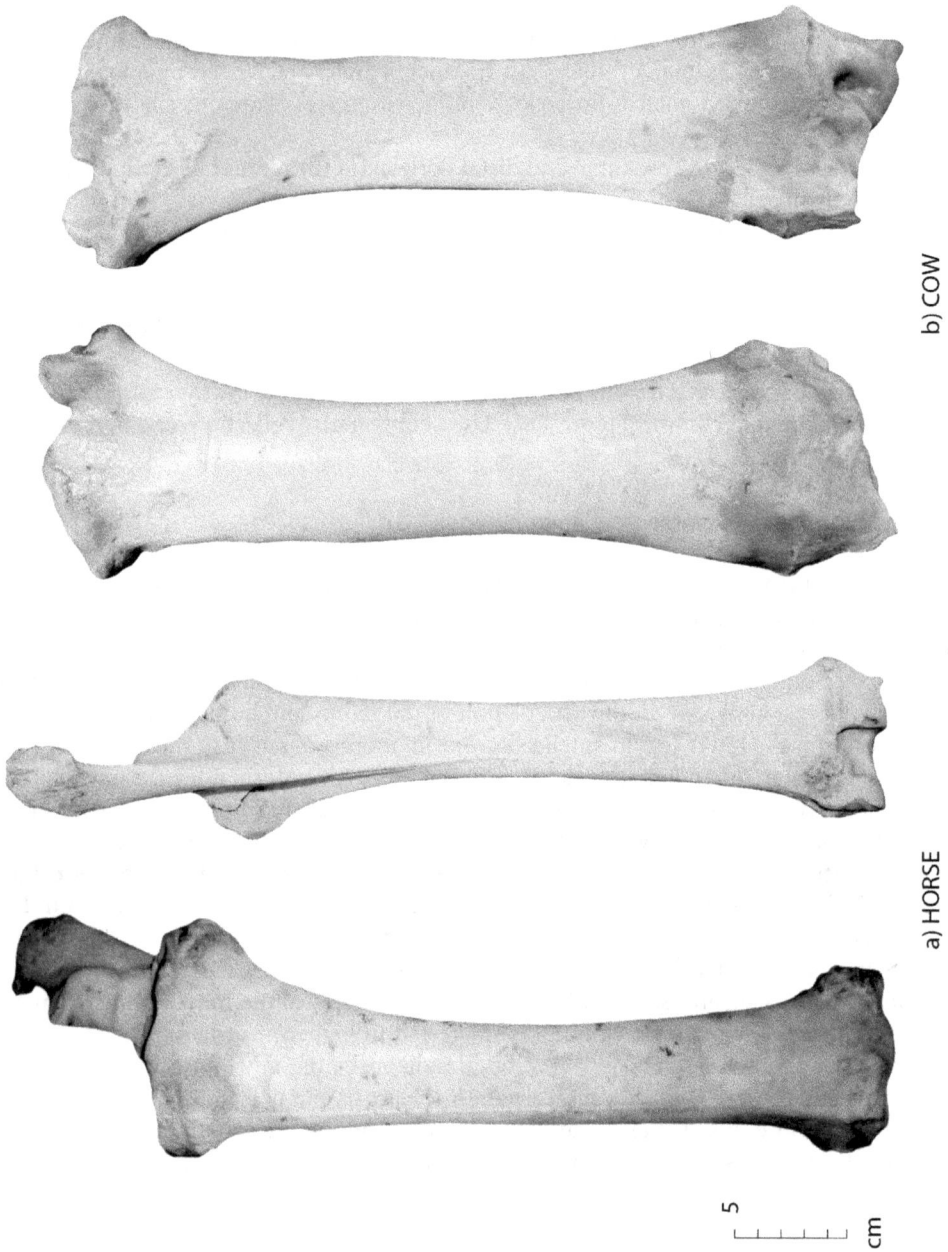

Figure 4.3: Posterior and anterior views of the fused radius and ulna of (a) horse and (b) cow.

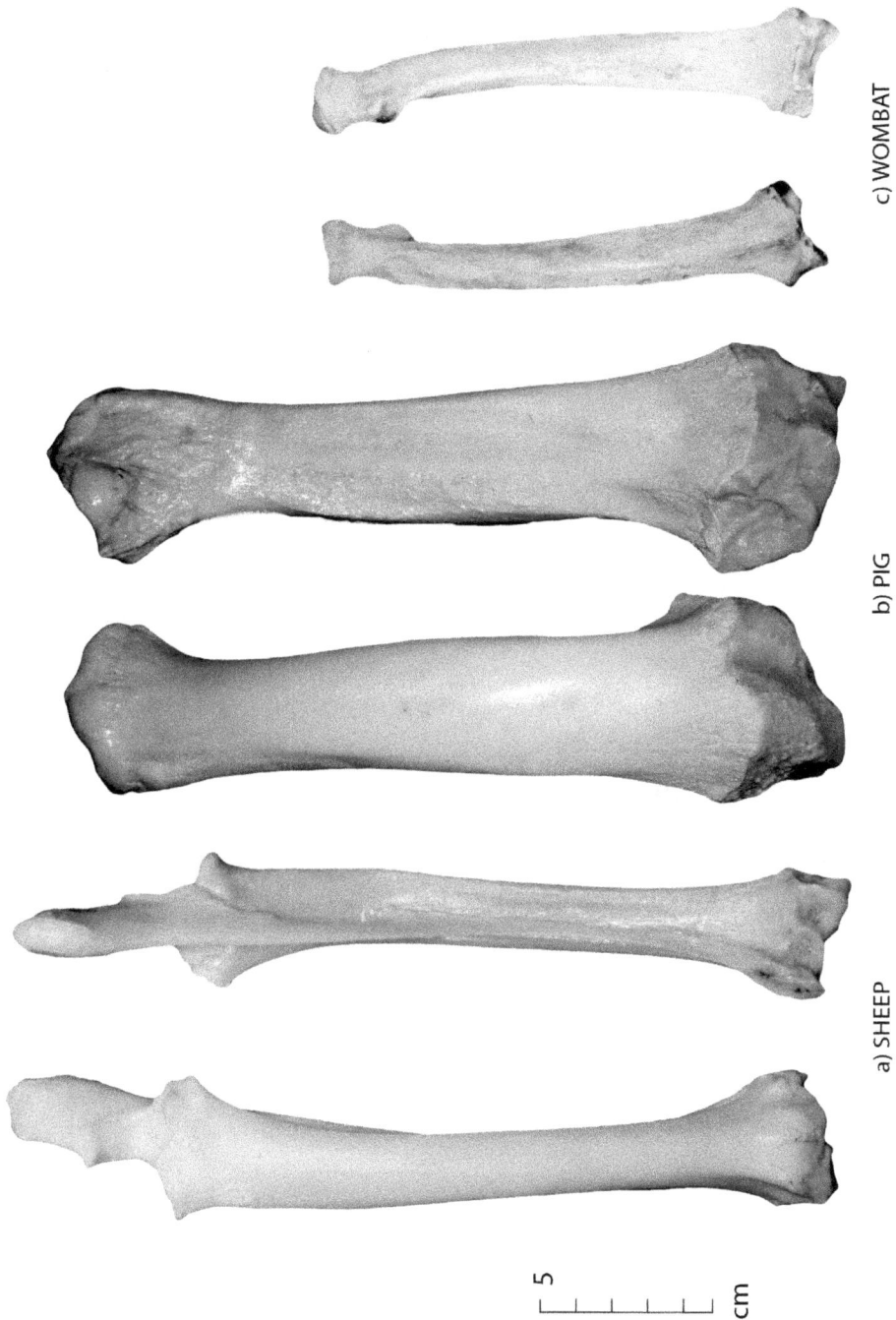

Figure 4.4: Posterior and anterior views of radii; (a) sheep radius with a fused ulna, (b) pig radius and (c) wombat radius. In quadrupeds the radius is more robust, and the set of ridges at the distal end that articulate with the metacarpal bones are visible on the pig and sheep.

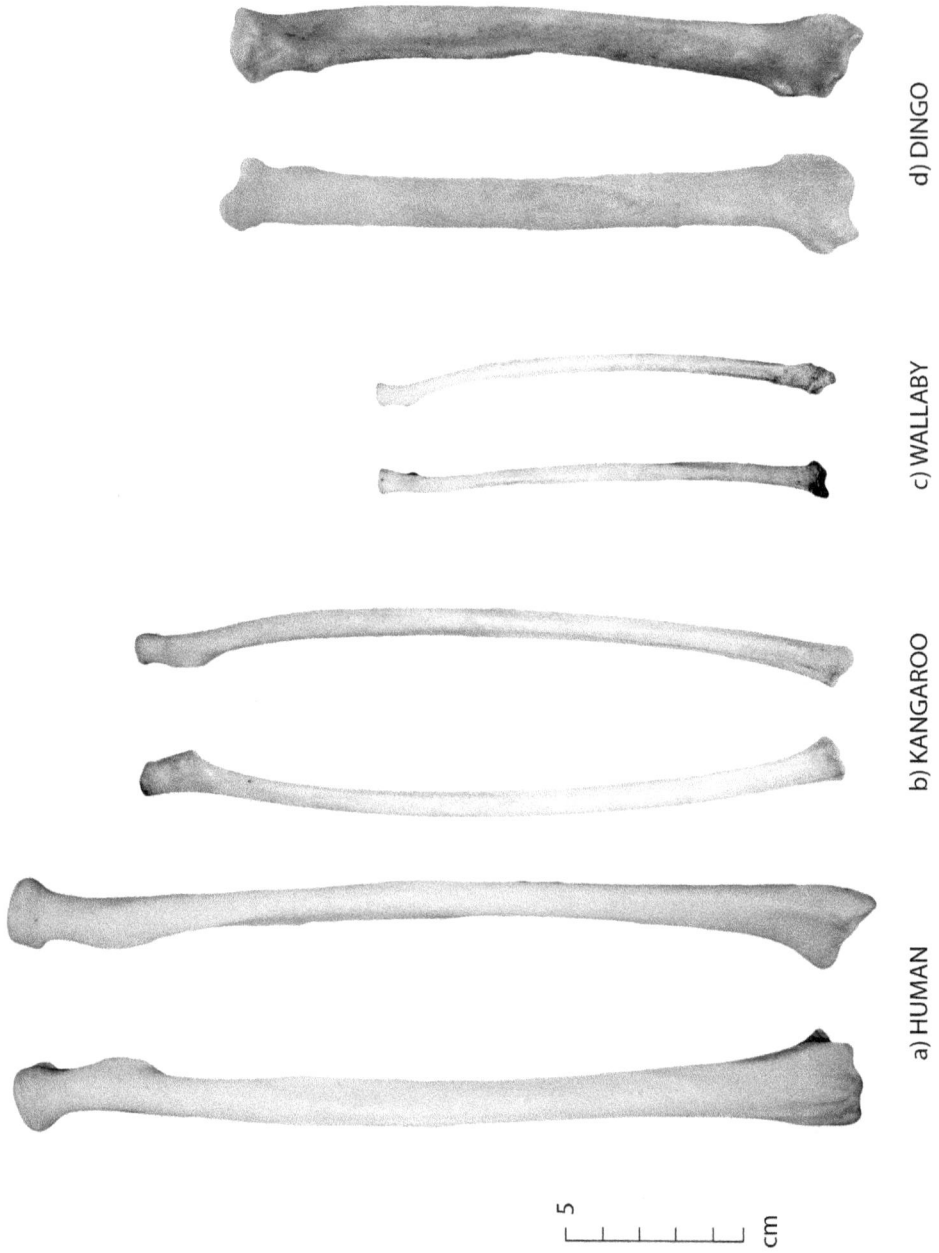

Figure 4.5: Posterior and anterior views of the radius; (a) human, (b) kangaroo, (c) wallaby and (d) dingo.

4 Radius

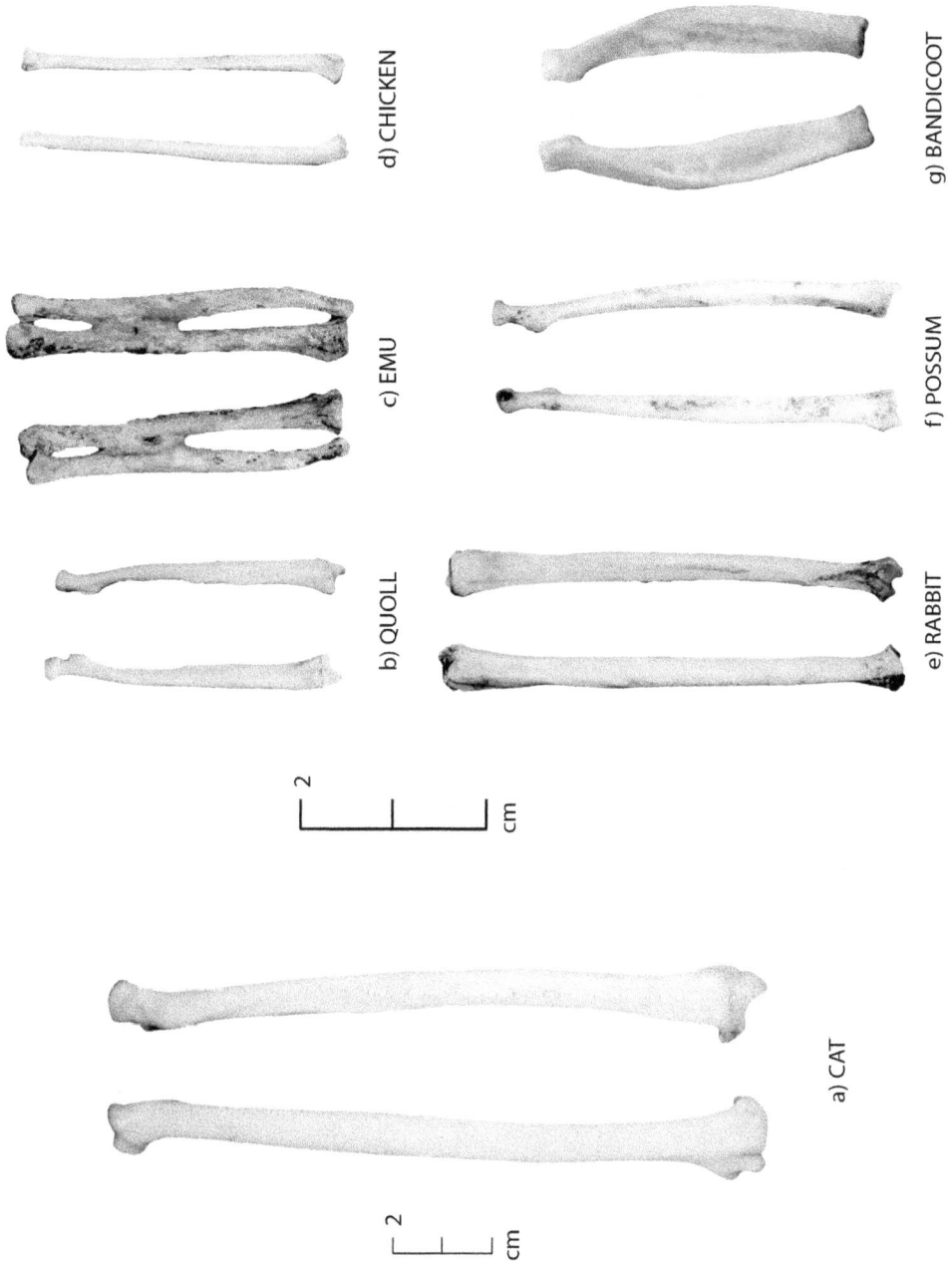

Figure 4.6: Posterior and anterior views of the radius; (a) cat, (b) quoll, (c) emu, (d) chicken, (e) rabbit, (f) brushtail possum and (g) bandicoot (unfused).

PROXIMAL RADIUS

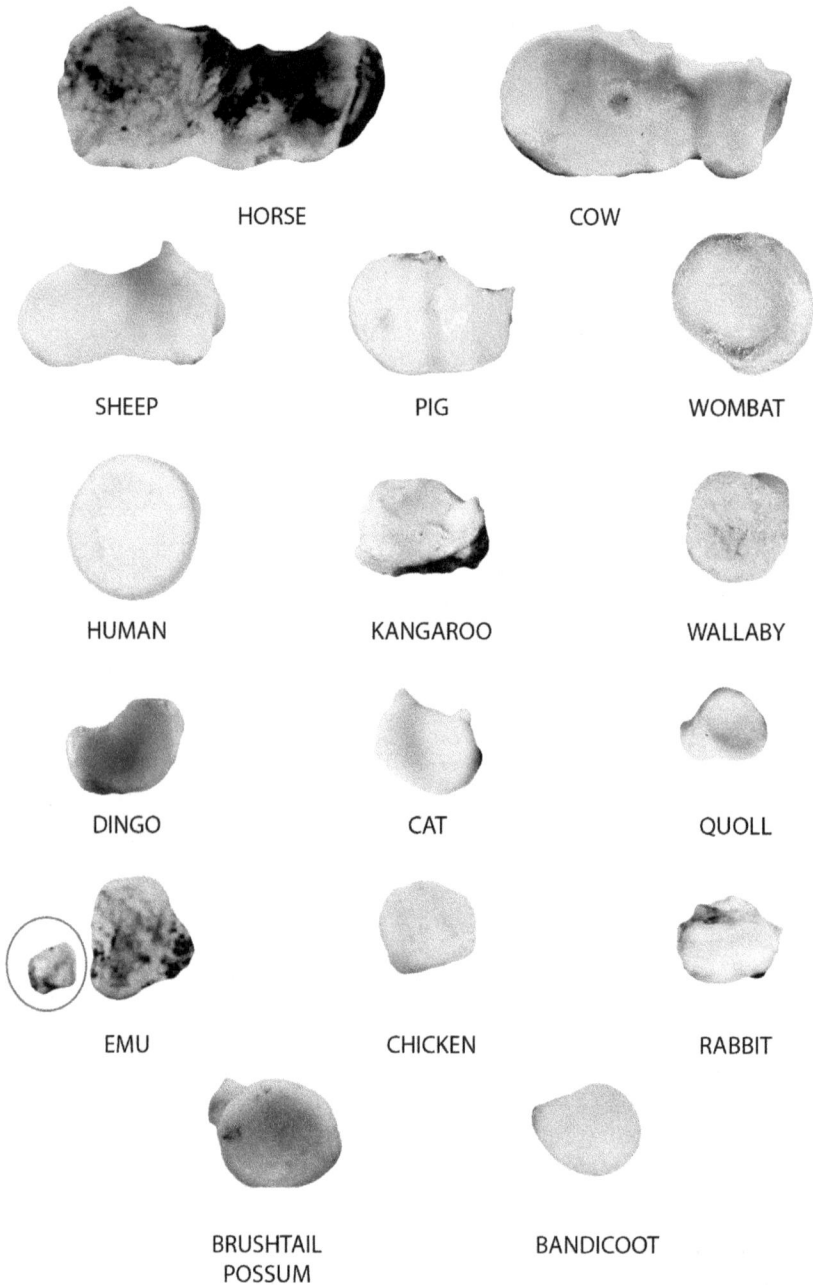

Figure 4.7: Proximal radius of all species (in order of decreasing size). The emu radius is circled.

DISTAL RADIUS

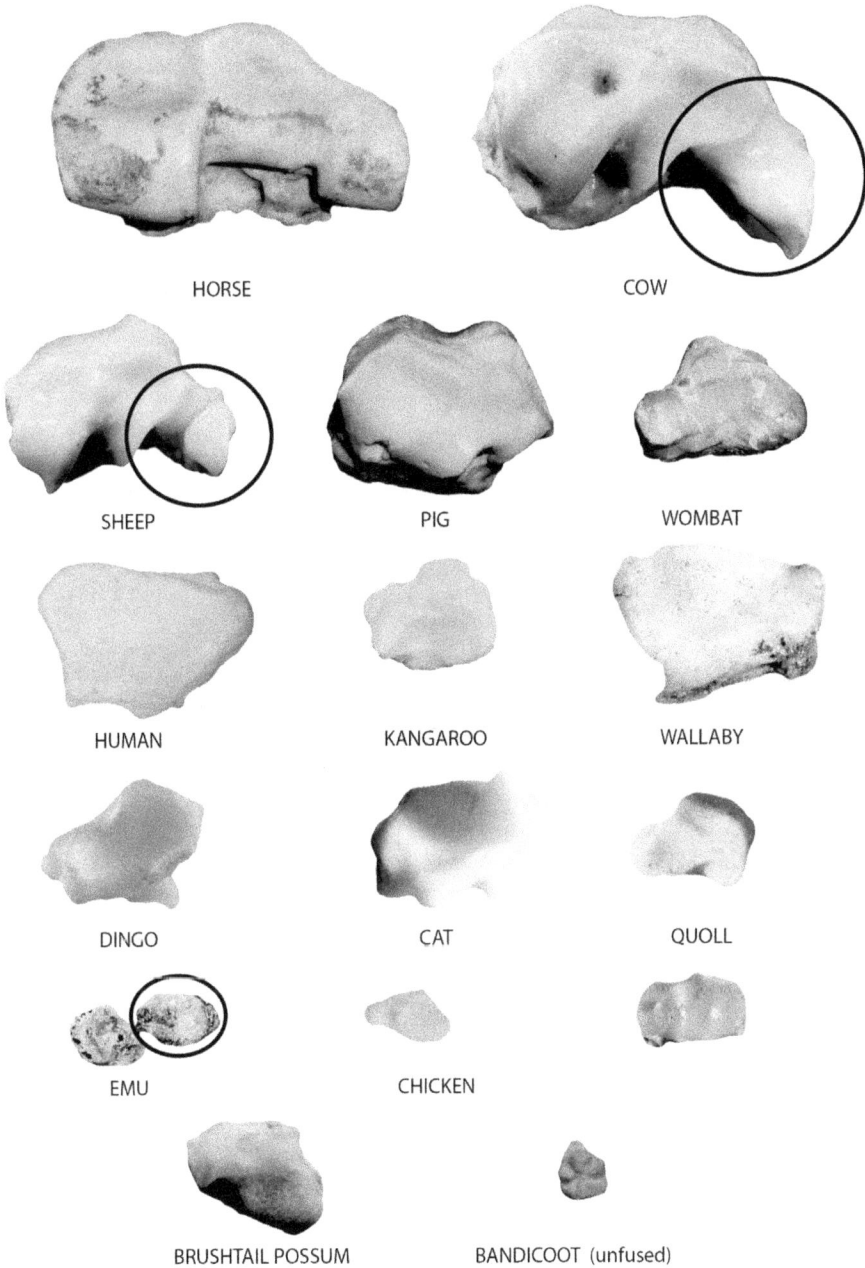

Figure 4.8: Distal radius of all species (in order of decreasing size). Those of smaller species are shown at an exaggerated size to show detail. The cow and sheep ulna remain attached and are circled. The emu radius is also circled.

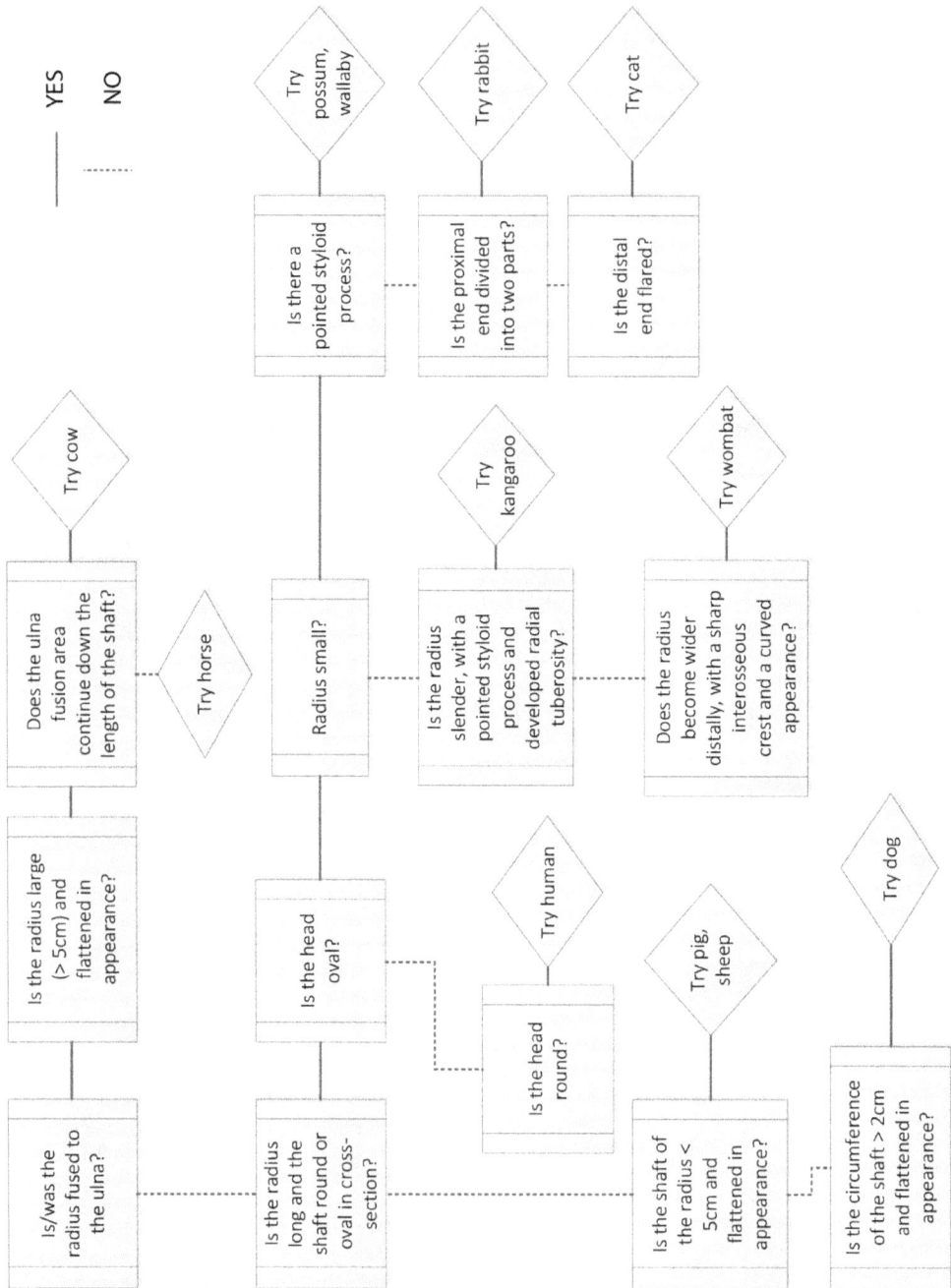

Figure 4.9: Radius decision process.

5
Ulna

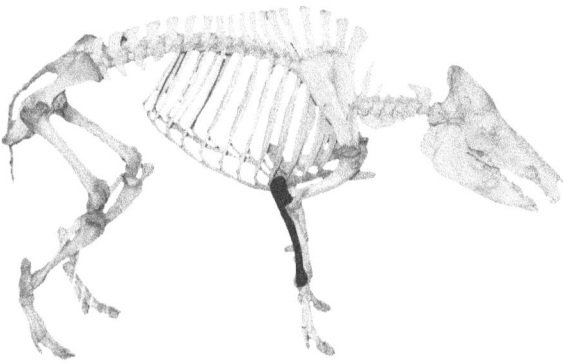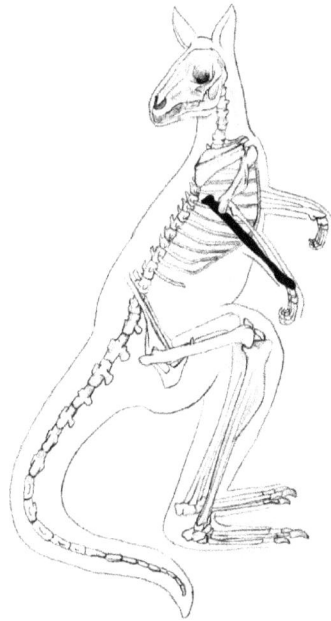

The ulna is generally the smaller of two paired bones that make up the fore limb (the other being the radius). It is responsible for flexion and extension, and forms a hinge with the humerus. In many species, the ulna is lateral to the radius, however in ungulates (hoofed animals), where it is often fused to the radius, it is posterior.

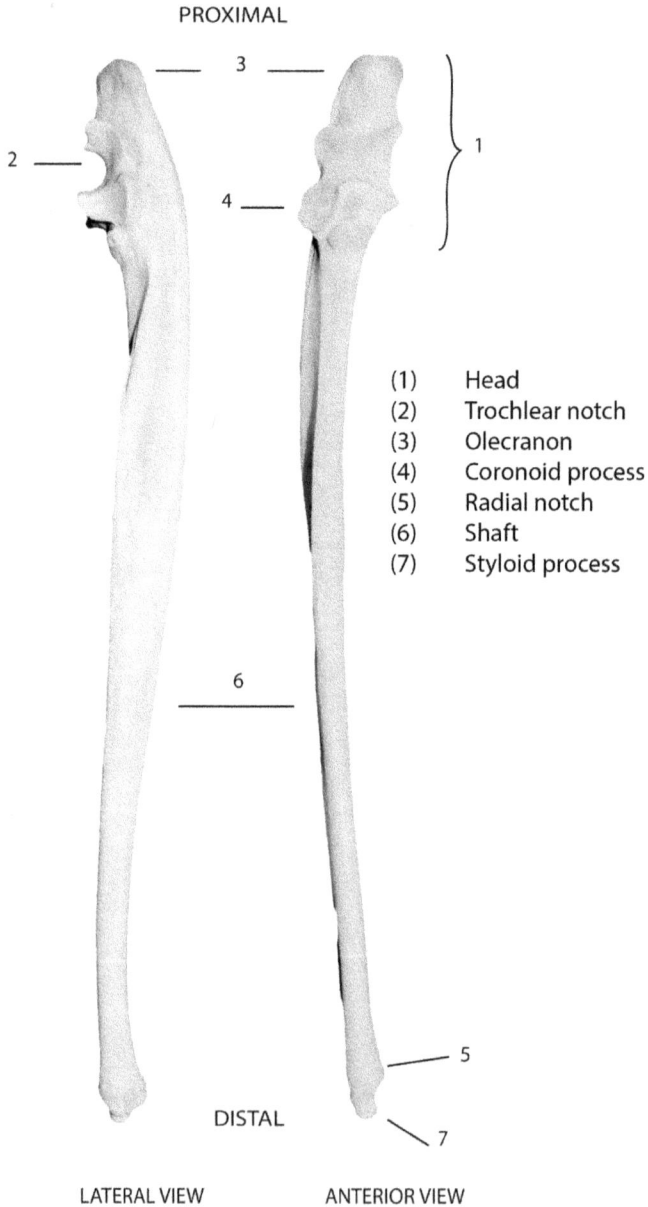

PROXIMAL

(1)   Head
(2)   Trochlear notch
(3)   Olecranon
(4)   Coronoid process
(5)   Radial notch
(6)   Shaft
(7)   Styloid process

DISTAL

LATERAL VIEW   ANTERIOR VIEW

Figure 5.1: Kangaroo ulna with diagnostic features labelled.

Diagnostic features

Diagnostic features of the ulna are shown in Figure 5.1. When complete, the ulna is easily recognised by its hook-like head (1), which is comprised of a **trochlear (semilunar) notch** (2) for articulation with the trochlea of the distal humerus, and often 'swollen-looking' proximal cap, the **olecranon process** (3). The **coronoid process** (4) projects from the distal portion of the trochlear notch, and fits into the coronoid fossa of the humerus. Some species also have a **radial notch** (5), projecting slightly on the lateral side of the trochlear notch, for articulation with the radius. The ulna has a thin, tapering **shaft** (6) that ends in a pointed **styloid process** (7) in many species. In adulthood, the ulna is fused to the radius in most ungulates, especially horses, cattle, sheep and often pigs (Figure 5.2). In these species, fusion results in a greatly reduced ulnar shaft. As for the radius, many of the images on the following pages depict both elements in these species. Note that in species with a fused radius/ulna, the two bones are generally separate in immature animals. Since the radius enables rotation of the forearm, in species in which it is fused to the ulna, no rotation of the fore limb is possible.

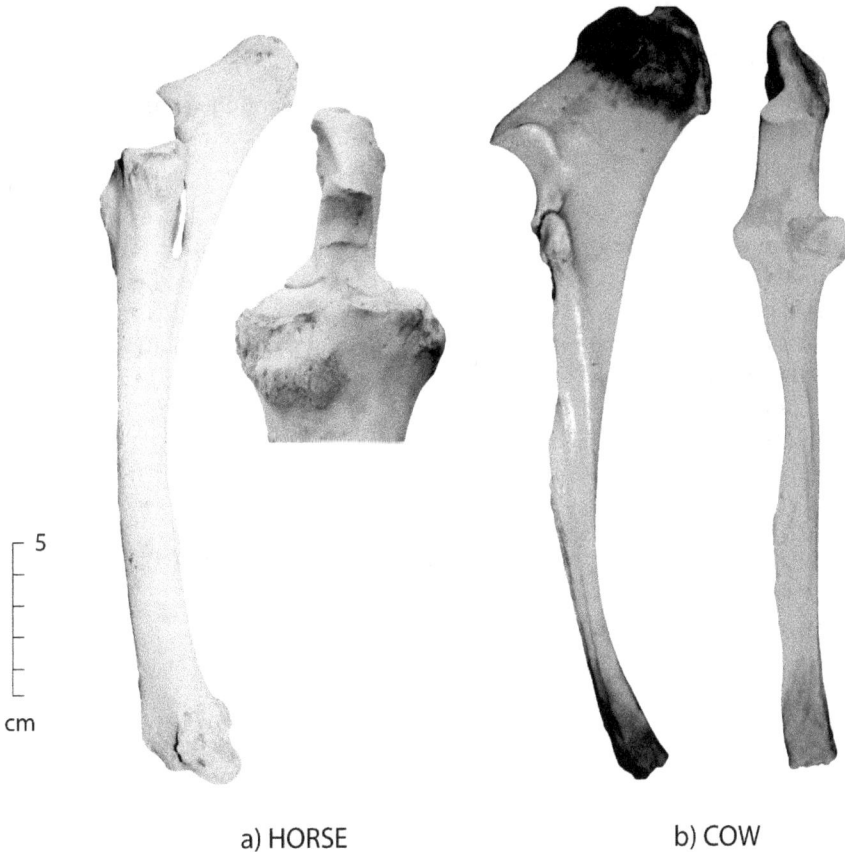

a) HORSE   b) COW

Figure 5.2: Lateral and anterior views of fused ulna/radius; (a) horse and (b) cow. The ulna and radius are fused in most adult ungulates.

Orientation and siding

To orient the ulna, the trochlear notch and olecranon process will be proximal and anterior (pointing up and forward), and the thin shaft will taper distally. In species with a distinct olecranon process, the curve can be used to indicate from which side the bone came. To side the ulna in this way, hold it with the trochlear notch facing you, and the olecranon process will 'curve' to the side from which it came. If the olecranon process is missing or less well developed, the morphology of the trochlear notch can be used. In this case (still holding the ulna with the trochlear notch facing you), the coronoid process will flare out on the side from which it came. Alternatively, you can hold the ulna in correct anatomical position, with the trochlear notch facing anteriorly, and side it by ensuring that the radial notch (if present) is lateral.

Species identification

Refer to Figures 5.2–5.6 for species identification using the ulna.

Distinguishing between human and macropod

The trochlear notches of both humans and macropods appear quite similar and the ulna of both species is rather long and thin. To differentiate between the two, it is often easiest to examine the proximal and distal ends of the ulna.

- Humans do not have a distinctive, well-developed olecranon process, but do have a slightly flared distal end right above a distinctive styloid process.
- Macropods have a well-developed olecranon process and a tapered (as opposed to flaring) distal end.
- Humans have a distinct sharp crest along the length of the ulnar shaft, which is only extant on the mid-shaft of macropods.
- In humans, the ulna has a teardrop-shaped mid-shaft section and is long and thin (Figure 5.3a).

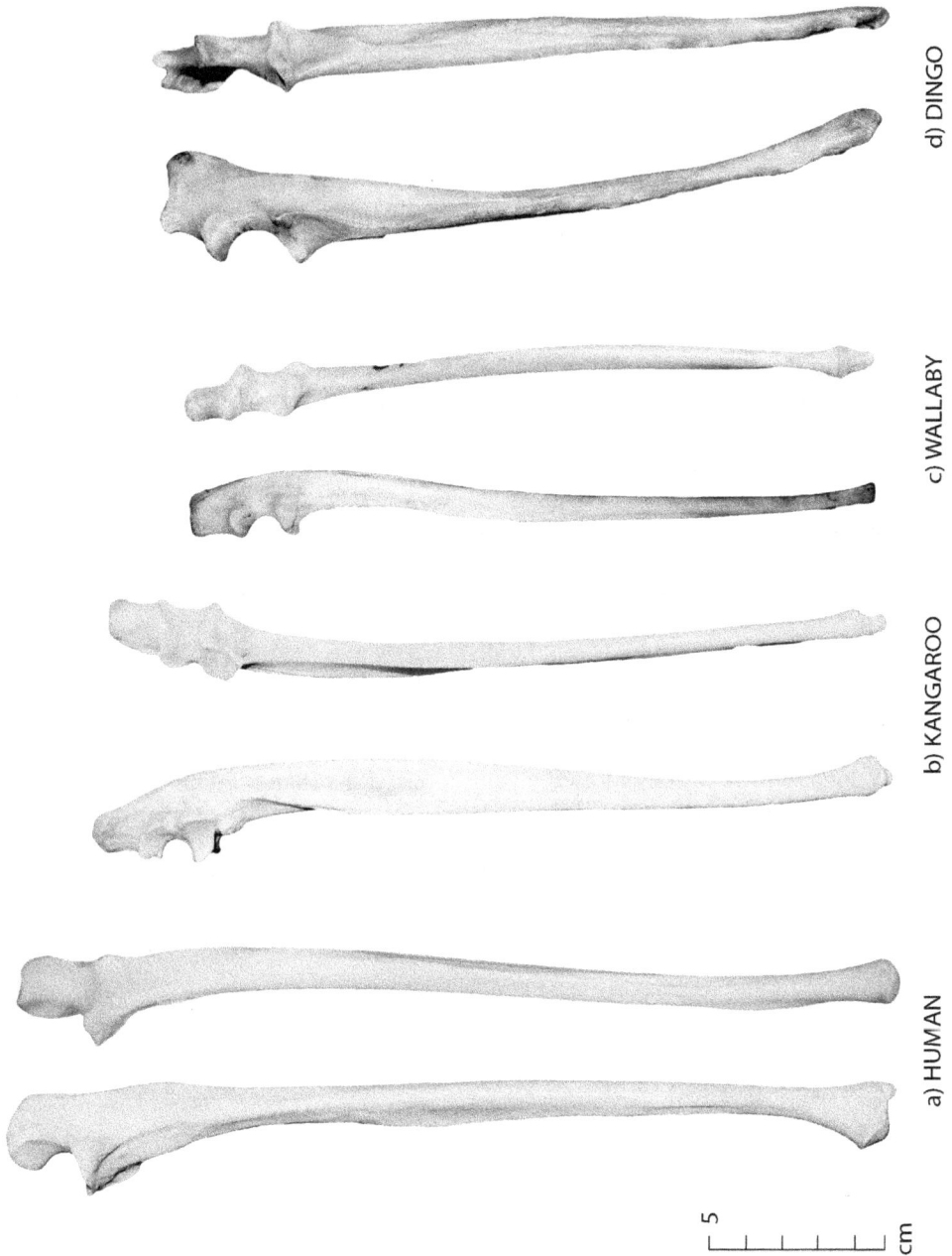

Figure 5.3: Lateral and anterior views of the ulna; (a) human, (b) kangaroo, (c) wallaby and (d) dingo. Note the close similarities but distinct size differences of the four species. The human ulna has a teardrop cross-section and is long and thin.

Differences between non-human species

- The ulna is distinguished by a 'flattened' appearance medio-laterally, with a shaft that becomes narrower distally.
- The ulna and radius are fused in most adult ungulates (horses, cattle, sheep and pigs).
- The distal ulna is severely reduced in most ungulates, especially horse.
- In species in which the radius and ulna do not fuse (humans, dingoes, cats, macropods, possums, quolls, bandicoots, wombats and rabbits), the ulnar shaft may be confused with a medial fibula shaft fragment.
- In adult horses, the ulna is so reduced in length the distal end tapers to a point that does not extend the full body of the radius.
- In dingoes and cats, the ulna has a prominent bulging mid-shaft tuberosity.
- To distinguish between cats and small dingoes, the distal ulna is rather small in dingoes and more prominent in cats; dingoes have a high olecranon process (distally) (Figure 5.4).
- Horses, cattle, sheep, pigs, macropods and wombats all have long and massive curved olecranon processes (Figure 5.5).
- Kangaroos, wallabies and possums all have very similar ulnar morphology. Use the size and curvature of the shaft to make a general distinction between most species of kangaroo and wallaby (kangaroos have a more pronounced anterior curve than wallabies) (Figure 5.3b and c).
- To differentiate between possums and wallabies, size may be used (wallabies are slightly larger), as well as robustness of the ulnar shaft. In general, the shaft is slightly more robust as it nears the distal end in possums, and more tapered in wallabies (Figures 5.6b and 5.3c).
- To distinguish between rabbits and possums, look at the shaft – rabbit ulnae curve anteriorly and have a deeper trochlear notch, whereas possums have a relatively straight shaft and a shallow trochlear notch (Figures 5.6a and b).
- To distinguish between wombats and pigs, look at the coronoid process, which flares outward in wombats (Figures 5.5b and c).

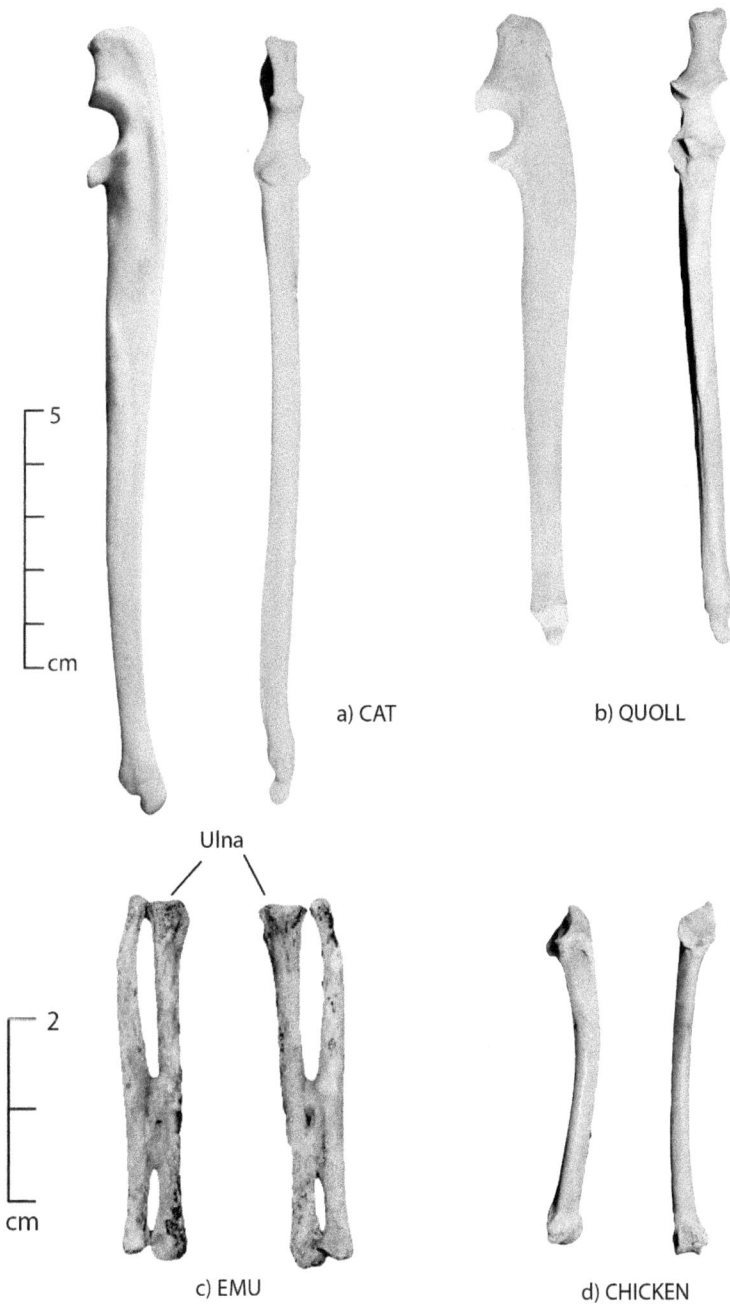

Figure 5.4: Lateral and anterior views of the ulna; (a) cat, (b) quoll, (c) emu and (d) chicken. The dingo (Fig. 5.3d) and cat ulna have a prominent and bulging mid-shaft tuberosity. To differentiate between the two, the distal portion of the dingo ulna is small, while that of the cat has a more prominent distal end.

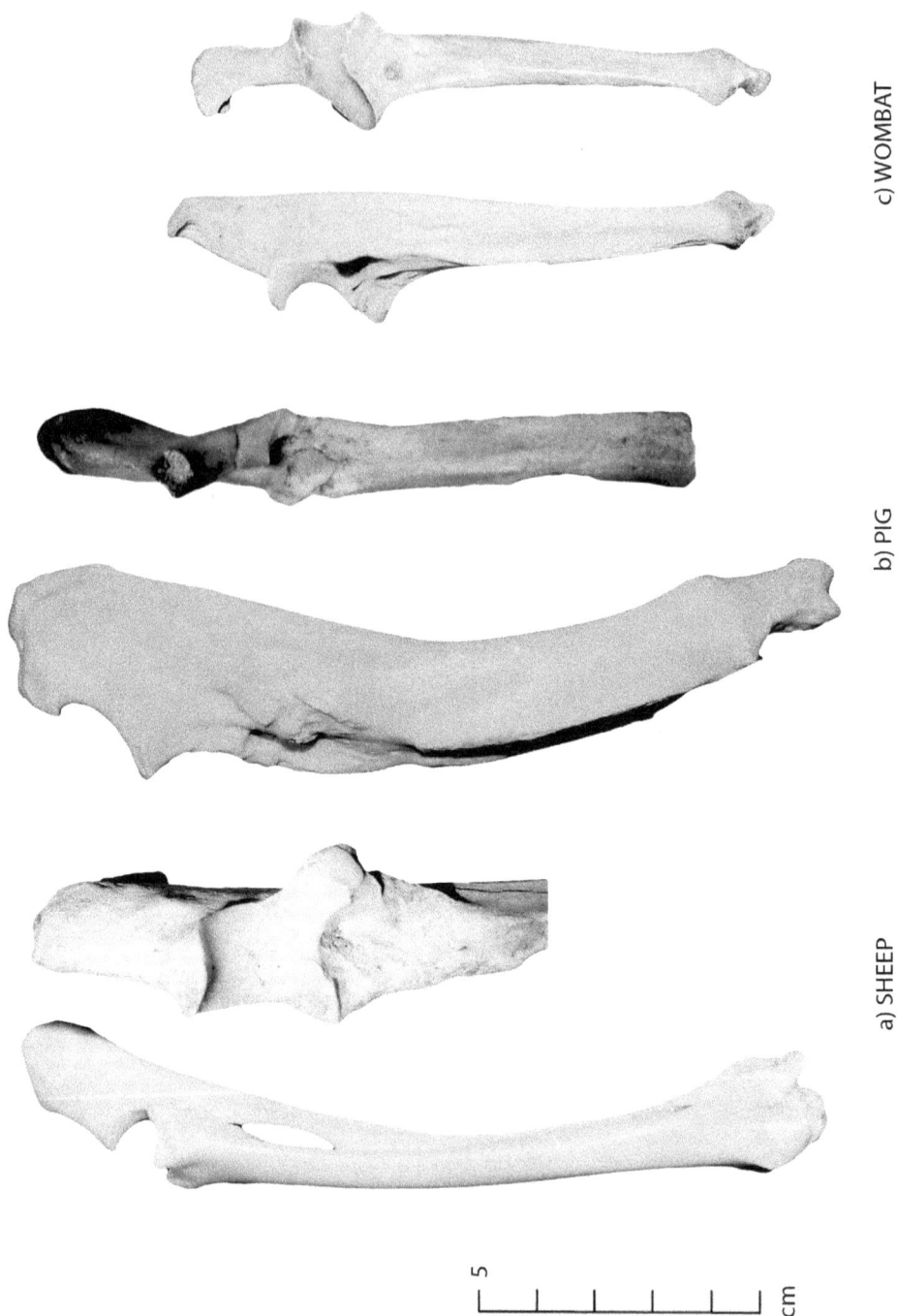

Figure 5.5: Lateral and anterior views of the ulna; (a) sheep, (b) pig and (c) wombat. The pig has a very large and curved olecranon, which is similar in morphology to wombat.

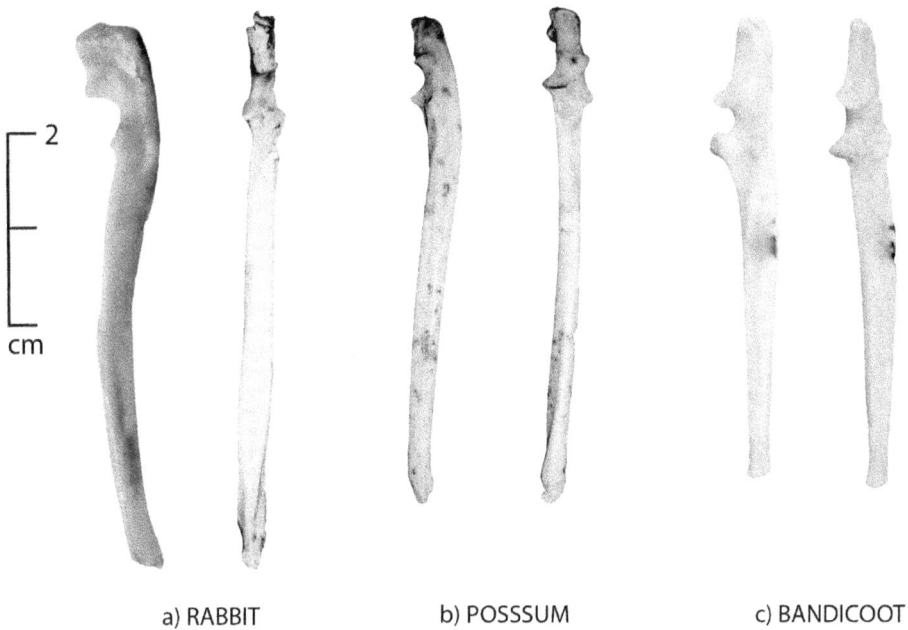

Figure 5.6: Lateral and anterior views of the ulna; (a) rabbit, (b) brushtail possum and (c) bandicoot.

Common state in archaeological assemblages

The ulna is frequently encountered in archaeological assemblages; however, it is very rarely complete. Generally, the relatively robust trochlear notch is extant, and can be used to identify species. The shaft is often broken, and even if extant, it is likely to be unidentified as it may be mistaken for a rib or fibula fragment. In species with a fused radius/ulna, part of a broken ulnar shaft may be extant on the posterior radial surface. The olecranon process is also often missing, as its proximal end is a fusion centre, and has an epiphyseal cap that may not be extant. This is especially prevalent in those species in which the olecranon process is more exaggerated and swollen-looking (i.e. horses, cattle, sheep, pigs, kangaroos and wallaby). In pigs, the ulna is generally found unfused in most historical archaeological assemblages due to the relatively young age at which pigs are slaughtered.

In species utilised for meat, primary butchery of a carcass tends to make an initial cut just above, or at, the articulation of the radius/ulna and humerus to disarticulate the upper from the lower fore leg. This often results in a cut mark through the trochlear notch. As is the case with the radius, the ulna is often left articulated with the humerus to form a leg cut (e.g. ham or lamb) that may be cooked with the bone. In rabbit, the ulna is often intact as rabbits are frequently not butchered prior to cooking; the same pattern is prevalent in poultry.

The reduced ulnae of some species are especially prone to different preservation and other taphonomic factors, such as scavenging. For example, emu ulnae are rarely found intact, as the wing is one of the first body parts to be scavenged. In macropods such as kangaroos and wallabies, there is little meat on this element, and it is commonly left behind by people interested in higher meat-bearing elements. In naturally accumulated assemblages, macropod ulnae are commonly found articulated with the entire hand or wrist (ulna, radius, carpals, metacarpals and phalanges), as even scavengers tend to ignore this element. The same pattern is commonly encountered in many species.

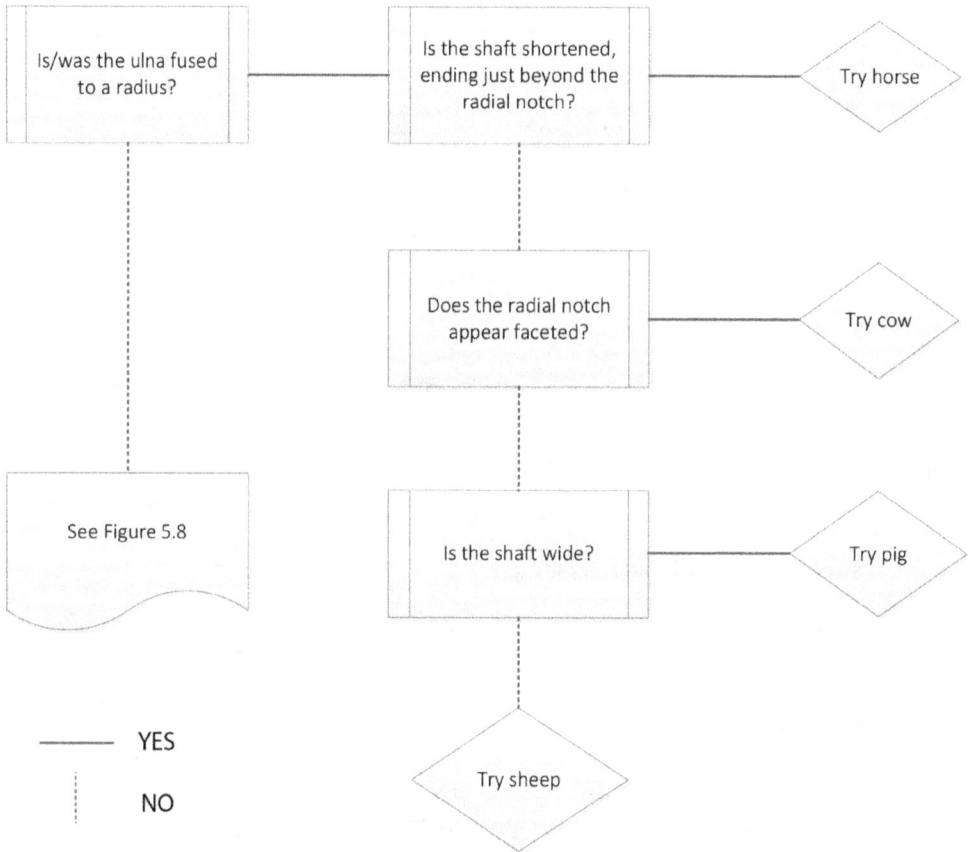

Figure 5.7: Ulna decision process 1. Ulna fused to radius.

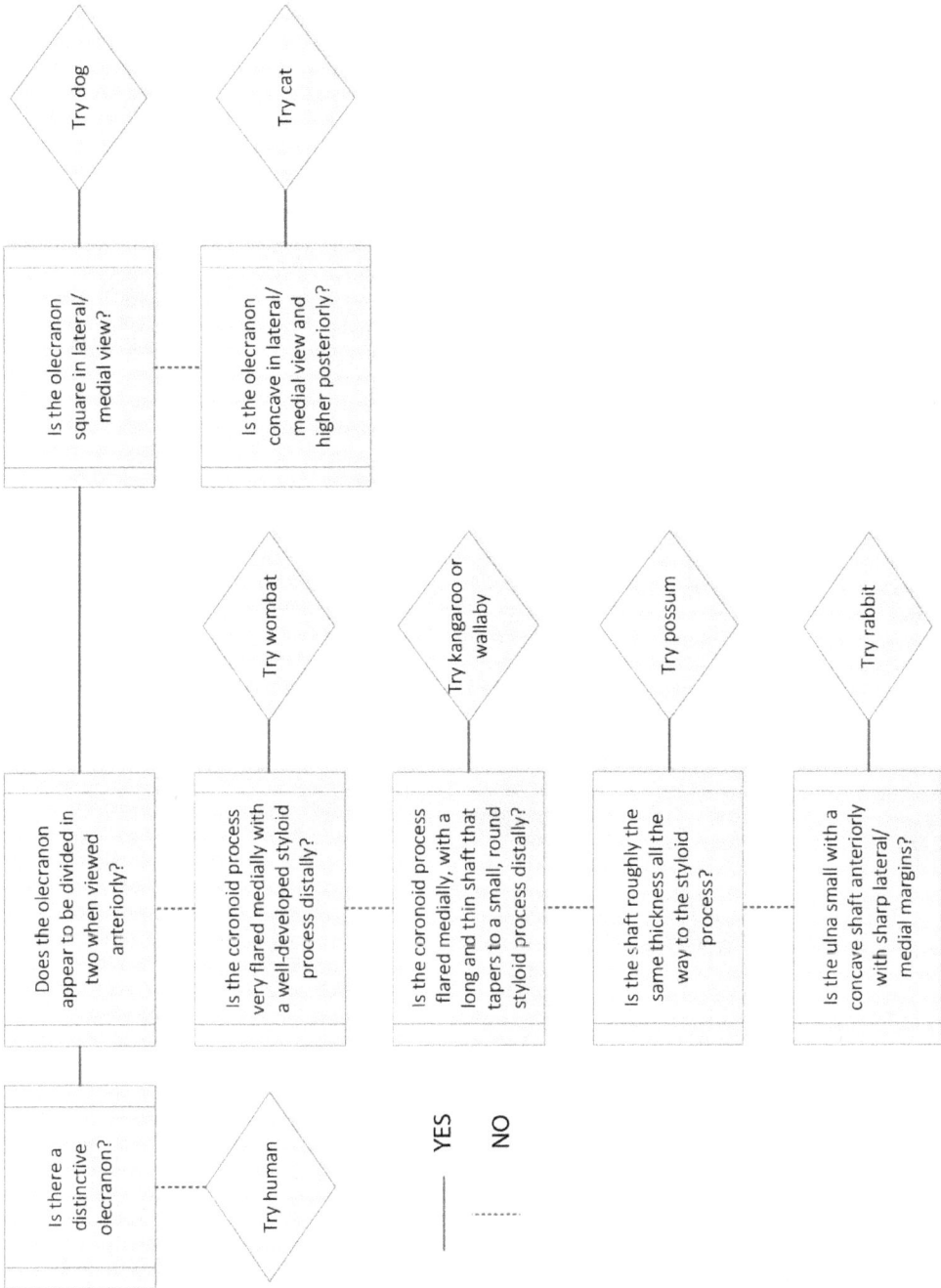

Figure 5.8: Ulna decision process 2. Ulna and radius not fused.

6
Pelvis

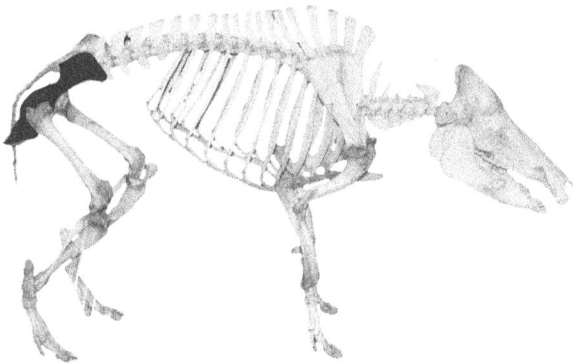

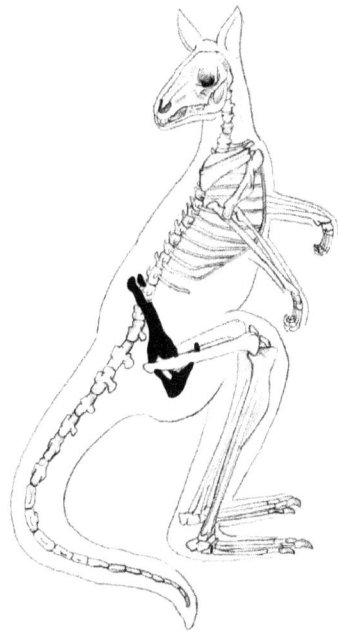

The pelvis is made up of three bones, a left and right **os coxa** (1) (more commonly referred to as the innominate) and the sacrum, which joins the two sides (see Figure 6.1). In most species, these three bones fuse together to form the hip or pelvic girdle, but are recovered disarticulated in the majority of archaeological contexts. Since the innominate is the most readily identifiable part of the pelvis, this bone will be the focus of discussion.

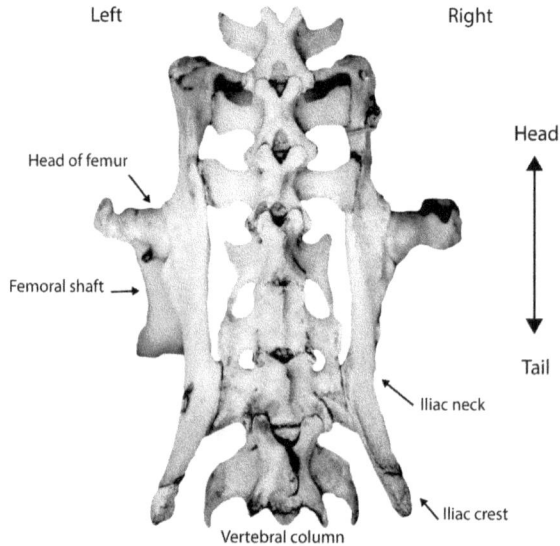

Figure 6.1: Articulated pelvis and sacrum of the quoll.

Diagnostic features

Diagnostic features of the pelvis are shown in Figure 6.2. Each innominate (or half) is comprised of three fused bones – the **ilium** (2), **ischium** (3) and **pubis** (4). One of the most diagnostic parts of the innominate is the **acetabulum** (5), or hip socket, and the **acetabular notch** (6), into which fits the head of the femur to form the hip joint. Due to its robust morphology, the acetabulum is nearly always intact if extant in archaeological assemblages. Less frequently, the entire innominate (left or right half) remains intact, in which case the shape of the **obturator foramen** (7), the **sciatic notch** (8), the **pubic symphysis** (9), the height of the **iliac neck** (10), the shape of the **iliac crest** (11) and the depth of the **supraacetabular fossa** (12) may also be used in species identification.

In addition to definitive species identification, the pelvis is also a key bone in the determination of sex and age, especially in humans. The biological ability to bear offspring has a direct effect on the morphology of the pelvis of nearly all mammalian adult females. Morphological differences are best identified with intact pelvic girdles, although it is often possible to sex even fragmentary elements. In humans, the size and shape of the ilium, opening of the pelvis girdle, and morphology of the pubic symphysis and sciatic notch are all indicators of sex. Age and number of births may also be determined by the morphology of the pubic symphysis. References that contain further information on ageing and sexing the pelvis can be found at the end of this manual.

(1) Os coxa
(2) Ilium
(3) Ischium
(4) Pubis

(5) Acetabulum
(6) Acetabular notch
(7) Obturator foramen
(8) Sciatic notch

(9) Pubic symphysis
(10) Iliac neck
(11) Iliac crest
(12) Supra-acetabular fossa

(13) Sacrum

a) KANGAROO

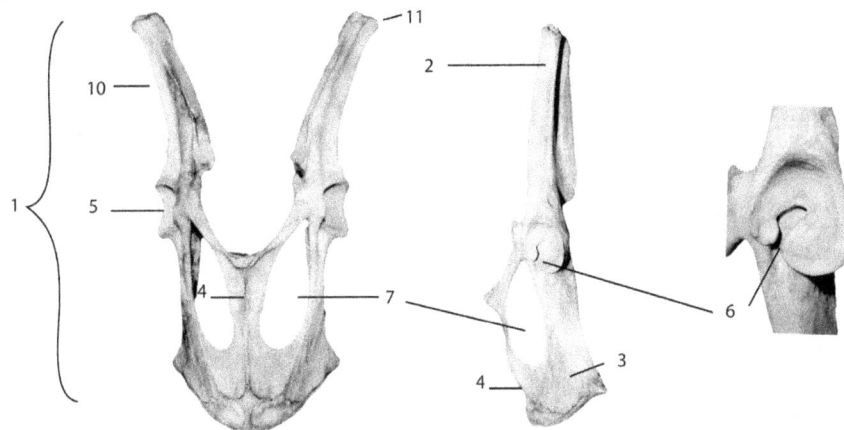

b) HUMAN

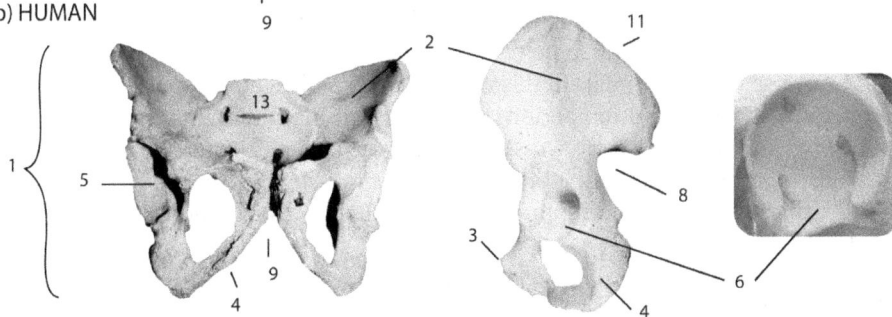

c) SHEEP

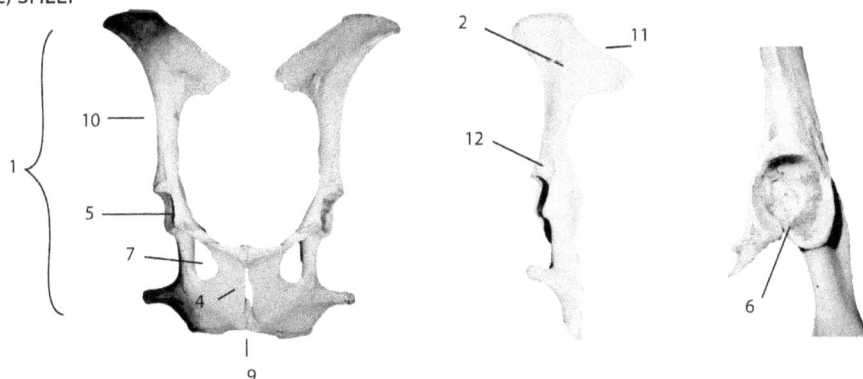

Figure 6.2: Pelves with diagnostic features labelled; (a) kangaroo, (b) human and (c) sheep. Details from left to right: articulated pelvis, os coxa and acetabulum. Note that the human pelvis has been rotated slightly and shown articulated with the sacrum.

Orientation and siding

To side and orient a complete pelvis, hold the pelvis with the fused pubic symphysis facing away from you (anterior), and the sacrum facing you (posterior). Orient the pelvis so the acetabula are facing laterally, and the ilia are pointing up (cranially). In this position, a left innominate will be on your left, etc. If just one innominate is extant, orient it by placing the ilium/iliac crest cranially, and the pubic symphysis/obturator foramen caudally. The acetabulum and ischium should be lateral, and the pubic symphysis medial.

Species identification

Refer to Figures 6.3–6.11 for species identification using the pelvis. Several morphological characteristics of the innominate facilitate species identification, however the most robust of these is the acetabulum. For this reason, the decision process at the end of this chapter is based on the morphology of this element. As with all bones, the size and shape of the pelvis is a reflection of the way in which an animal moves and the degree to which their young are born altricially (incapable of moving around) or precocially (quickly mobile). Altricial human babies are born with large heads relative to the rest of their bodies, due to larger brain size. The need to fit a grapefruit-sized object through a narrow opening, coupled with bipedal locomotion (walking on two legs), is a governing factor in the relatively low, rounded shape of the human pelvis (which translates into a wide ilium in the innominate). Conversely, most animals in this manual are precocial quadrupeds that bear young with relatively short maturation periods and smaller heads and brains. These traits are exemplified by tall, narrow, and often distally flared iliac blades, among other characteristics. Marsupials, who bear undeveloped pouch young, have epipubic bones (see Figure 0.6 in 'Bone identification 101'). The depth of the acetabulum is also an indicator of locomotion and habitat.

As the size and general shape of the pelvis varies considerably between species due to all of these factors (and more), several different views of the pelvis are depicted here. The acetabulum and iliac neck and crest is shown for every species, and also included are views of several articulated pelves to illustrate variability in size and shape across a variety of species (Figure 6.3).

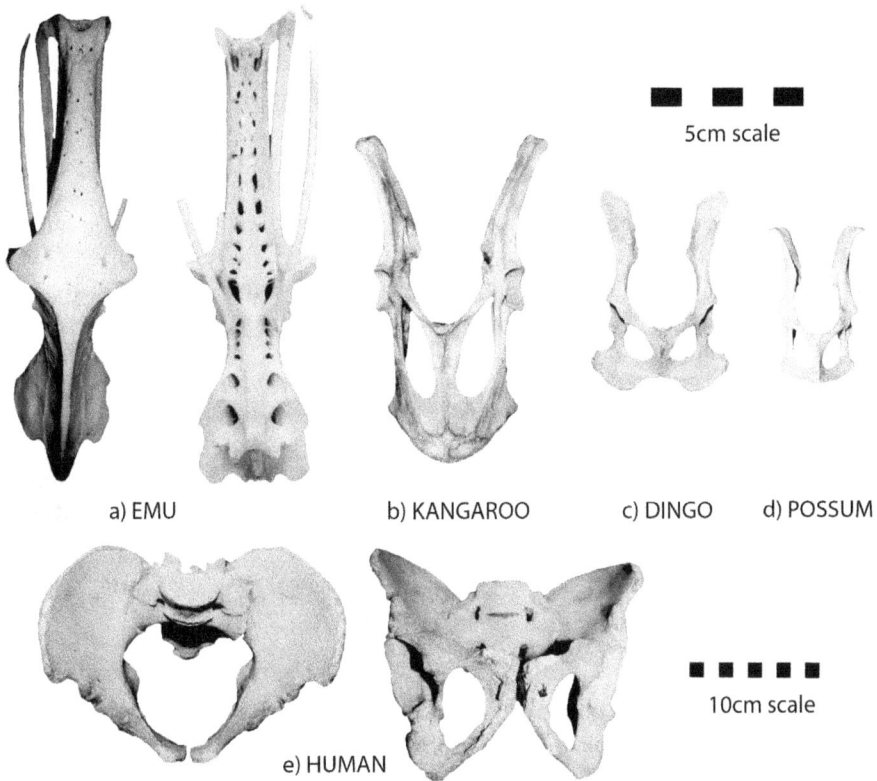

Figure 6.3: A size and shape comparison of several different articulated pelves; (a) emu, (b) kangaroo, (c) dingo, (d) possum and (e) human.

The following are some specific morphological distinctions (refer to Figures 6.4–6.11).

Acetabular notch

- The acetabular notch is open for humans (see Figure 6.6a), horses (Figure 6.4a), wombats, dingoes, cats and possums.
- The acetabular notch is almost closed for cattle (see Figure 6.4b), sheep, pigs, kangaroos, wallabies and rabbits (Figure 6.5).
- The acetabular notch is widely open, giving the acetabulum a U-shaped outline in humans (see Figure 6.6a), dingoes (Figure 6.6c) and cats.
- The acetabulum lacks a 'notch', and is smooth and round, resembling a ring in emus (see Figure 6.4c) and chickens.
- Cattle and horses have a large acetabulum (> 50 mm in diameter), the acetabulum of pigs, humans and kangaroos is medium (30–50 mm), the acetabulum of wallabies, wombats, sheep and dingoes are small (15–30 mm), and those of cat, rabbit and possum are all very small (generally < 15 mm).
- Pigs have a very raised acetabular rim when viewed from the side, with a very deep fossa.

Supra-acetabular fossa

- Cattle and sheep have a deep, slit-like supra-acetabular fossa, however in other species the supra-acetabular fossa is very shallow and more like a depression than a fossa.

Pelvic neck and blade

- The neck of the ilium is broad relative to its length, terminating cranially in a rounded, paddle-shaped iliac crest in dingoes, cats and rabbits (see Figures 6.8c, d and f).
- The neck of the ilium is long and thin, terminating in a flared, almost triangular iliac crest: horse, cow, sheep and pig (see Figures 6.9 and 6.10b).
- The neck of the ilium is long and tapers gradually toward a narrower iliac 'crest' in kangaroos, wallabies and possums (see Figures 6.8a, b and g).
- In wombats, the neck of the ilium is long, slender and terminates in a sickle-shaped iliac blade that curves laterally (Figure 6.10c).
- The innominate is long and irregularly shaped, curved cranially and characterised by many holes ventrally (resembling a 'Swiss cheese' appearance), with a rounded acetabulum in the centre in emus and chickens (Figure 6.11).

Differentiating between marsupial and placental mammals

- If a complete innominate is present, marsupials are relatively easy to distinguish from placentals by the long, thin, cranially tapering ilia.

Common state in archaeological assemblages

Innominates are frequently recovered from archaeological assemblages, but generally in a fragmentary state. When incomplete, parts of the pelvis are commonly mistaken for other elements. For example, the ischium of some species is often confused with the mandibular ramus, while the neck and iliac crest can be confused with the scapula. In these cases, use of a comparative collection is the best way to make a positive identification. The pelvis is almost always broken as a result of either natural (scavenging, post-depositional disturbance) or anthropogenic factors (for example, butchery). In naturally accumulated faunal assemblages, scavenging species tend to disarticulate and break the pelvis early on when accessing a carcass. Carnivore damage often results in a broken ilium, resulting from gnawing and accessing the internal organs. The ischium and pubis may also be broken during these processes. The acetabulum generally survives due to its general robustness. In historic anthropogenic (human-accumulated) faunal assemblages, portions of the innominate are often recovered as they form part of common leg meat cuts (along with the femur and tibia). In prehistoric assemblages, the bone is also frequently extant. Cut marks may be found in or around the acetabulum as a result of the disarticulation of the femur, as well as on the iliac blade if skinning has occurred. Band saw cuts are also commonly found on either side of the acetabulum.

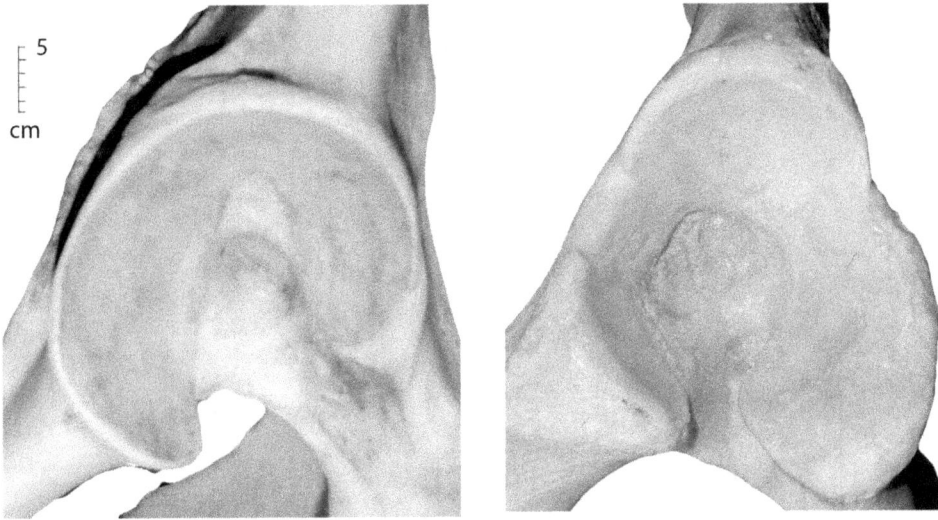

a) HORSE

b) COW

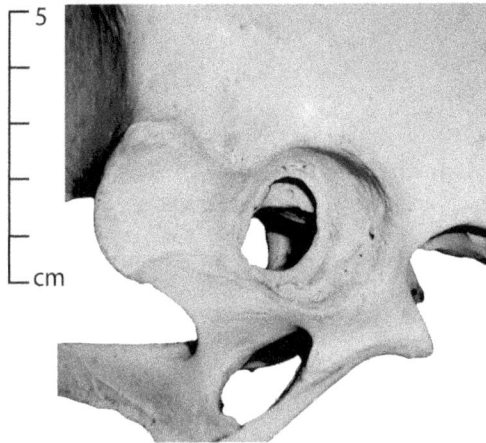

c) EMU

Figure 6.4: A detail image of an acetabulum; (a) horse, (b) cow and (c) emu; illustrating an open acetabular notch (a) and an almost closed acetabular notch (b).

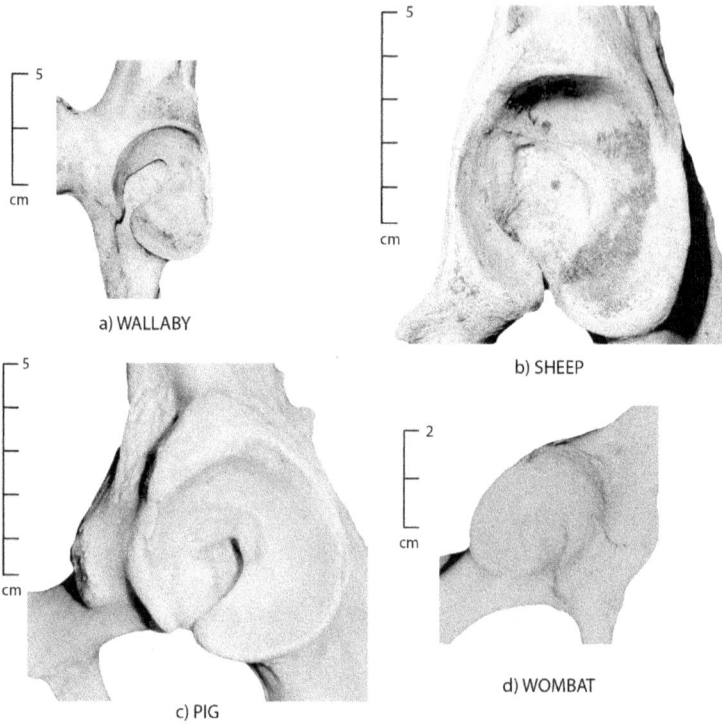

Figure 6.5: A detail image of an acetabulum; (a) wallaby, (b) sheep, (c) pig and (d) wombat; illustrating the lack of an acetabular notch, and the smooth, round shape.

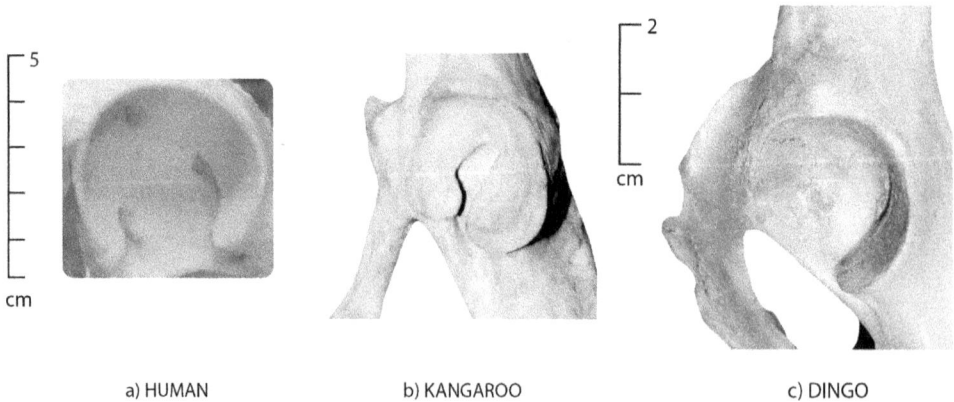

Figure 6.6: A detail image of an acetabulum; (a) human, (b) kangaroo and (c) dingo; illustrating a widely open acetabular notch (a) to an almost closed acetabular notch (b).

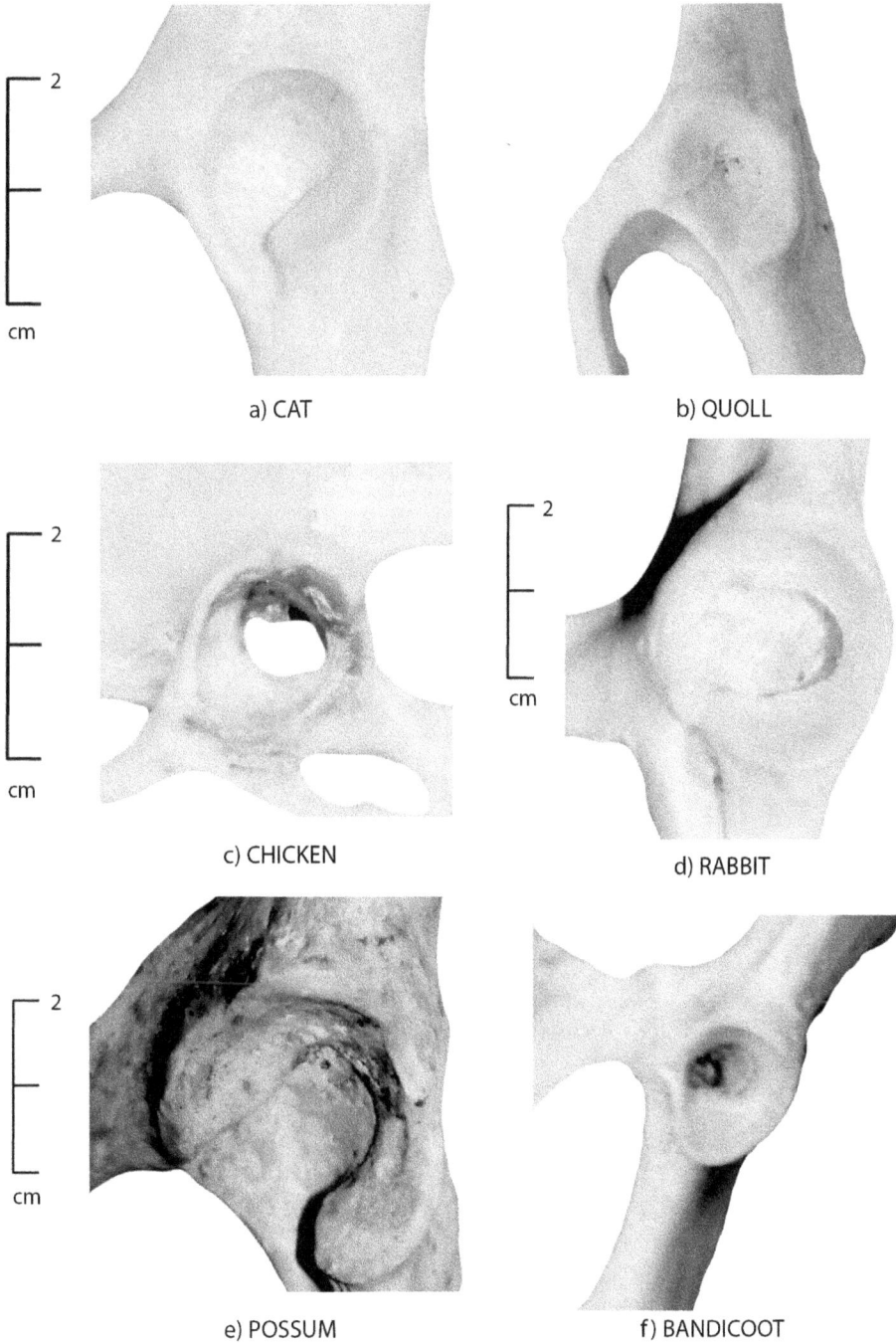

Figure 6.7: A detail image of (a) cat, (b) quoll, (c) chicken, (d) rabbit, (e) brushtail possum and (f) bandicoot acetabulum.

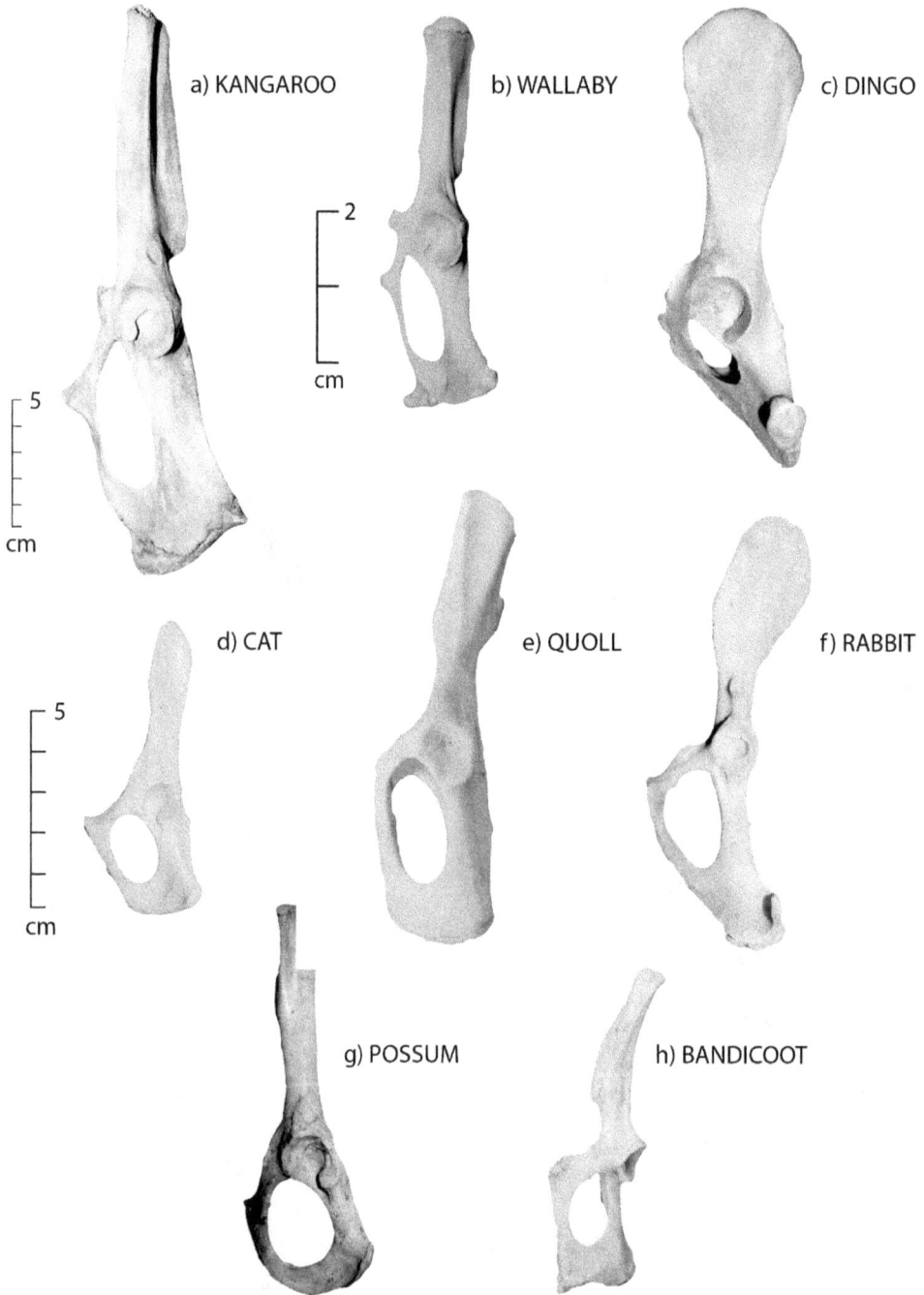

Figure 6.8: Innominate positioned to show the shape of the neck and blade; (a) kangaroo, (b) wallaby, (c) dingo, (d) cat, (e) quoll, (f) rabbit, (g) brushtail possum and (h) bandicoot. Note the long, thin tapering blade of the marsupials and the sickle-shaped hook of the wombat in Figure 6.10c. The dingo has a rounded blade.

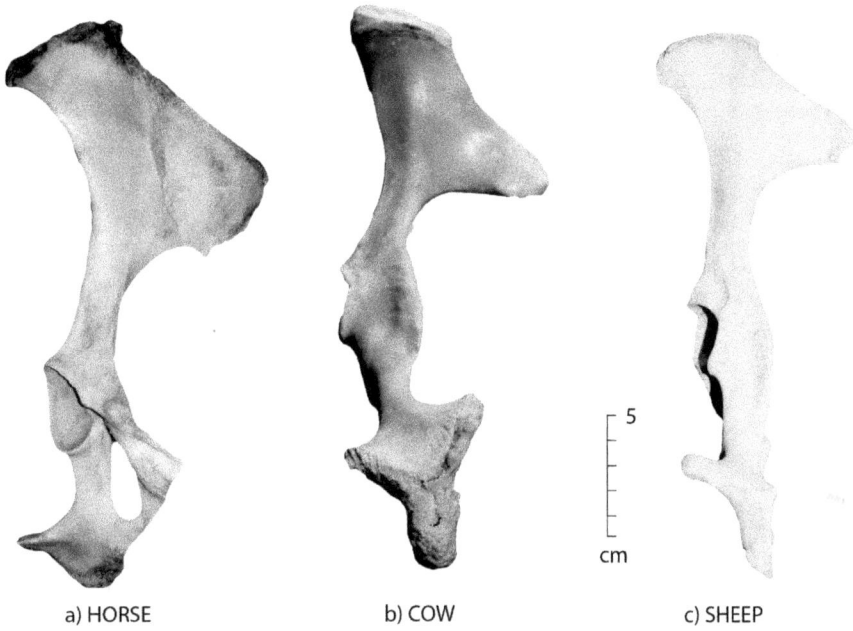

Figure 6.9: Pelvis positioned to show the morphology of the neck and the blade, especially the triangular crest of the ilium; (a) horse, (b) cow and (c) sheep.

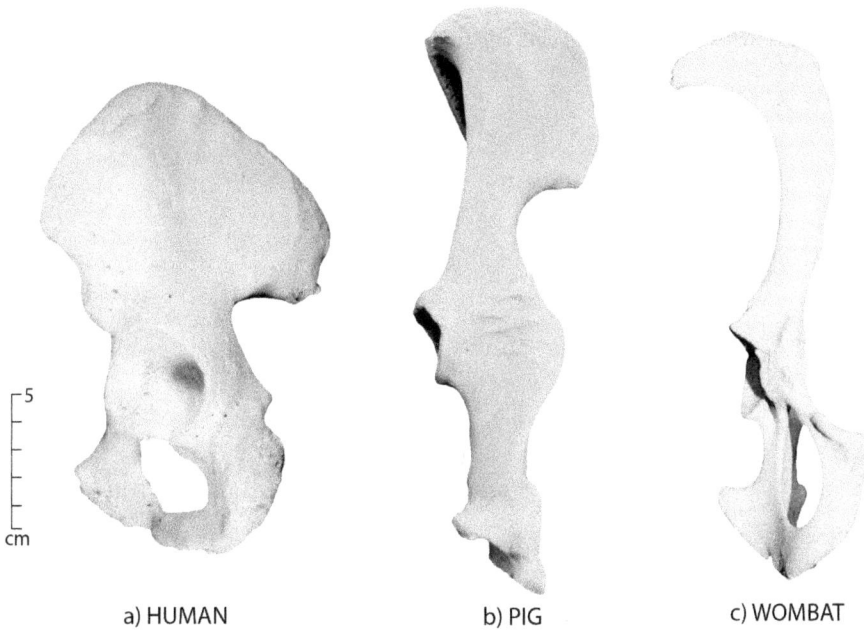

Figure 6.10: Pelvis positioned to show the morphology of the neck and the blade; (a) human, (b) pig and (c) wombat. The raised acetabulum of the pig is clear when compared to the shallower depression in the human.

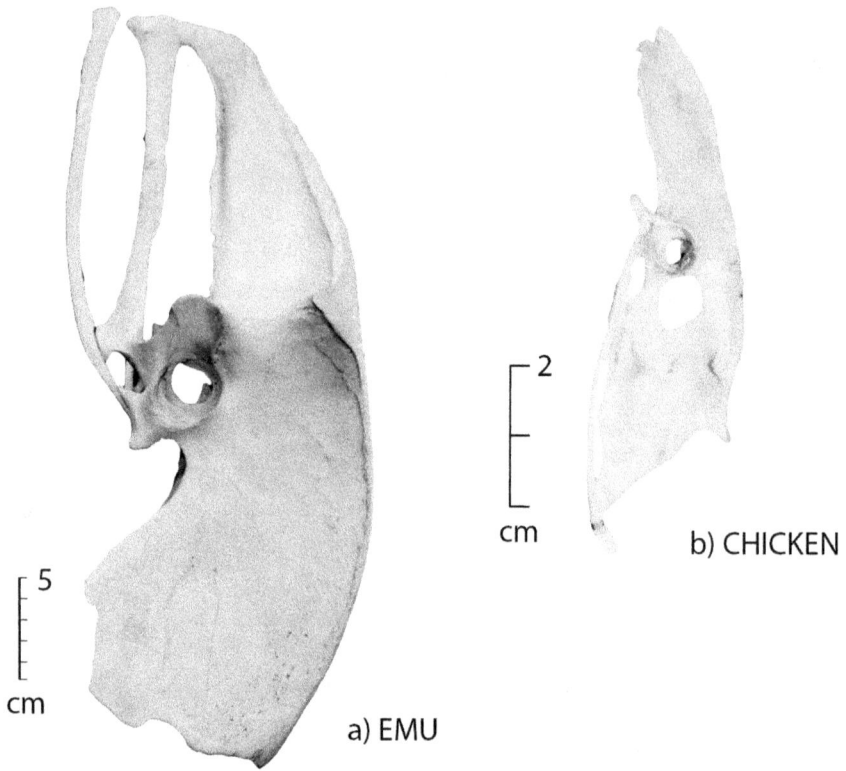

Figure 6.11: Articulated pelvis; (a) emu and (b) chicken.

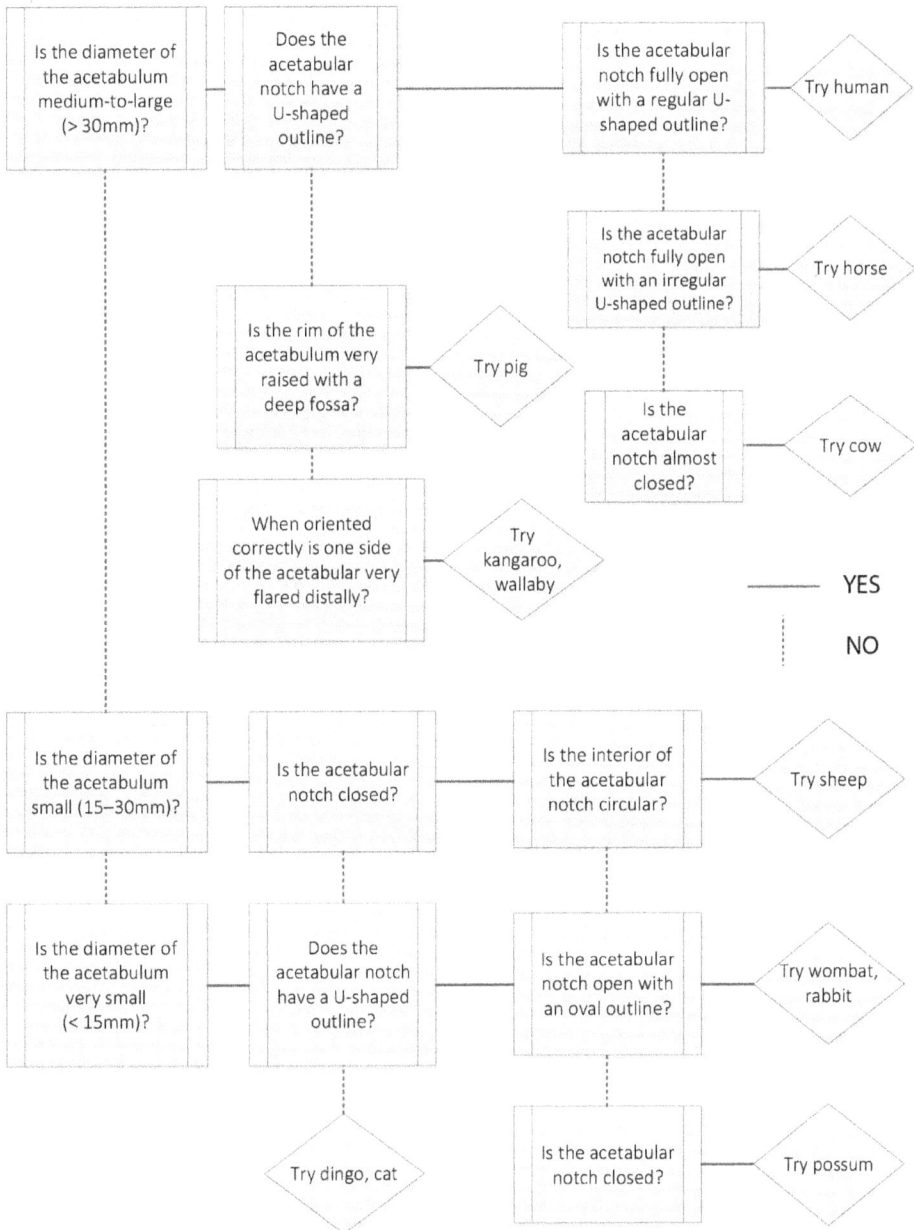

Figure 6.12: Pelvis decision process. Since the pelvis is generally fragmented in an archaeological assemblage, this decision process uses the morphological features of the acetabulum for species identification.

7
Femur

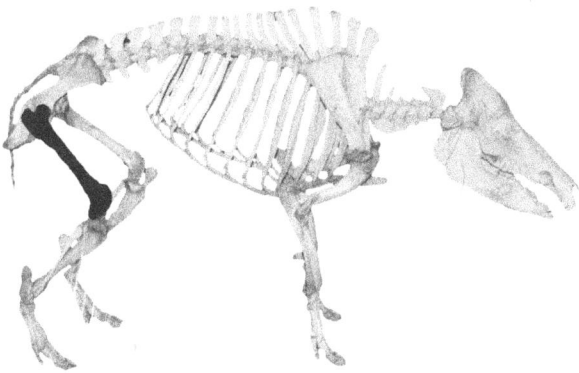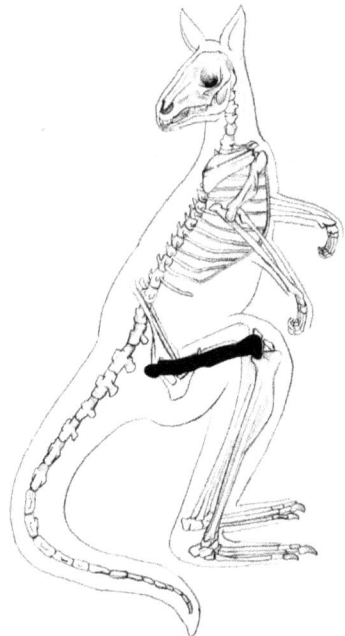

The femur (thigh bone) is the largest of the long bones. It is long relative to its diameter, with a fairly robust shaft.

Diagnostic features

Diagnostic features of the femur are shown in Figures 7.1 and 7.2. The **head** (1) of the femur has a round, ball-like shape that articulates with the acetabulum of the pelvis proximally to form the hip joint. Distally, the **medial** (2) and **lateral condyles** (3) articulate with the tibia, and the **patellar surface** (4) articulates with the patella (knee cap), forming the knee joint. The curvature (or lack thereof) of the femoral **shaft** (5) can be used in species and element identification. The **linea aspera** (6), a prominent line that runs along the length of the shaft on the posterior side and branches as it nears the distal end, is also a diagnostic feature. At the proximal end, the **greater trochanter** (7) (most proximal), **lesser trochanter** (8) (medial), and in some species **third trochanter** (9) (lateral) is also useful for species identification. The **trochanteric fossa** (10) is a deep depression that lies just below the femoral head and **neck** (11) on the posterior side, and its depth is also useful in species identification.

A complete femur is frequently confused with a humerus, due to the similarity of their rounded proximal ends. The femoral head, however, is a complete ball, whereas the humeral head has only a rounded articular surface. To identify a femur based solely on a shaft fragment, consider that the femoral shaft is generally quite round in cross-section, whereas the cross-section of the humeral shaft is irregular, and that of the tibial shaft is triangular.

Orientation and siding

To side the femur, orient it by placing the head and neck proximally (up) and the condyles distally (down). The head is medial and the intertrochanteric fossa is posterior (anatomical position). If oriented using these criteria, the side from which the femur came should also be apparent, as the medial head will fit into the pelvis. If unclear, one trick that often works with complete femurs is to 'stand' them on their condyles on a flat surface (with the intertrochanteric fossa facing you). In quadrupeds (and most macropods), the femur will generally slant slightly **away** from the side from which it came. In humans the distal end will slant **toward** the side from which it came (due to the bicondylar angle, which facilitates bipedal locomotion).

Species identification

Refer to Figures 7.3–7.9 for species identification using the femur. If faced with a complete femur, identification to species is straightforward, and can be accomplished using a combination of the following morphological characteristics: a) size of the femoral neck, b) depth of the intertrochanteric fossa, c) height of the greater trochanter, d) size and position of the lesser trochanter, e) presence of a third trochanter, f) rugosity of the linea aspera, and g) general morphology of the distal articulation.

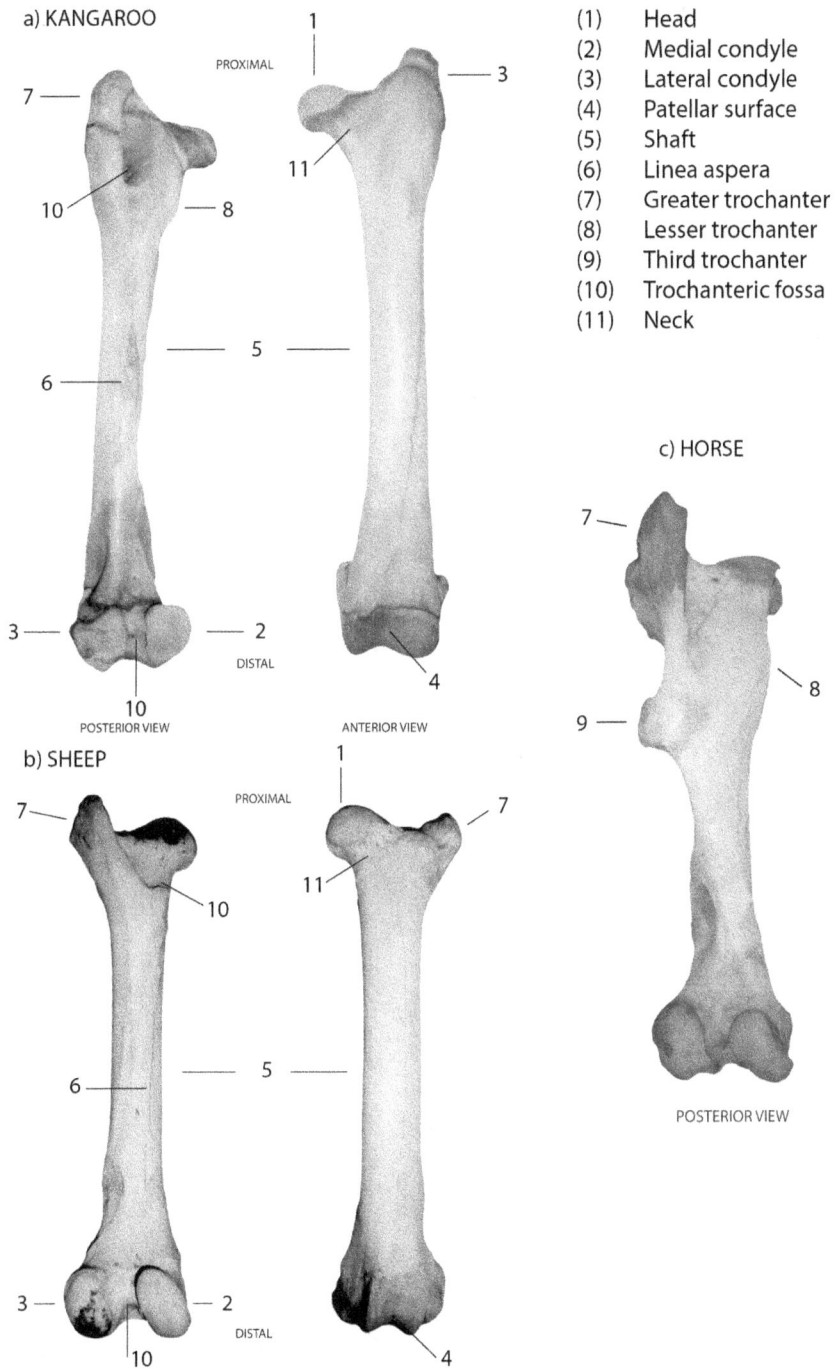

a) KANGAROO

(1) Head
(2) Medial condyle
(3) Lateral condyle
(4) Patellar surface
(5) Shaft
(6) Linea aspera
(7) Greater trochanter
(8) Lesser trochanter
(9) Third trochanter
(10) Trochanteric fossa
(11) Neck

c) HORSE

b) SHEEP

Figure 7.1: Femur with diagnostic features labelled; (a) kangaroo (b) sheep and (c) horse.

Head ⟷ Tail

Pelvic blade

Articulation of the head of femur
and the acetabulum

Greater trochanter

Femur

Patella

Tibia

Calcaneus

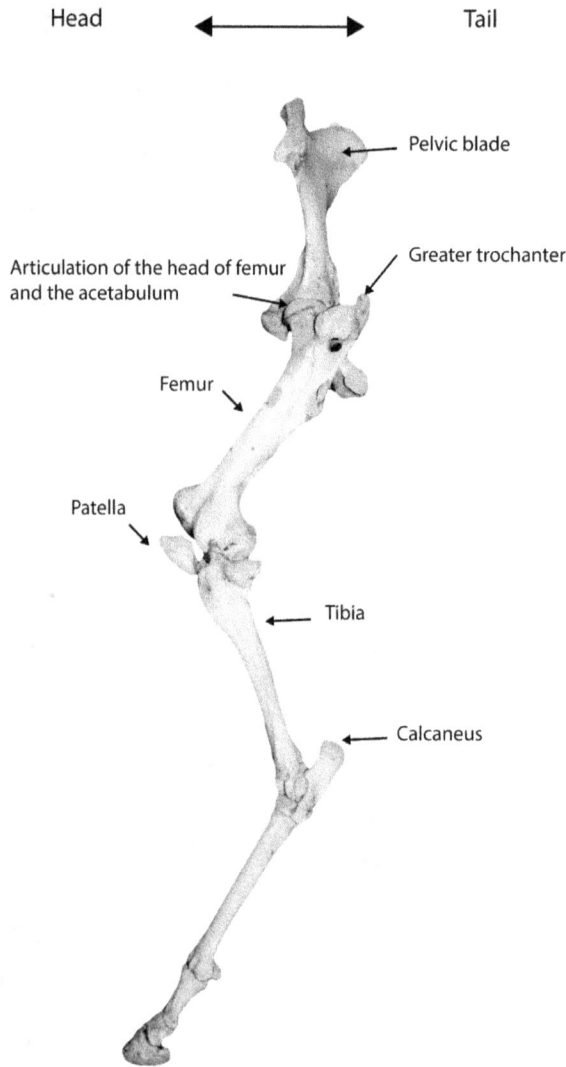

Figure 7.2: Horse hind limb (left, rear), illustrating joint articulation.

Inter-species distinctions

- Horses (Figure 7.3a) and rabbits have a third trochanter laterally.
- Marsupials and rabbits have well-developed lesser trochanters that give the proximal femur a fan-shaped appearance.
- The femoral shaft is straight in horses, cats, pigs, cattle, wombats and possums.
- The femoral shaft is curved convex anteriorly in rabbits, sheep, dingoes, wallabies, kangaroos and humans.
- Marsupials and horses have a long, 90-degree slit-shaped intertrochanteric fossa posteriorly.

- The lesser trochanter of marsupials begins as a rounded knob and terminates in a lipped trough.
- The lesser trochanter of horses is long and stretched in appearance.
- The lesser trochanter of wombats is triangular proximally when viewed from an anterior perspective; when viewed posteriorly, it appears as a distinctive knob that protrudes medially (Figure 7.4c).
- The femoral head has a triangular notch (fovea) in horses.
- Dingo and cat femurs are similar in form (but not in size) to human femurs, but can be distinguished from human femurs by their shorter necks.

Differentiating between humans and macropods

Large kangaroo femurs are frequently mistaken for human femurs. However, closer inspection of the proximal end reveals several key differences.

- In macropods the intertrochanteric fossa is deep, slit-like and angled at 90 degrees, while in humans it is shallow and angled (Figures 7.5b and c).
- In macropods, the knob-like lesser trochanter is followed distally by a lipped trough, whereas in humans there is no trough.
- Macropods have a greater trochanter that extends higher than the femoral head, whereas in humans the femoral head is higher and the greater trochanter is reduced.
- Medially, the human femoral shafts are slender with a long, thread-like, raised linea aspera.
- The linea aspera of kangaroos is very knobby and rugose and is found on the posterior mid-shaft.
- Distally, when viewed posteriorly, human femurs have a shallow patellar groove, whereas in kangaroos the patellar groove is quite deep.

Common state in archaeological assemblages

The femur is frequently encountered in many different types of faunal assemblages across time and space. Its high economic utility as a prime meat-bearing bone in food species is one contributing factor in its frequency (and popularity). Another factor leading to its increased survivability is the femur's general robustness and density compared with other bones of the body. The femur is often found complete or as shaft fragments. Cut marks are frequently found on the femoral head and neck, resulting from the disarticulation of the leg from the pelvis (hip joint). Similarly, cut marks may be visible on the distal condyles resulting from the disarticulation from the lower leg at the knee joint. When fragmented in historical assemblages, femoral shafts often bear cut marks from butcher's band saws. In prehistoric assemblages, the shaft may be smashed and broken open for marrow extraction. In the presence of carnivores, the femoral head is often missing (having been chewed), and the distal condyles are frequently gnawed.

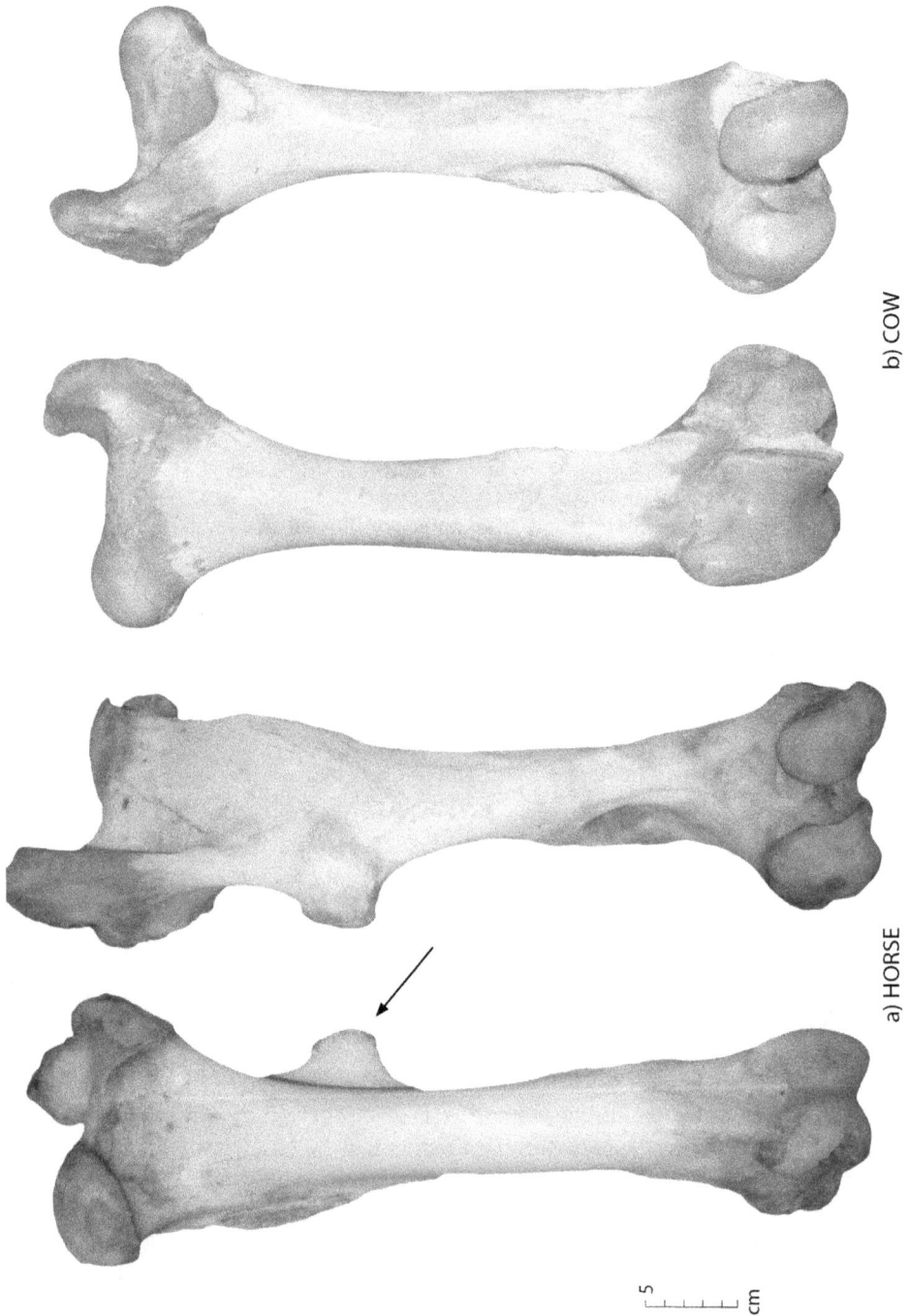

Figure 7.3: Anterior and posterior views of the femur; (a) horse and (b) cow. The third trochanter is visible on the horse (arrowed).

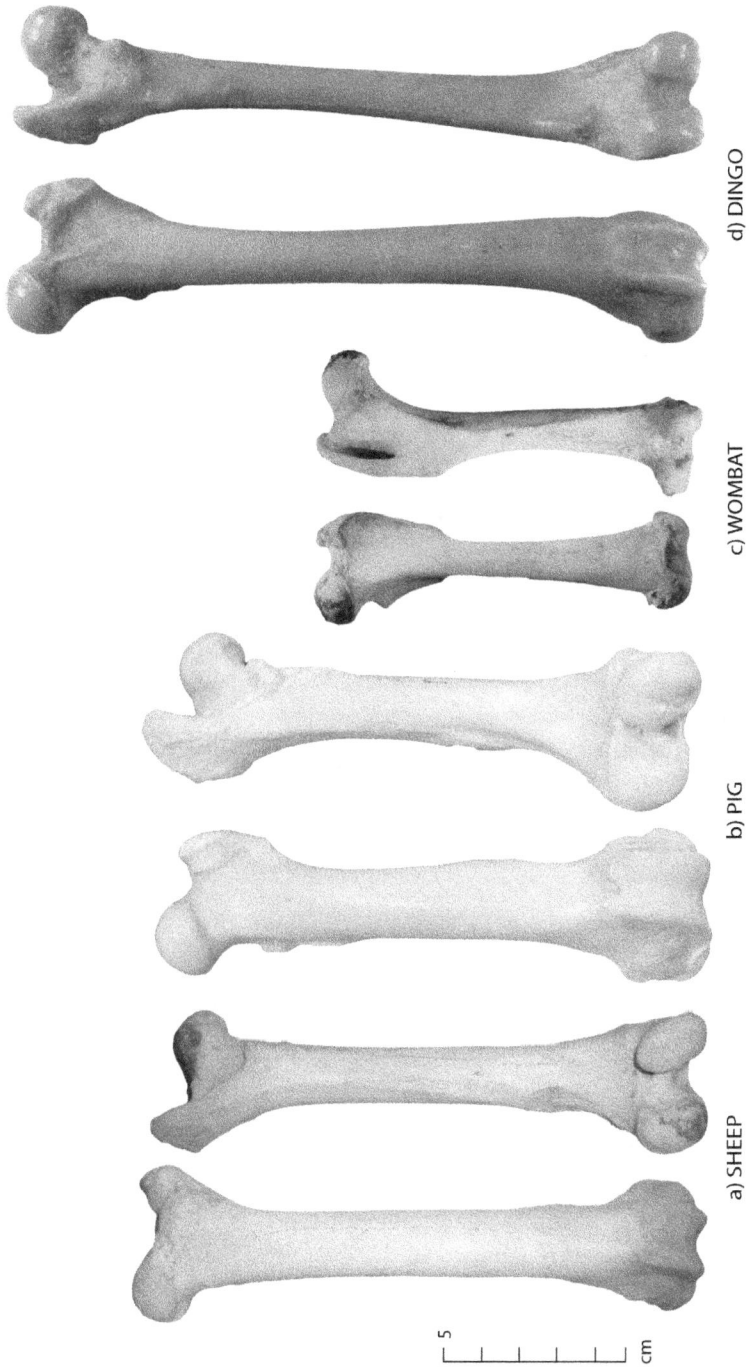

Figure 7.4: Anterior and posterior views of the femur; (a) sheep, (b) pig, and (c) wombat and (d) dingo.

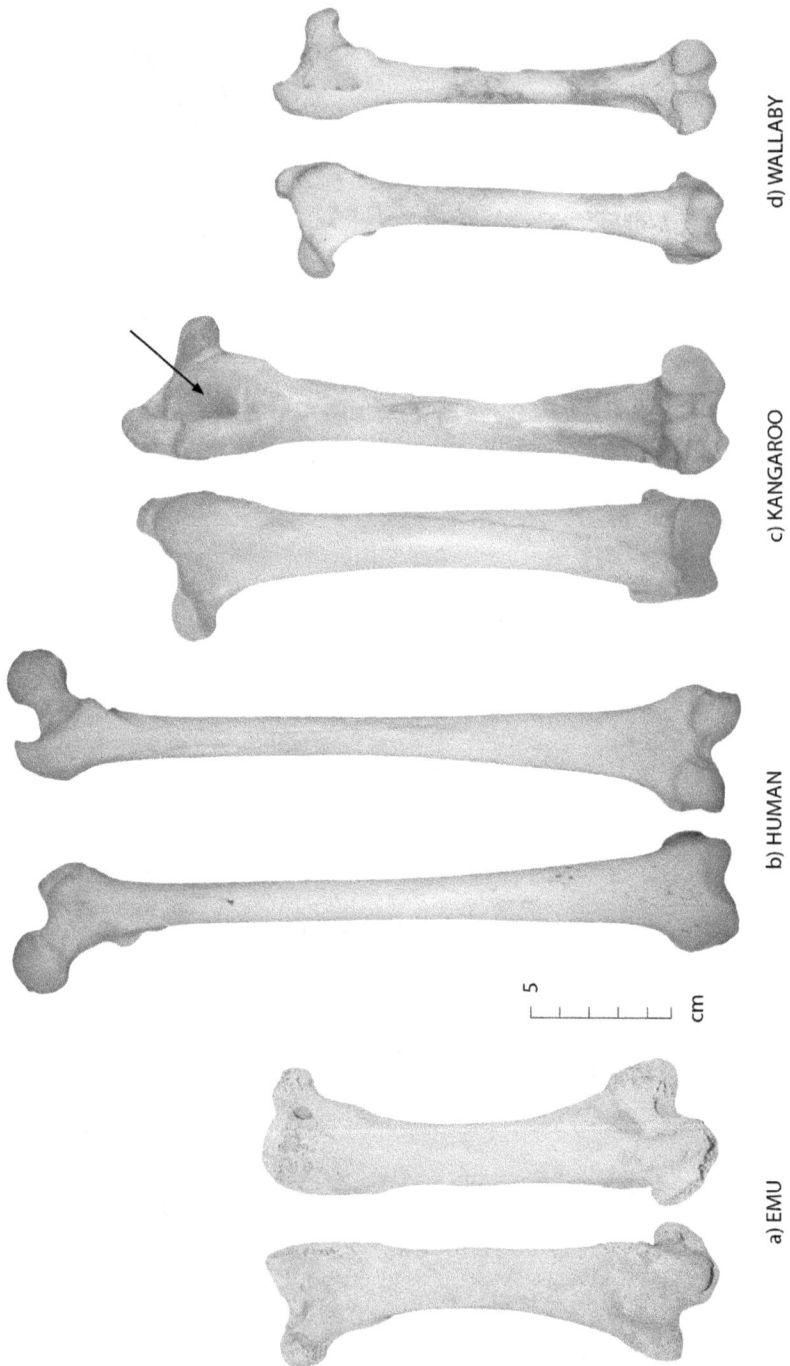

Figure 7.5: Anterior and posterior views of the femur; (a) emu, (b) human, (c) kangaroo and (d) wallaby. Note the 'slit' on posterior kangaroo femur, arrowed.

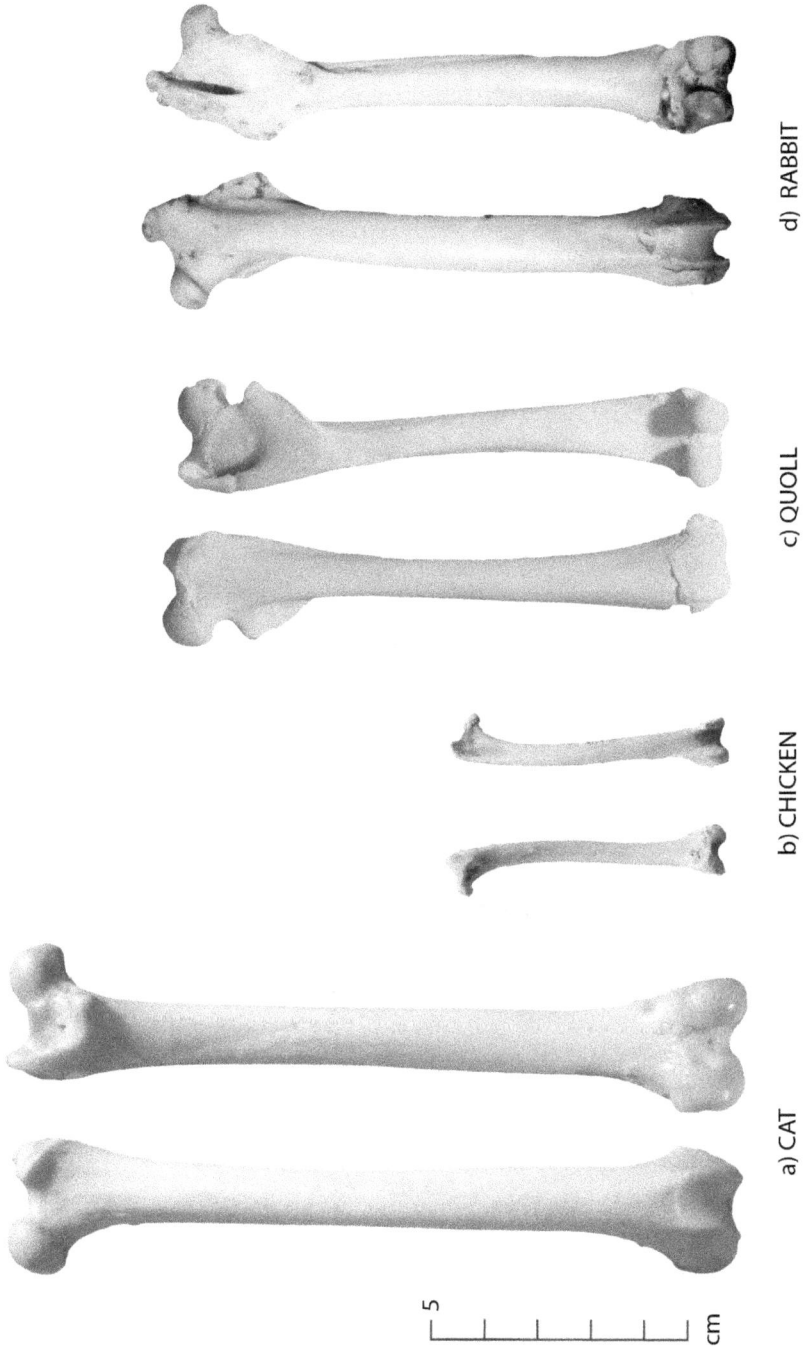

Figure 7.6: Anterior and posterior views of the femur; (a) cat , (b) chicken, (c) quoll and (d) rabbit.

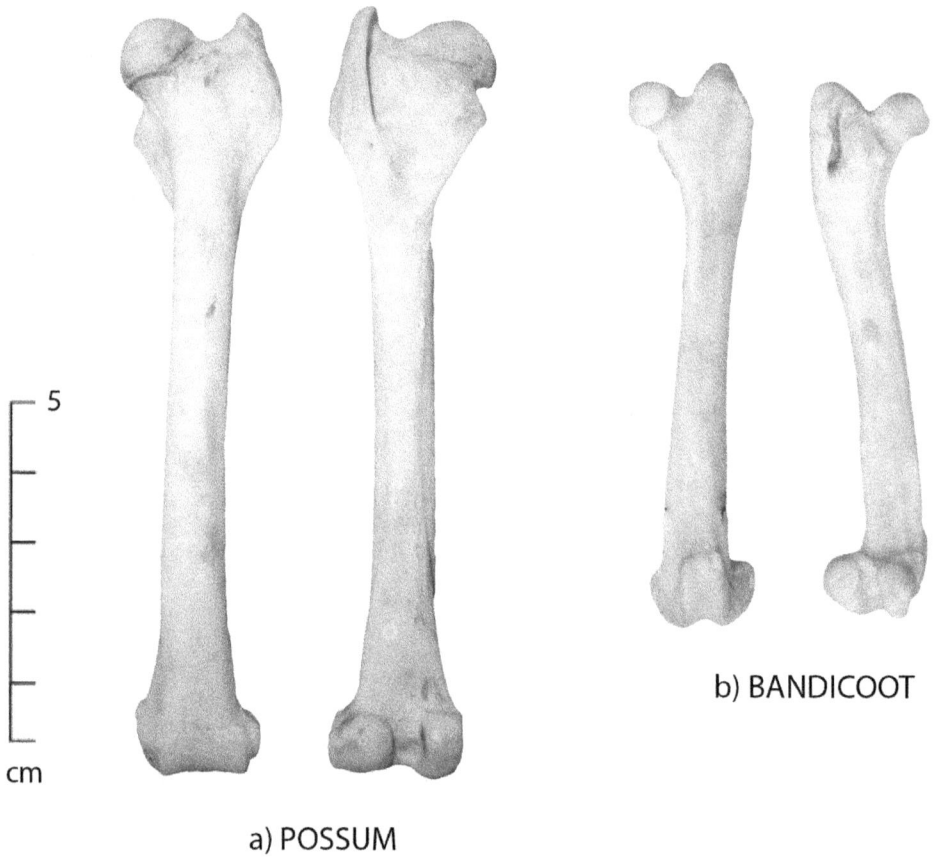

Figure 7.7: Anterior and posterior views of the femur; (a) brushtail possum and (b) bandicoot.

PROXIMAL FEMUR

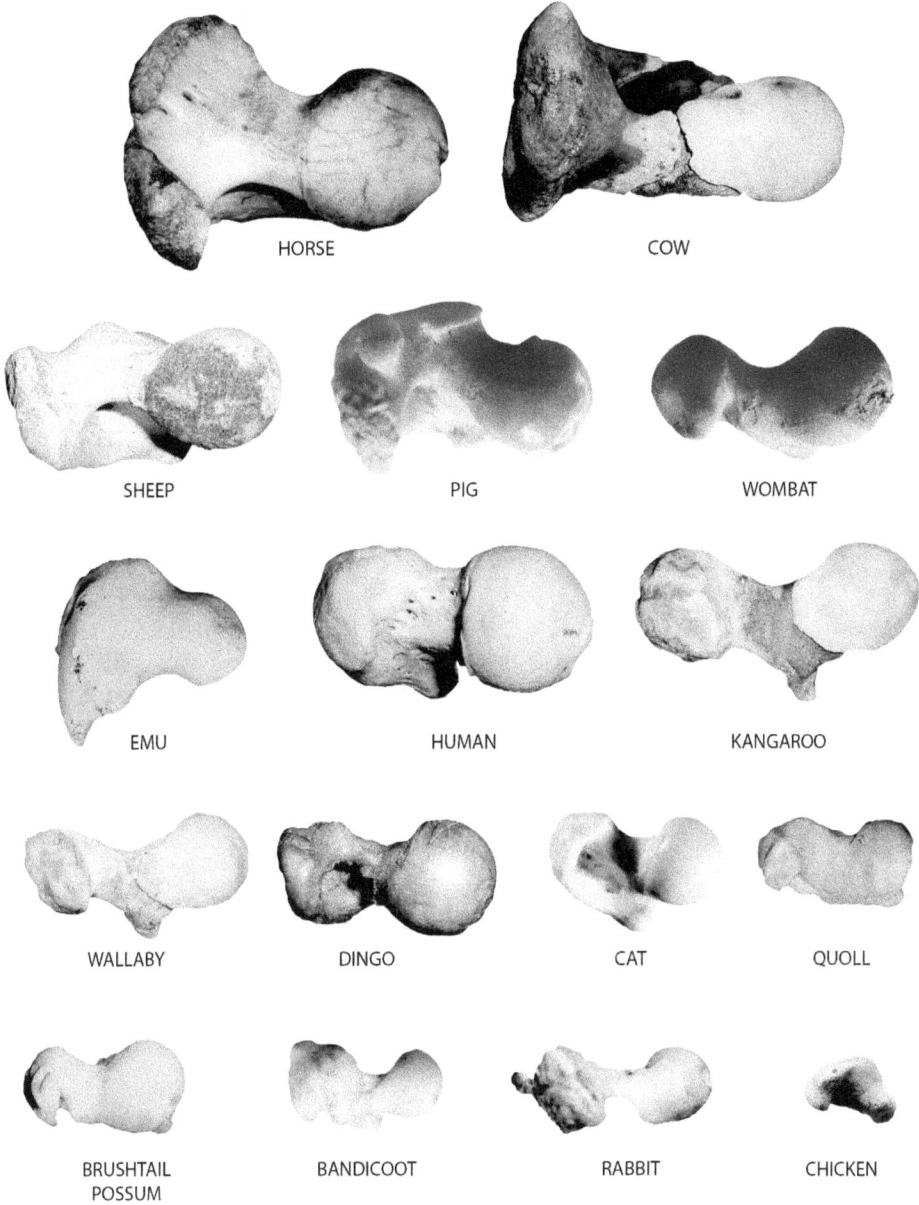

Figure 7.8: Proximal femur for all species (in order of decreasing size). Smaller species are exaggerated in size to show detail.

DISTAL FEMUR

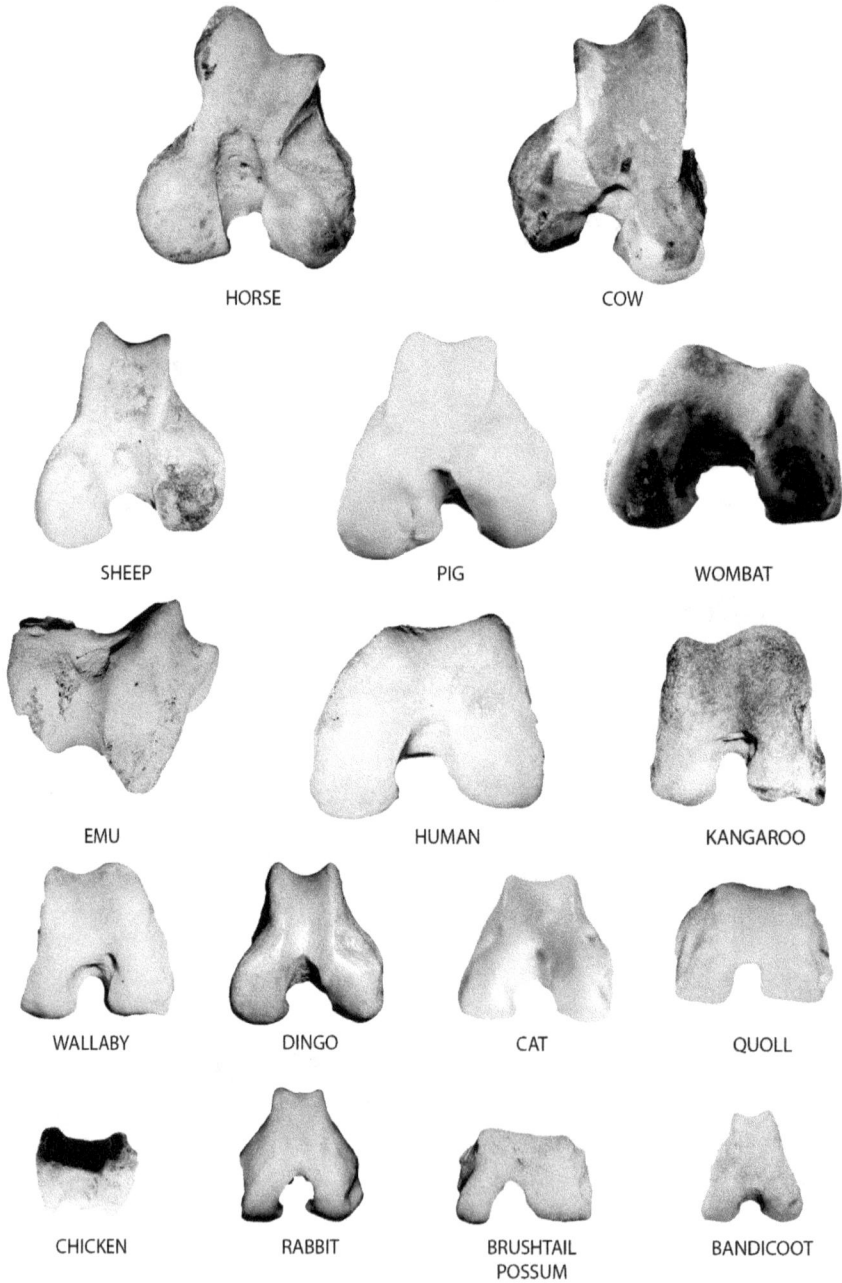

HORSE   COW

SHEEP   PIG   WOMBAT

EMU   HUMAN   KANGAROO

WALLABY   DINGO   CAT   QUOLL

CHICKEN   RABBIT   BRUSHTAIL POSSUM   BANDICOOT

Figure 7.9: Distal femur for all species (in order of decreasing size). Smaller species are exaggerated in size to show detail.

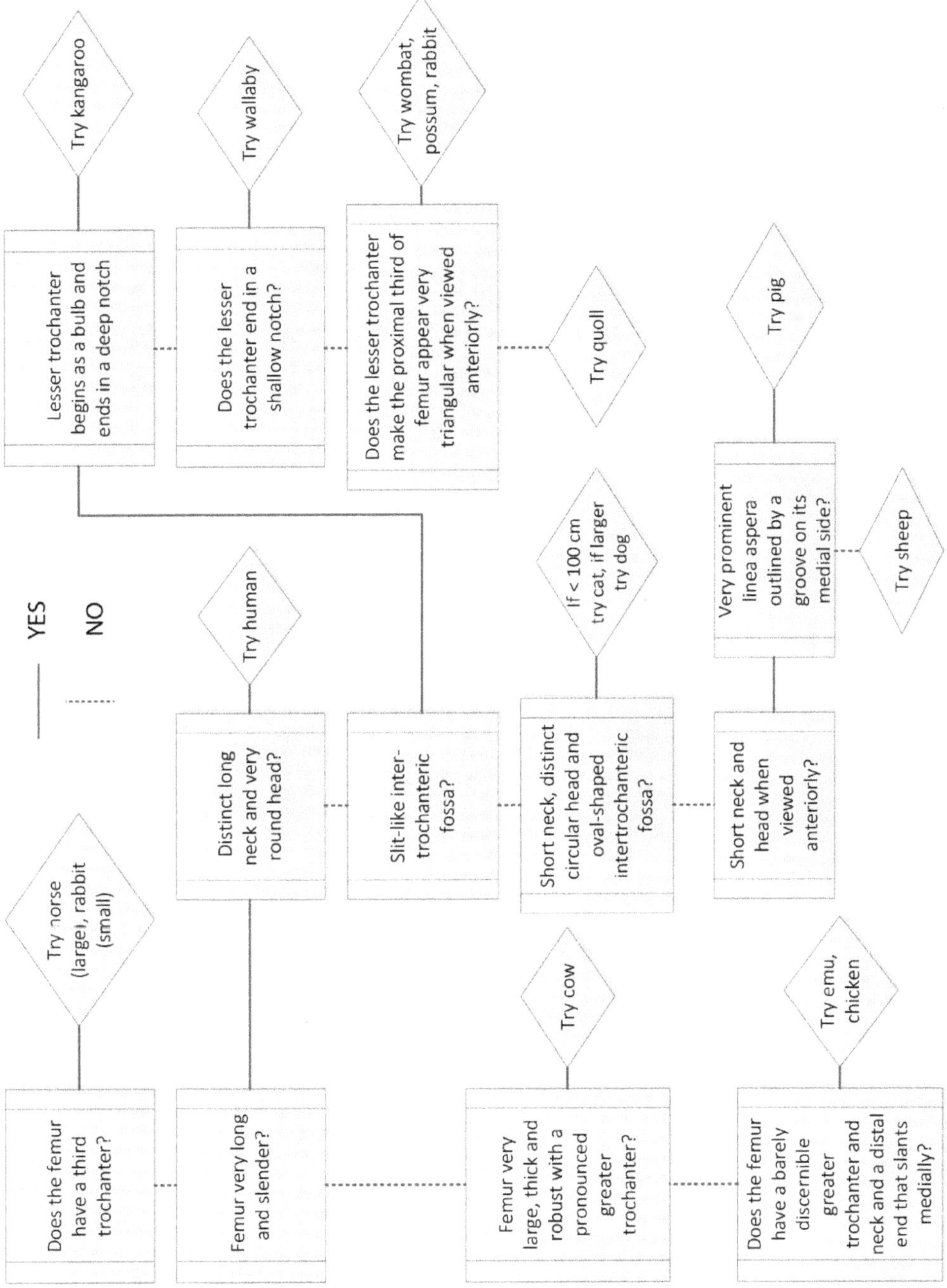

Figure 7.10: Femur decision process.

8
Tibia

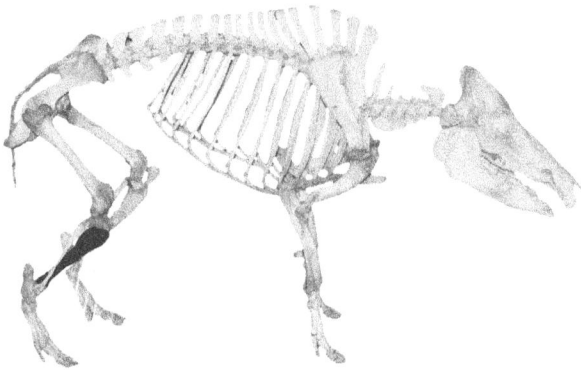

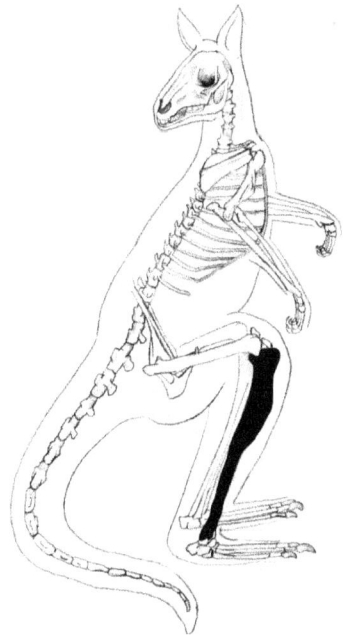

The tibia, or shin bone, is one of the longest bones in the skeleton of most mammals, and one which is commonly recovered from a variety of faunal assemblages. Together with the smaller fibula, the two bones make up the lower leg, and are analogous to the radius and ulna of the fore limb. In some animal species, the tibia and fibula become fused during adulthood, while in others the fibula has become significantly shortened. The fibula is typically long and thin, and frequently broken in archaeological contexts. While an important bone typically used in the manufacture of bone points, on its own the fibula is difficult to identify without the help of a comparative collection. For this reason, the fibula has been omitted from this manual.

Diagnostic features

Diagnostic features of the tibia are shown in Figure 8.1. The tibia is readily identifiable in bone assemblages due to the unique morphology of its proximal and distal articulations, and the shape of its shaft cross-section. The proximal tibia articulates with the distal femur to form the knee joint. This key weight-bearing joint is reflected in the morphology of the broad proximal tibial surface, specifically in the **medial** (1) and **lateral condyles** (2), and the **intercondylar eminence** (3). The **tibial tuberosity** (4) rises from the anterior proximal shaft (5) and runs down the length of the bone as a crest, giving the tibia a triangular shape when viewed in cross-section. Distally, the tibia has a swollen appearance for articulation with the either the talus or calcaneus to form the ankle joint of many species. The distal articular surface is trough-like, and is characterised by the **medial malleolus** (6), a small protrusion or process that in humans forms the 'bump' on the inside of the ankle.

Orientation and siding

The tibia is one of the easiest bones to orient and side, due to the distinctive crest, the tibial tuberosity, on its anterior surface. To orient the tibia, place the broad, wide articular surface up or proximal, and the small, trough-like depression down, or distal. Next, place the tibial tuberosity facing away from you – or anterior. When placed in this way (anatomical position), the crest will lean toward the side from which it came.

Species identification

Refer to Figures 8.2–8.7 for species identification using the tibia. While the tibia is one of the easiest bones to identify, it is also one of the harder ones to correctly assign to species as a result of its remarkable uniformity. This said, the two best areas on which to base species identifications are the proximal and distal articular surfaces – with the distal articulation being the 'easiest'. As with all elements, the morphology of the tibia is a reflection of the way in which an animal moves. This means that the tibias of most quadrupeds will appear similar, as will those of most bipeds. In Australian sites, this translates into kangaroo tibias being frequently mistaken as human. The following list contains some specific inter-species distinctions.

| (1) | Medial condyle | (3) | Intercondylar eminence | (5) | Shaft |
| (2) | Lateral condyle | (4) | Tibial tuberosity | (6) | Medial malleolus |

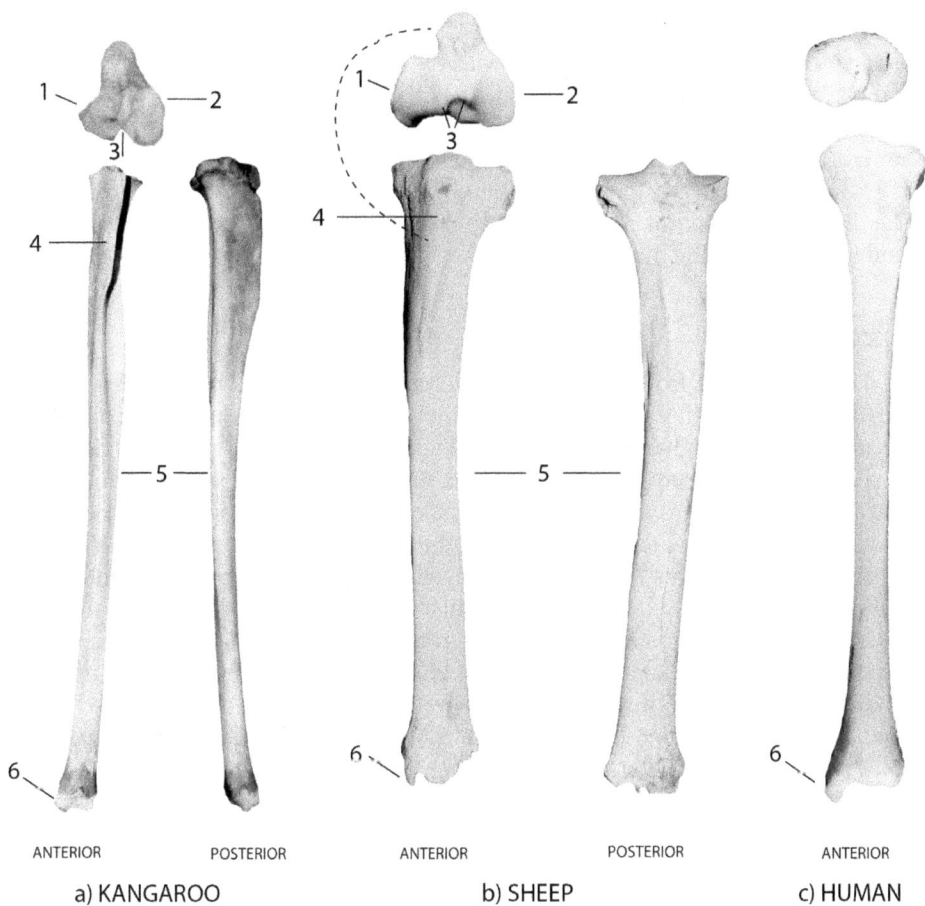

ANTERIOR   POSTERIOR   ANTERIOR   POSTERIOR   ANTERIOR

a) KANGAROO   b) SHEEP   c) HUMAN

Figure 8.1: Anterior and posterior views of the tibia, labelled: (a) kangaroo, (b) sheep and (c) human.

Distinguishing between humans and animals

- The proximal condyles of the human tibia are rounded in appearance, while they are triangular in most other species (including macropods) (Figure 8.3).

Distal articulation

- The distal articulation of a human tibia is triangular in outline, with very shallow, less pronounced 'troughs' for articulation with the ankle (talus). There is a prominent medial malleolus (see Figure 8.3b).
- The distal articulation of a macropod tibia (kangaroos and wallabies) is similar to the human, but has a rectangular outline, rather than a triangular outline (Figures 8.3c and d).
- The distal articulation of cows and sheep has an additional twin-lobed protrusion extending laterally of the main articulation.

Other comparisons

- To distinguish cattle from horses: horses have a groove on the upper-most portion of the tibial tuberosity that produces two distinct 'swollen' areas, whereas in cows this area has just one very roughened swollen area (Figure 8.2).
- To distinguish pigs from sheep: pigs have a very short, thick tibia that is robust in appearance and has a pronounced medial malleolus (because pigs have a fibula). Sheep have long, thin tibias with a flared distal end on both sides (Figures 8.4a and b).
- To distinguish wombats from pigs: distally, wombats have a very pronounced medial malleolus that extends beyond the articular surface. Pigs have a pronounced tibial tuberosity, whereas wombats have a sharp crest that extends two-thirds of the way down the shaft, giving the tibia a very flattened, twisted appearance (Figures 8.4b and c).
- To distinguish dingoes from sheep: both have long, thin tibias, but the dingo has a pronounced medial malleolus balanced by a smooth, knob-like lateral end, whereas the distal sheep tibia flares laterally.
- To distinguish rabbits from possums: possums have a proximal surface that is rounded in outline, in contrast to the triangular outline of rabbits. Distally, the rabbit tibia is flared on both sides, whereas the possum tibia ends in a pronounced medial malleolus that has a knob-like appearance.
- The fibula is fused to the tibia in rabbits (Figure 8.5d). It is unfused but greatly reduced in horses, emus and chickens. The fibula is also unfused in kangaroos, wallabies, wombats, humans, pigs, dingoes, cats and possums. The fibula is absent in cows and sheep.
- The tibia of a bird is often referred to as a tibio-tarsus, and is easily recognisable by a distinctive morphology that includes a rounded, spool-shaped distal articulation and a very prominent tibial crest that often rises higher than the proximal articular surface.

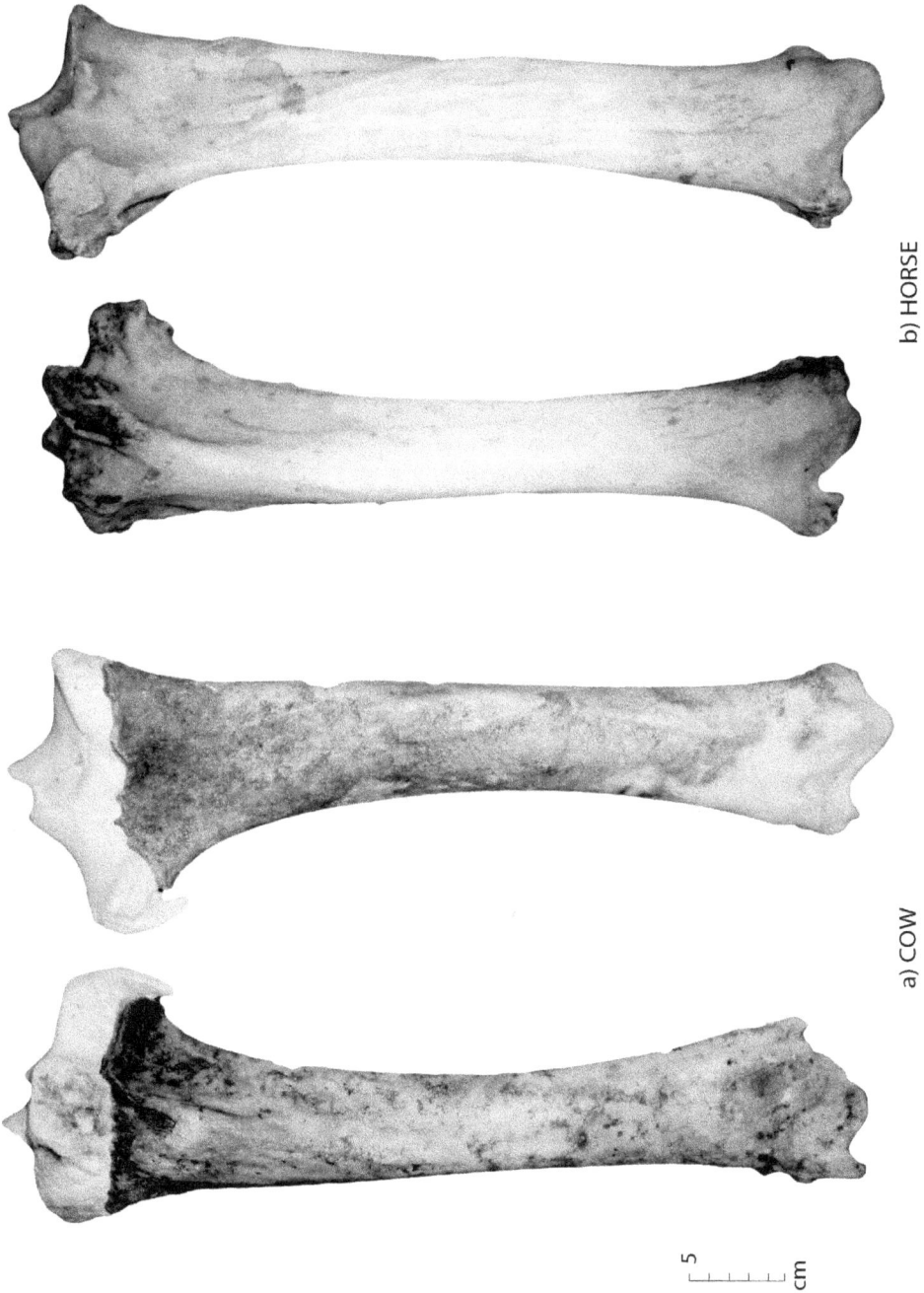

b) HORSE

a) COW

Figure 8.2: Anterior and posterior views of the tibia; (a) horse and (b) cow. Note the groove on the upper part of the tibial tuberosity of the horse that gives two protruding areas.

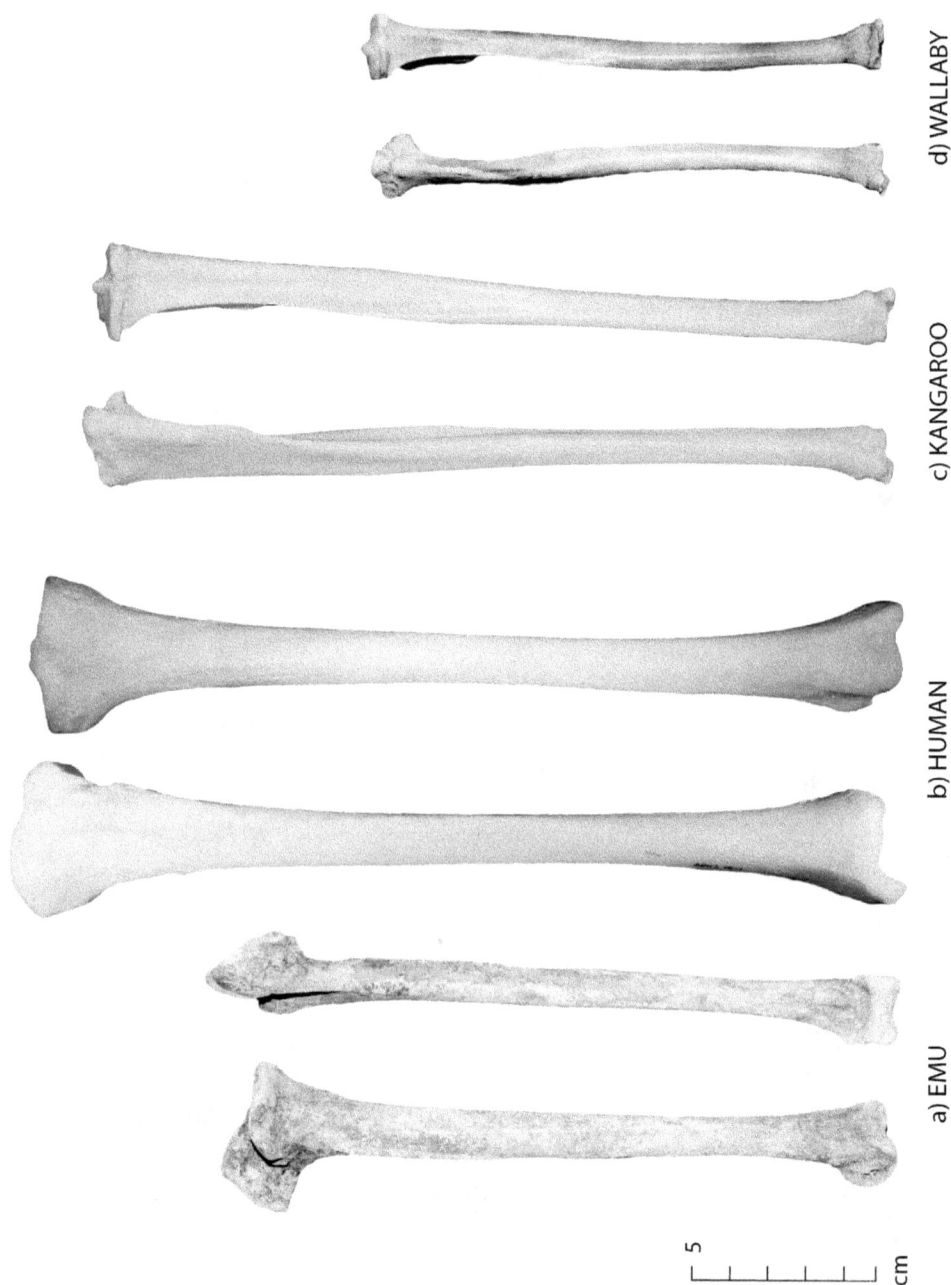

Figure 8.3: Anterior and posterior views of the tibia; (a) emu, (b) human, (c) kangaroo and (d) wallaby. The human tibia is long and slender, with rounded proximal condyles; however, in most other species, the proximal end is triangular.

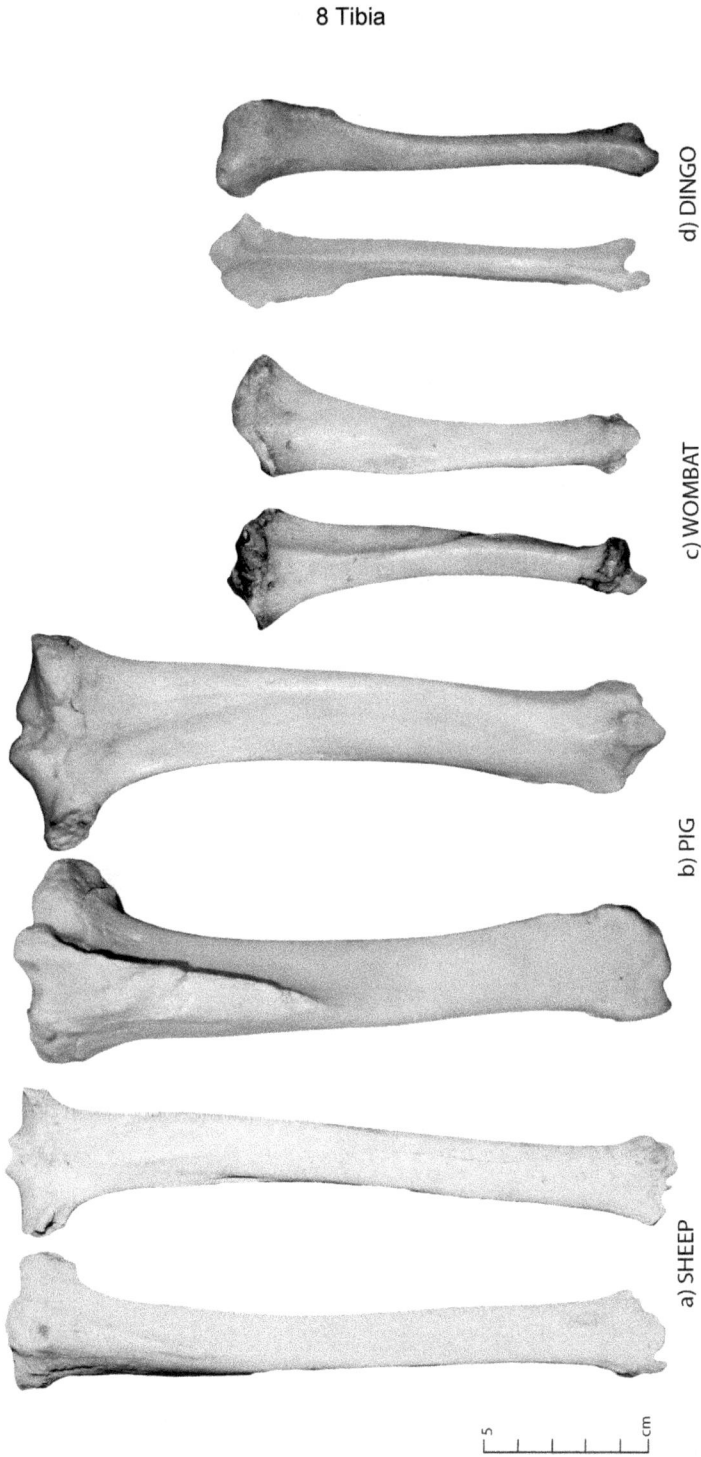

Figure 8.4: Anterior and posterior views of the tibia; (a) sheep, (b) pig, (c) wombat and (d) dingo.

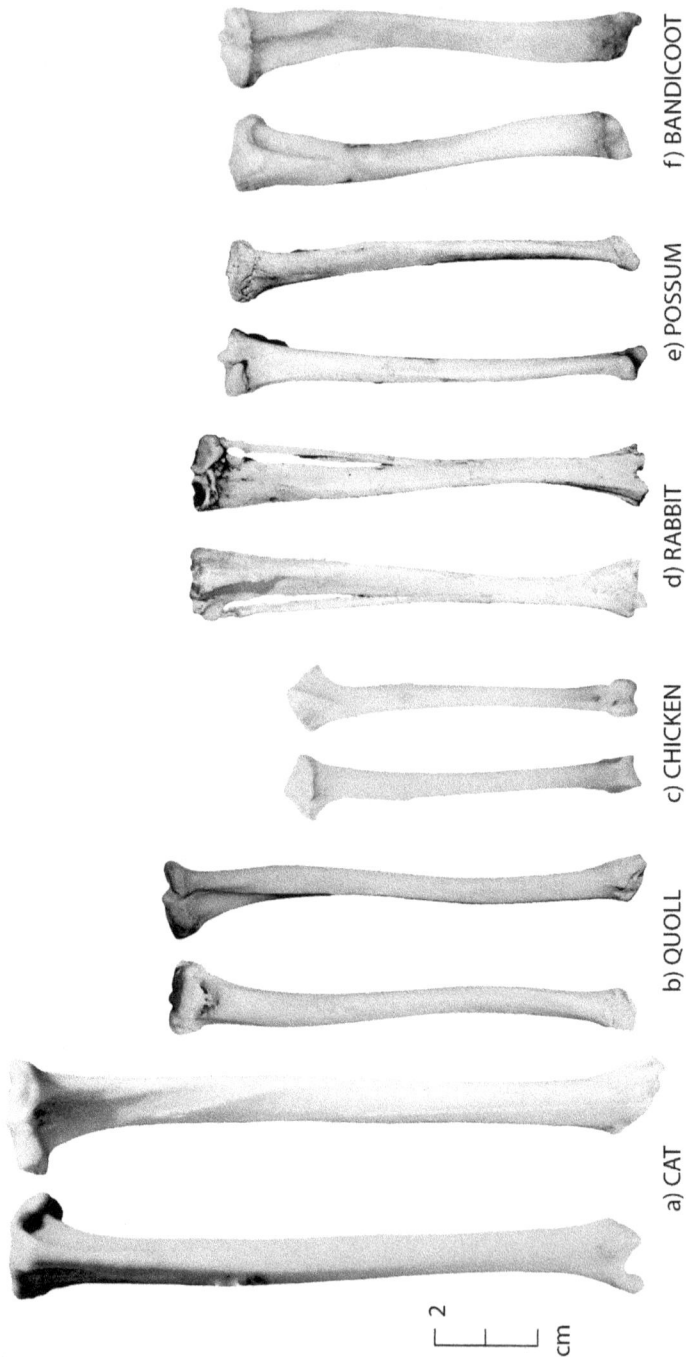

Figure 8.5: Anterior and posterior views of the tibia; (a) cat, (b) quoll, (c) chicken, (d) rabbit, (e) brush-tail possum and (f) bandicoot.

PROXIMAL TIBIA

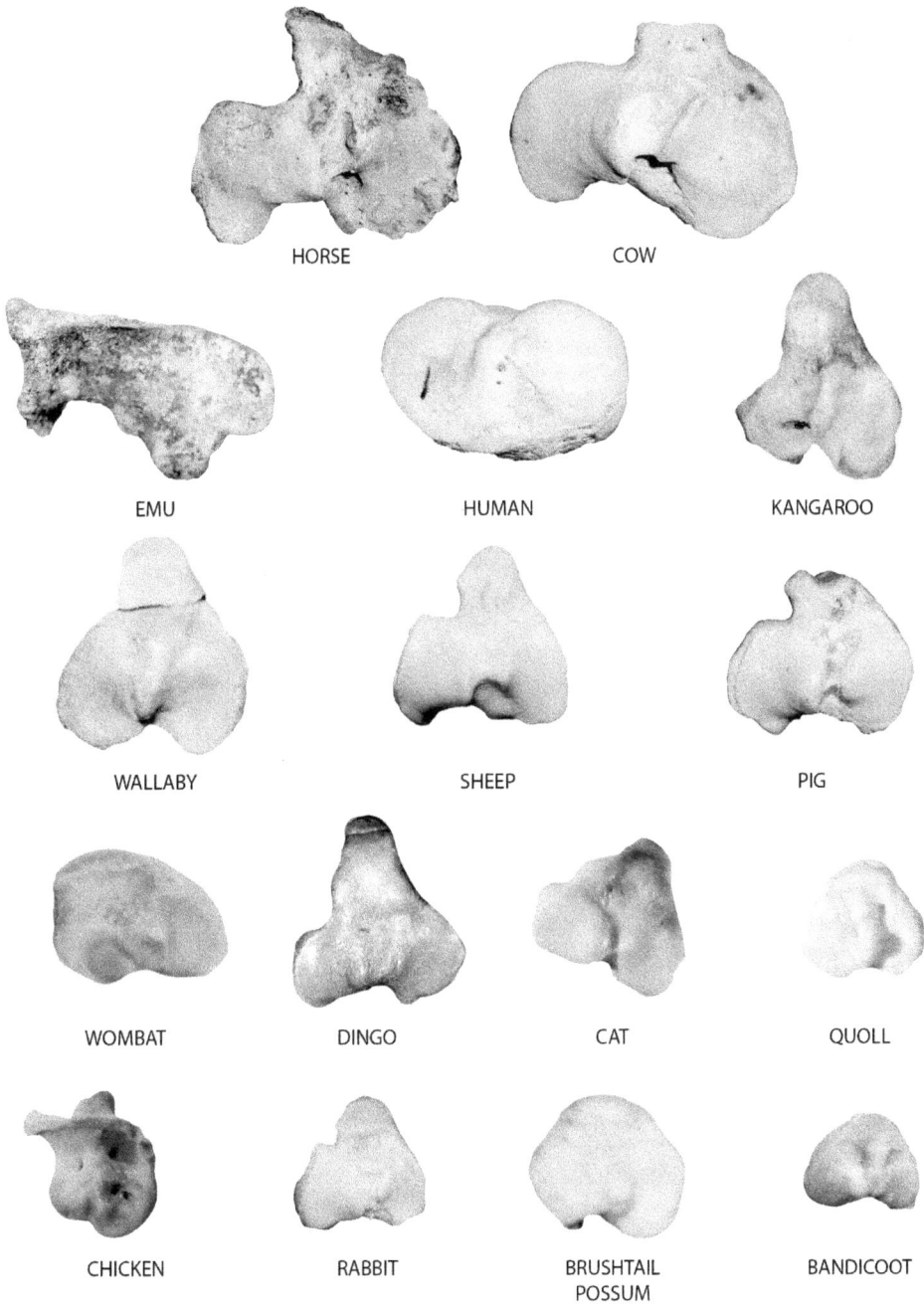

Figure 8.6: Proximal tibia of all species (in order of decreasing size). Smaller species are shown at an exaggerated size to show detail.

DISTAL TIBIA

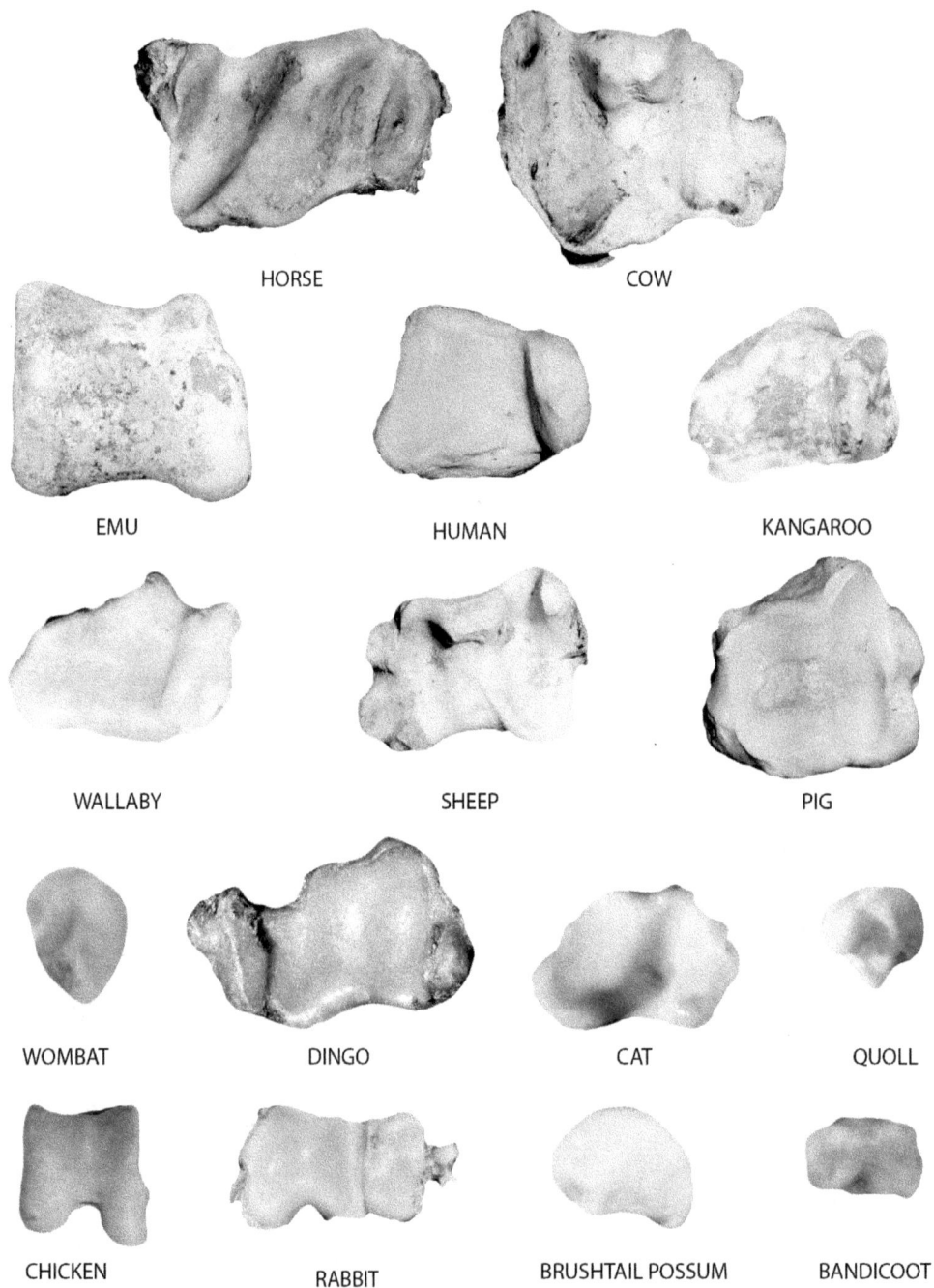

Figure 8.7: Distal tibia of all species (in order of deceasing size). Smaller species are shown at an exaggerated size to show detail.

Common state in archaeological assemblages

The tibia is one of the few bones that may be recovered complete from many archaeological contexts. This may be due to its general robustness or tendency to remain articulated with the ankle and foot bones (especially in macropods and birds). When broken, the fragmentation of the tibia in most species follows a similar pattern. The proximal articulation is often missing, as it is also an epiphyseal cap that in young species may not be fully fused at the time of death. In marsupials, the proximal surface fuses very late in life, and often not at all. The distal articulation of the tibia is also late fusing in marsupials, and often missing unless the bone remained articulated with the foot. In most other species, the tibia may be broken in two around the mid-shaft, frequently resulting in medio-distal fragments that can be identified on the distal morphology and the triangular cross-sectional shape of the shaft.

The relative completeness of the tibia varies between types of sites and assemblages. For example, in naturally accumulated assemblages in which an animal may have died without human agency, the tibia often remains articulated with the foot. This results in the recovery of medio-distal tibia with intact distal articulations. This pattern is common, whether the animal has died from being bogged in soft mud or was killed and scavenged by predators. In prehistoric Indigenous assemblages, the tibia may remain articulated to the foot of many species, especially in large kangaroos and emus, as there is little to no edible meat on this body part. However, tibias in Indigenous assemblages may also be reduced to small fragments as a result of being smashed open for marrow extraction. In historic assemblages, the tibia is frequently cut through the shaft, with traces of the easily identifiable striations of a butcher's band saw. The placement of the cut is dependent upon the portion of meat desired, and may vary between urban and rural contexts.

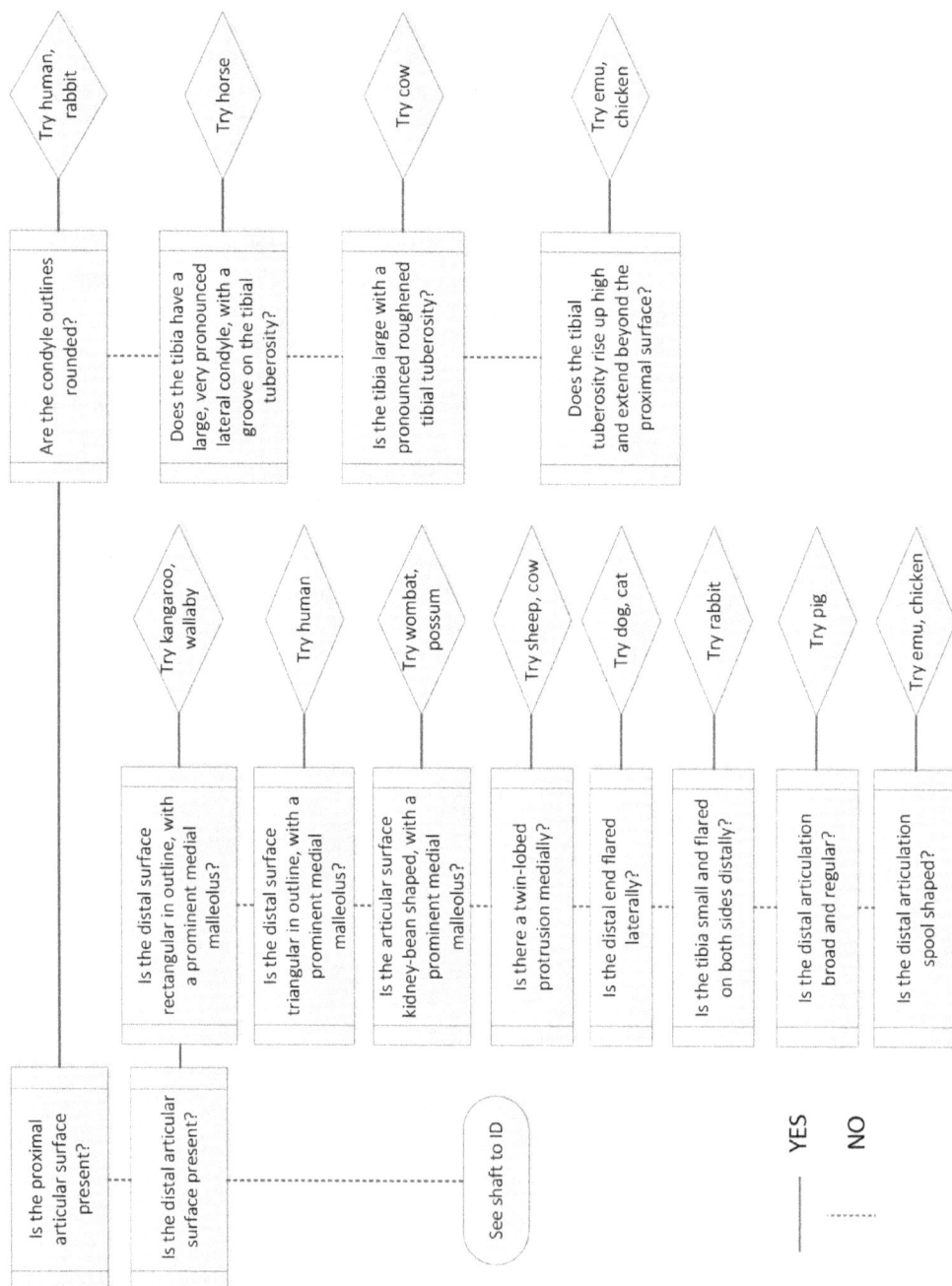

Figure 8.8: Tibia decision process 1. Use this decision process if you have the proximal or distal articular surface of the tibia.

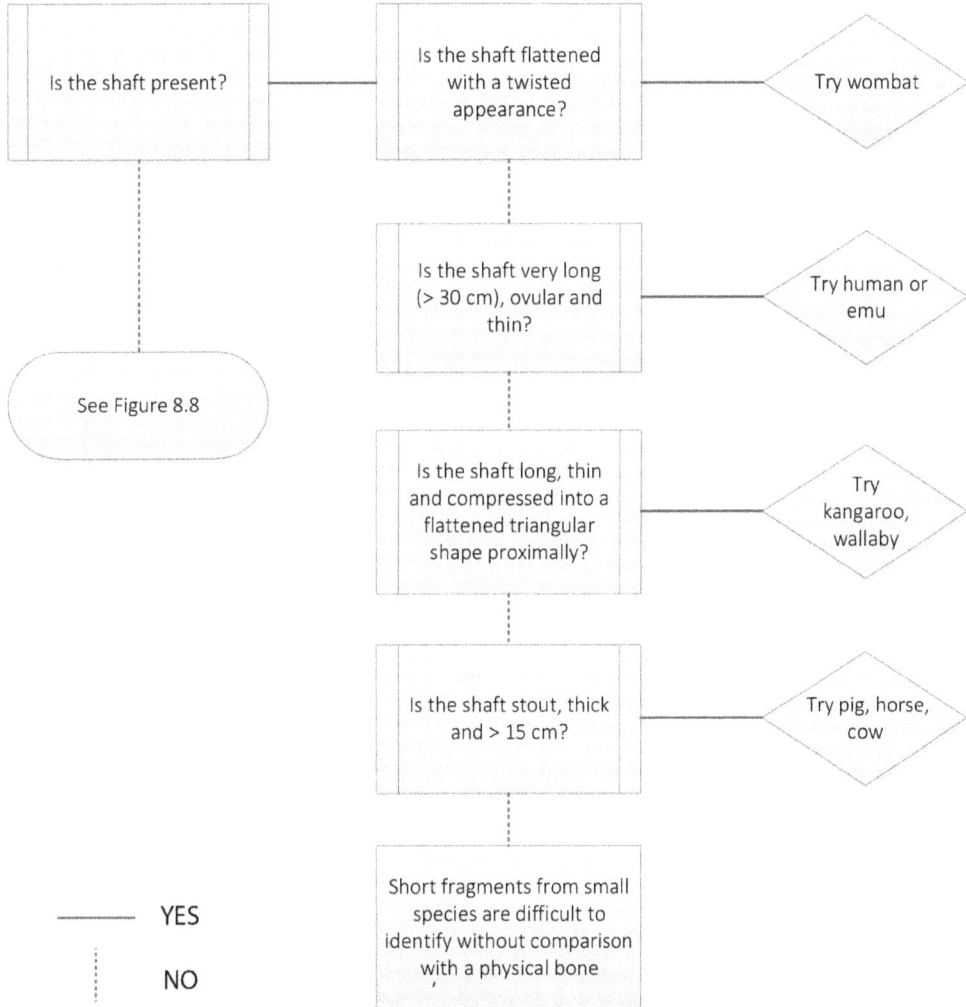

Figure 8.9: Tibia decision process 2. Use this decision process if you have the tibia shaft.

9
The extremities: hands and feet

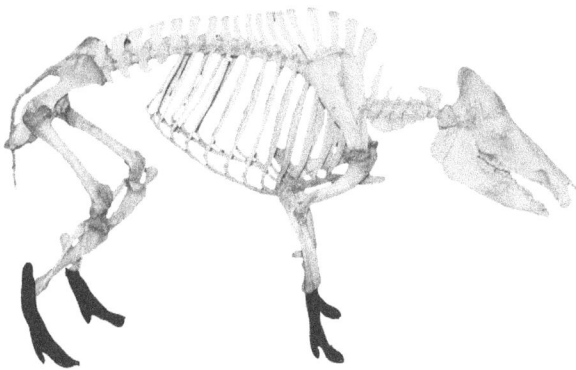

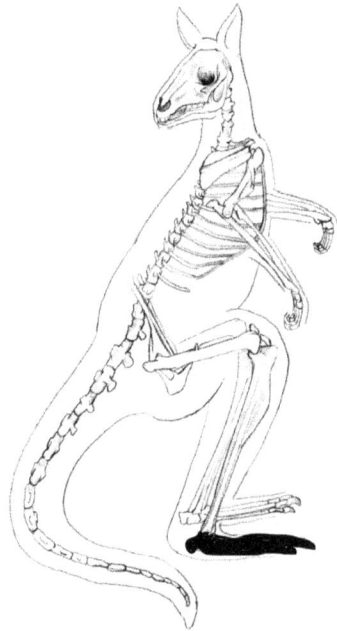

The bones of the extremities (hands and feet), often generically termed 'metapodials' are numerous, some with confusingly similar morphologies. This chapter provides a generalised discussion of both fore and hind limb elements as a starting point. Two bones, the astragalus (talus) and calcaneus are discussed in detail, since both are found in all species, are easy to identify, and are commonly recovered intact from archaeological contexts. The remaining bones are discussed more generally. Photos of articulated extremities of each species are included to augment this discussion. The combination of text and photos provides a starting point that should permit you to at least identify a bone as coming from the hand or foot, and hopefully enable you to identify its type (e.g. metatarsal, phalanx). As you are by now no doubt aware, finer identification to species necessitates a good comparative collection and consultation with a specialist.

'Hands' versus 'feet'

Many of the major bones of the extremities of the major quadrupeds are virtually indistinguishable, while there are greater differences among bipeds (in this manual, humans and macropods). The major bones of the fore leg (hand) are the carpals (wrist), metacarpals (knuckles) and phalanges (fingers) (Figure 9.1). The major bones of the hind leg are the calcaneus, astragalus, tarsals (all three make up the ankle joint), metatarsals and phalanges (toes) (Figure 9.2). From an evolutionary perspective, there is a successive reduction in the number of bones, beginning with humans. For example, the human foot has 26 bones (and there are 27 in the human hand), and horses have 12 foot bones.

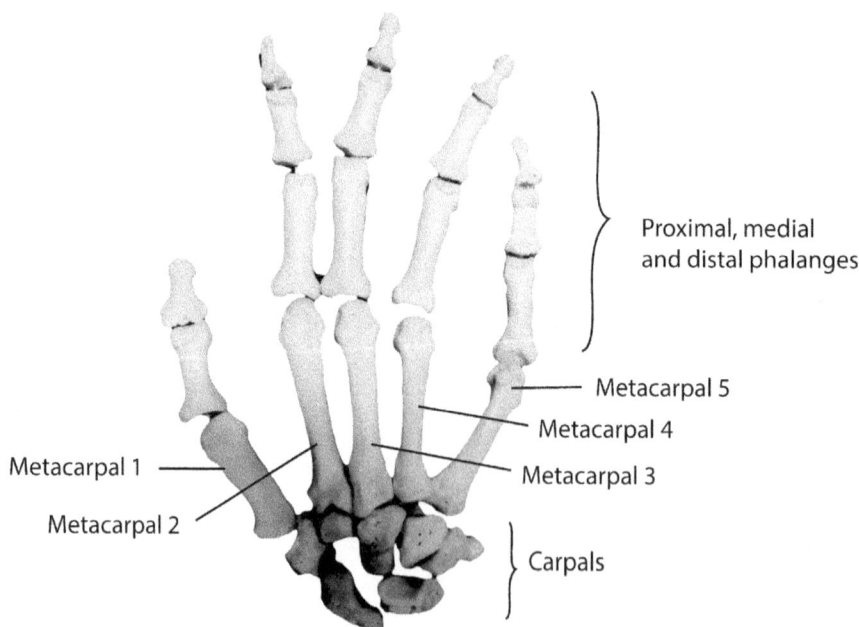

Figure 9.1: Human hand with major bones labelled.

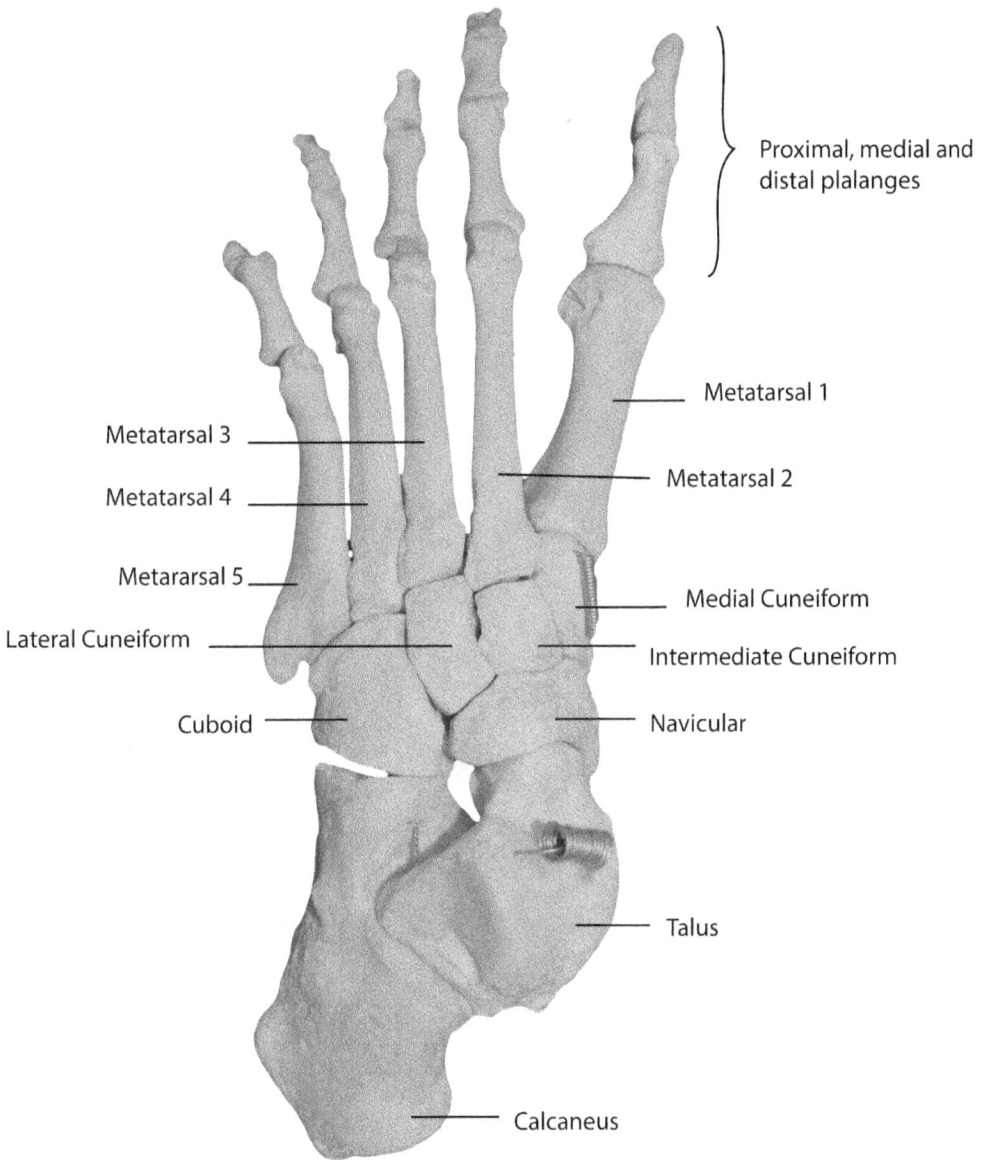

Figure 9.2: Human foot with major bones labelled.

Types of bones in the extremities

Carpals are the small, irregularly shaped bones that make up the fore limb ankle joint (or wrist in bipeds). The number of carpals varies by species, ranging from seven in humans to just two in cattle and sheep. The name of each varies according to position and whether the nomenclature followed is for humans or animals (see Hillson 1992).

Tarsals are the hind limb (ankle) equivalent to carpals, and they too vary in shape, number and morphology. The maximum number of tarsal bones is seven (found in most species) to two (found in cattle and sheep). The astragalus (talus) and calcaneus are the largest, and most easily recognisable of the tarsal bones, and are discussed and depicted in greater detail below (Figures 9.8–9.9).

The astragalus is one of two main bones in the ankle joint (Figure 9.3). It has two main articular facets, the superior, which is either saddle or pulley-shaped, for articulation with the distal tibia, and a second inferiorly, which varies in morphology, for articulation with the central tarsal bone.

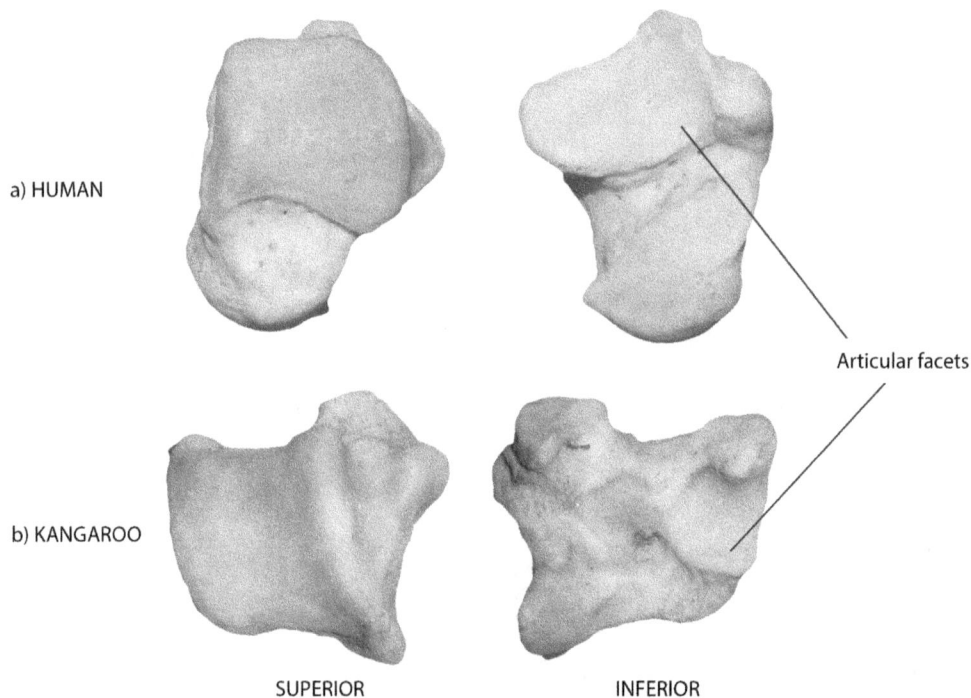

a) HUMAN

b) KANGAROO

Articular facets

SUPERIOR   INFERIOR

Figure 9.3: Astragali with the articular facets labelled in the superior and inferior views; (a) human, (b) kangaroo.

The calcaneus (the heel bone) is easy to recognise due to its distinctive morphology, which includes a square to triangular-shaped distal end with several articular facets (Figure 9.4). Proximally, the calcaneus has a swollen, roughened **head** (1), to which the Achilles tendon is attached. The **shaft** (2) varies in length and thickness, and the distal articulation contains a series of smaller articular surfaces for joints with the astragalus and central tarsal bones. There is a roughened protrusion on the medial size of the distal articulation, the **sustentaculum tali** (3), which forms the main articulation with the astragalus.

(1) Head   (2) Shaft   (3) Sustentaculum tali

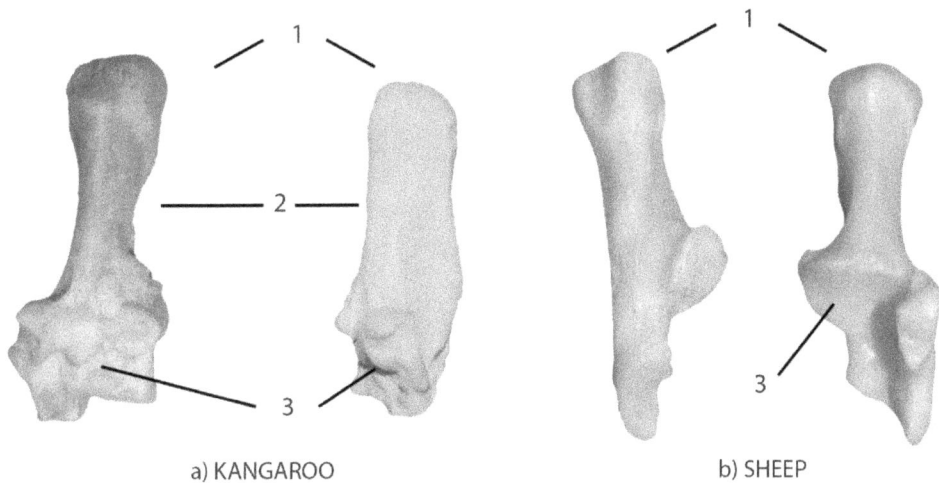

a) KANGAROO   b) SHEEP

Figure 9.4: Calcanei with diagnostic features labelled in the anterior and medial views; (a) kangaroo, (b) sheep.

Metacarpals and metatarsals (collectively termed metapodials) are the long, tubular bones that connect the wrist or ankle joint with the phalanges (toe bones). Most species have four, but again their number is variable (Figure 9.5). They are larger than, but morphologically similar to phalanges, and have two articular surfaces (proximal and distal). In some species, such as cattle, sheep and horses, the metacarpals and tarsals are reduced in number, reflected in their morphology. In cattle and sheep, the metapodials are reduced to two (the third and fourth metapodials), which fuse together early in life, forming one wide, thickened bone with a characteristic double pulley-shaped distal end (Figure 9.5). In macropods, the metacarpals are similar to humans, but the metatarsals are changed. Macropods have evolved to have one large, central metatarsal, the fourth (IV), with varying numbers of smaller metatarsals. Kangaroos and wallabies have four metatarsals in total, the second and third (II, III) are greatly reduced, long and thin, while the fifth (V) is intermediate in size between the large fifth and smaller second and third (Figure 9.6). The changes in the metatarsals of macropods are an adaptation to their unique pattern of locomotion (i.e. hopping). A selected example of articulated fore and hind limbs have been included at the end of this section.

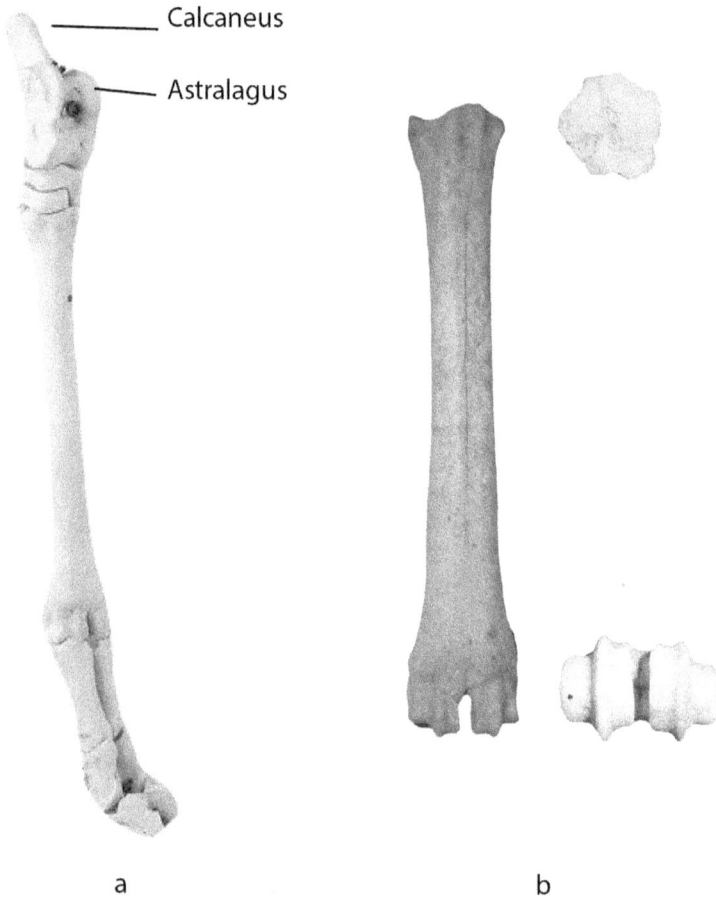

Figure 9.5: (a) Articulated sheep hind foot with calcaneus and astragalus labelled; (b) sheep metatarsal, note the spool-shaped distal end.

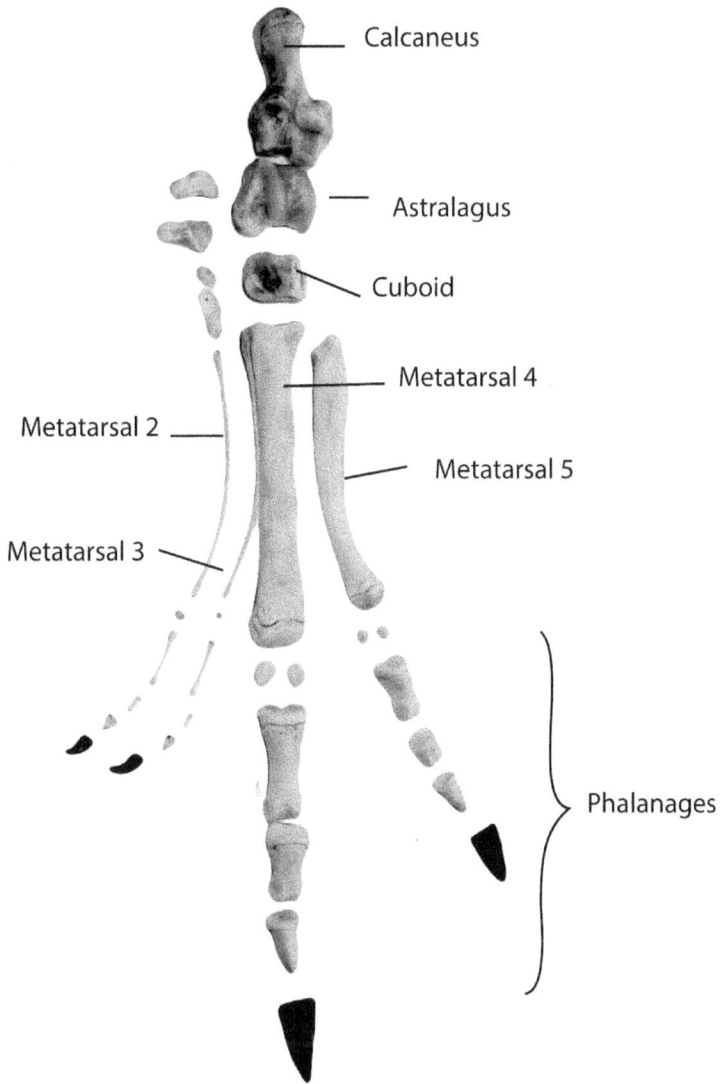

Figure 9.6: Semi-articulated kangaroo foot.

Phalanges (finger and toe bones) follow similar evolutionary patterns as the metapodials. In most species, each digit is comprised of three phalanges (singular, phalanx) (Figure 9.7). These are often referred to as either the first, second or third phalanx, or the proximal, intermediate or distal phalanx. The third, or distal, phalanx of most species is a claw or hoof. It is often very difficult to distinguish between phalanges from the hand and foot, and to avoid certain frustration, this should not be attempted without additional resources.

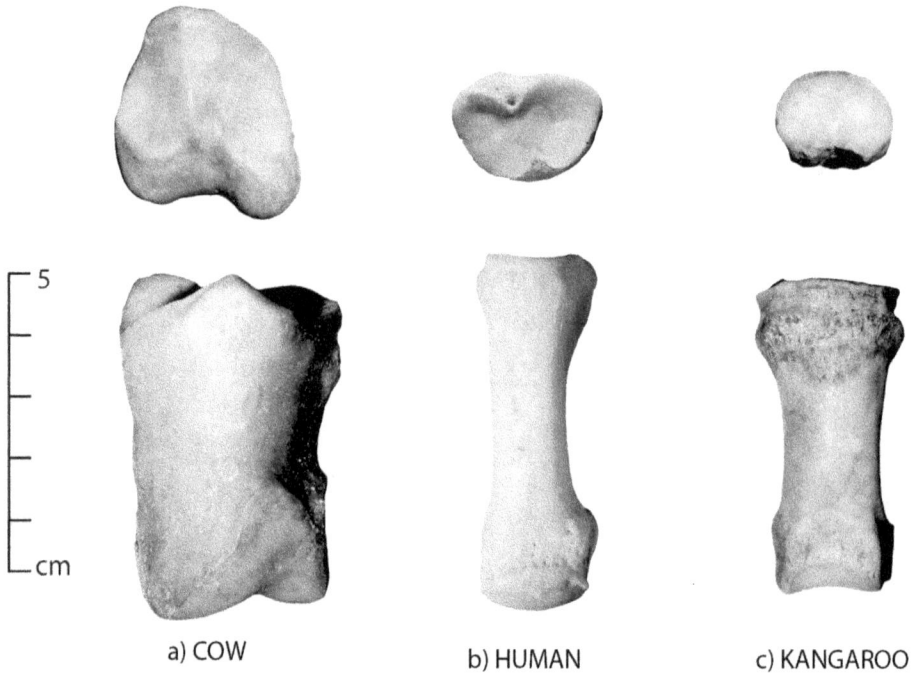

Figure 9.7: Morphological comparison of the first phalanx from (a) cow, (b) human and (c) kangaroo.

Common state in archaeological assemblages

As you can imagine, the morphological variation between the different bones of the extremities plays a role in their preservation. In general, smaller carpals, tarsals and pha-langes survive well; however, they are often the subject of recovery bias if an assemblage is not sieved (as smaller bones may be missed when recovered by eye). From the perspec-tive of subsistence, hands and feet are typically less desirable than other, meatier bones such as femurs. This results in variable patterns of consumption, in which their presence or absence can have different interpretations. An absence of extremities, coupled with the presence of long bones, might suggest offsite butchery. In a settlement context, this pattern might also have implications for status. The presence of extremities alone could represent waste or it could represent consumers of lower socio-economic rank if the bones show signs of cooking/butchery.

There are also many uses of metapodial bones in contexts outside of subsistence. In industrial contexts involving hide-working such as those associated with tanning, the large metapodials of many species (cattle, sheep, horse) were left intact with the skin to be used as handles to aid in processing hides. Large metapodials (such as those of sheep, cattle or horses) have had many uses, including roof repair. Astragali were used in gaming in the ancient world (often drilled and filled with iron to weigh them down), and they were even used as paving for floors (along with metapodials). Tools, implements, buttons and all sorts of smaller items have been made from metapodials. Cut marks on most are rare, with the most common being encircling marks on the proximal metacarpals or tarsals, representing skinning. Cut marks may also be found on astragali, resulting from the disarticulation of the foot from the lower leg. Phalanges and smaller carpal or tarsal bones rarely contain marks.

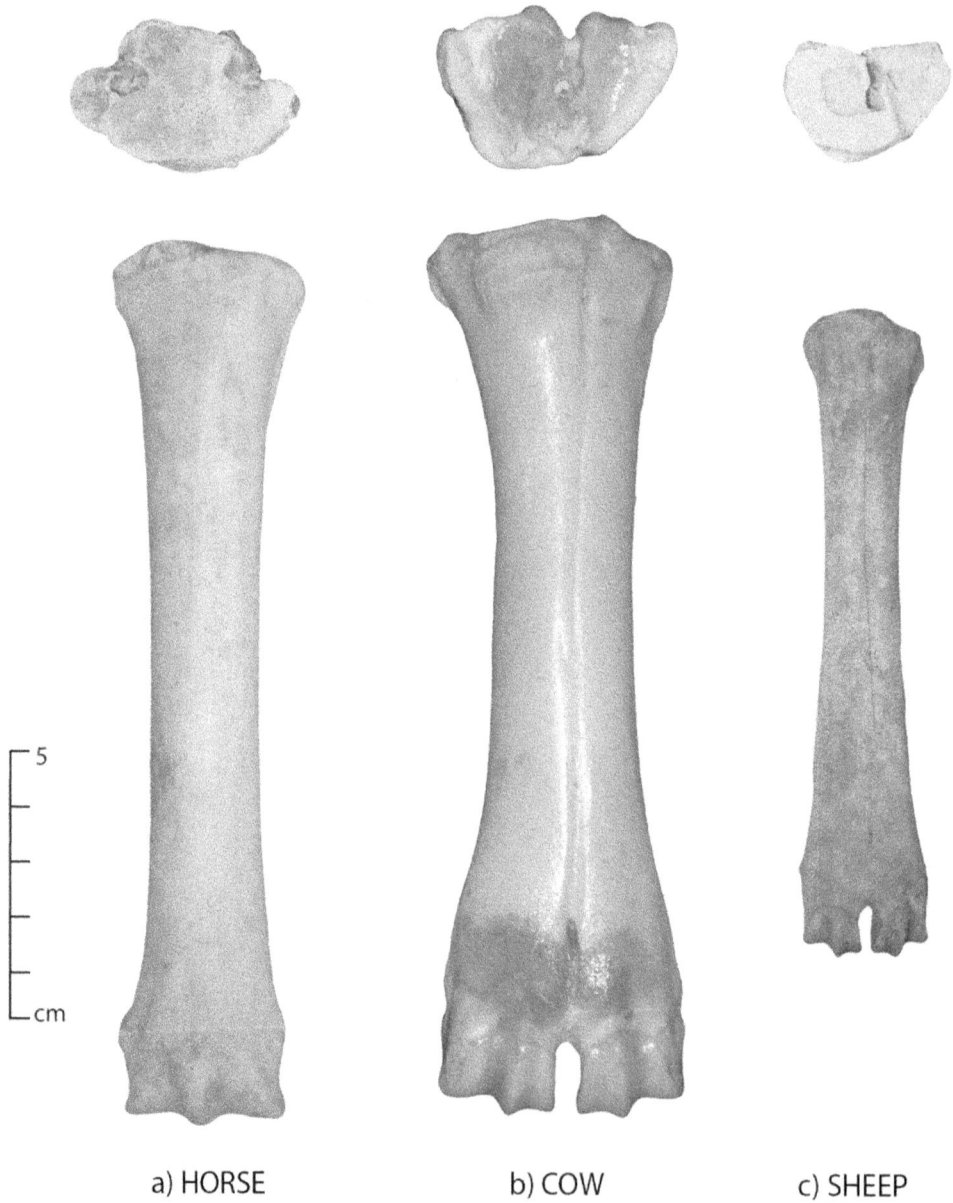

Figure 9.8: Metacarpals; proximal view (top) and anterior view (bottom); (a) horse, (b) cow and (c) sheep. See Figure 2.2 for an image depicting cow metacarpal articulation with the surrounding bones of the fore limb.

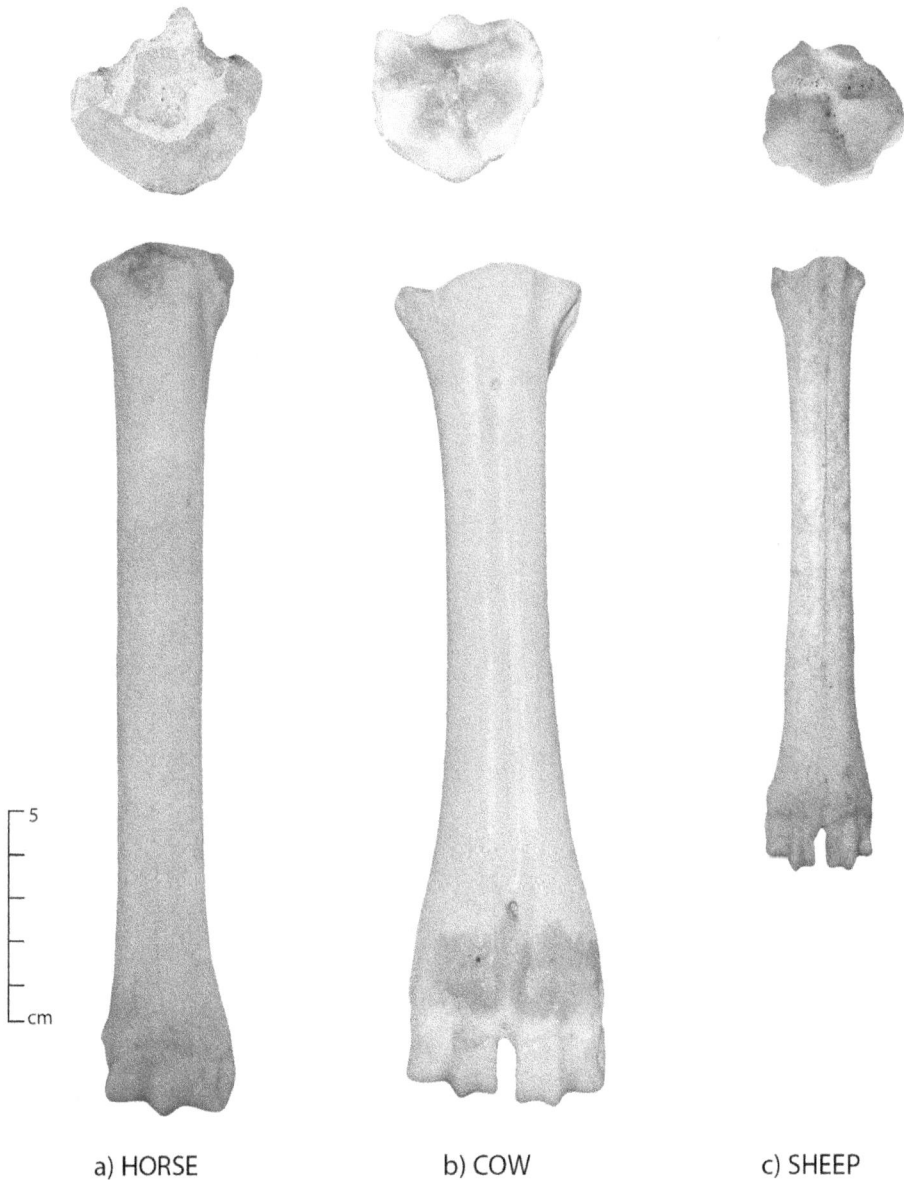

Figure 9.9: Metatarsals; proximal view (top) and anterior view (bottom); (a) horse, (b) cow and (c) sheep. See Figures 9.12–9.14 for images depicting metatarsal articulation with the surrounding bones of the hind limb.

CALCANEUS

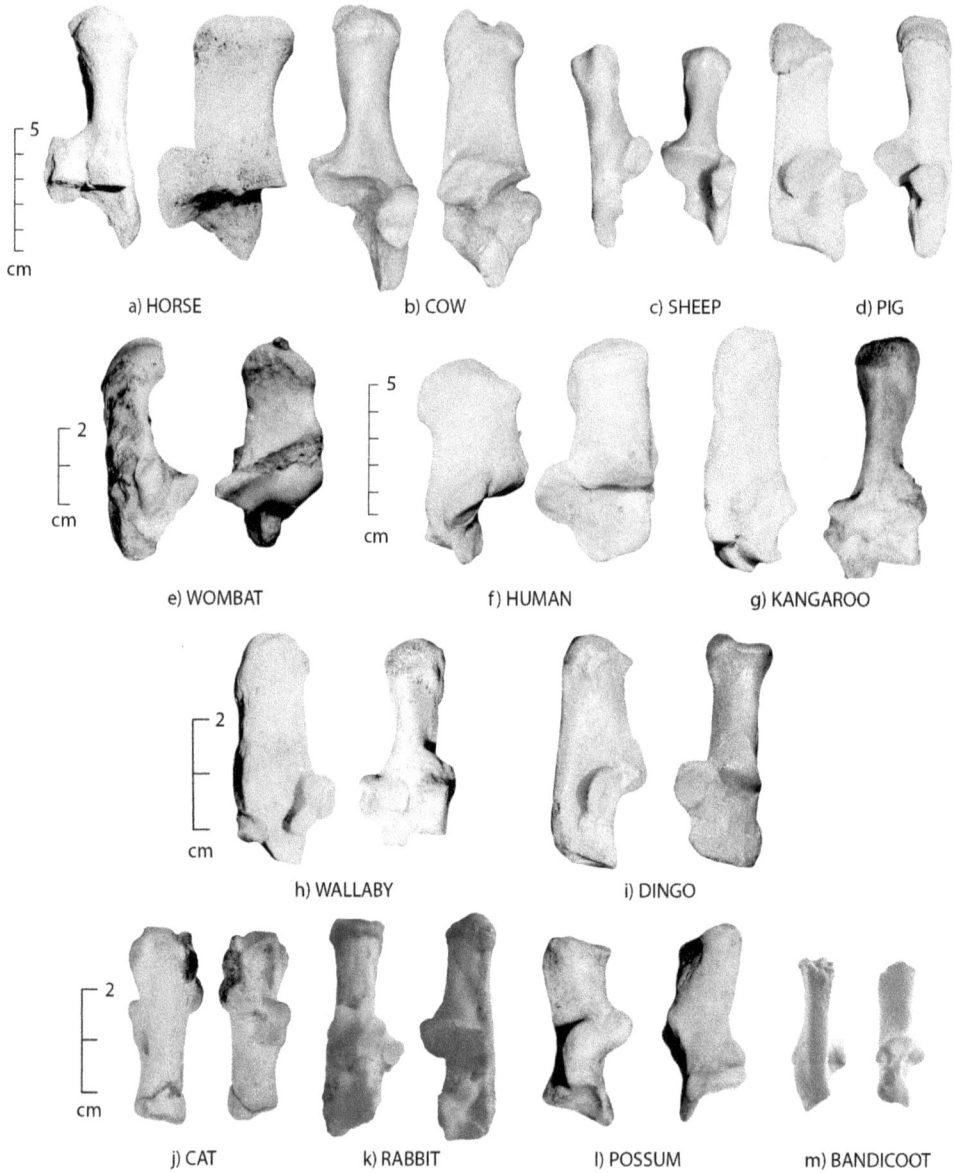

Figure 9.10: Calcanei; medial view (left) and anterior view (right); (a) horse, (b) cow, (c) sheep, (d) pig, (e) wombat, (f) human, (g) kangaroo, (h) wallaby, (i) dingo, (j) cat, (k) rabbit, (l) brushtail possum and (m) bandicoot.

ASTRAGALUS

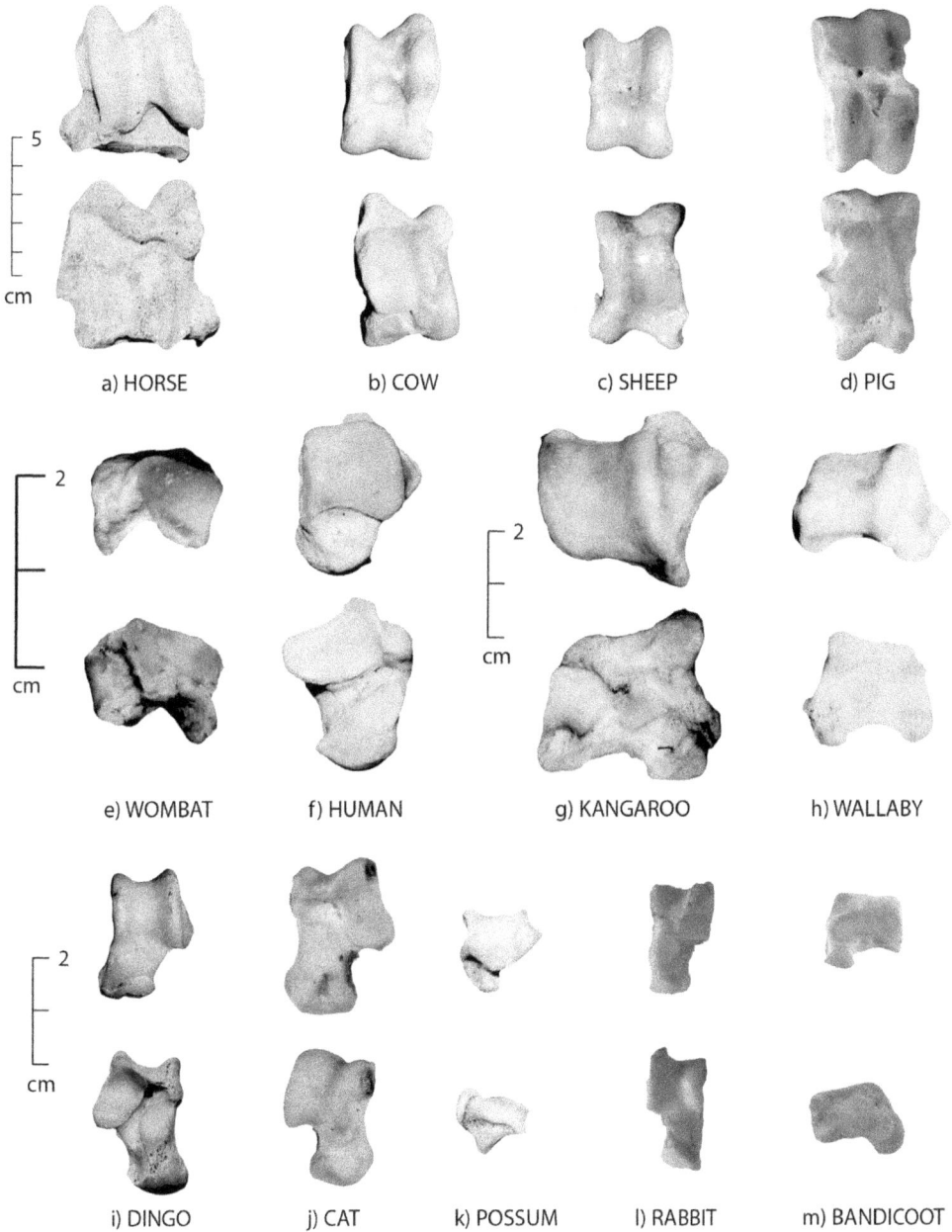

Figure 9.11: Astragali; superior view (top) and anterior view (bottom); (a) horse, (b) cow, (c) sheep, (d) pig, (e) wombat, (f) human, (g) kangaroo, (h) wallaby, (i) dingo, (j) cat, (k) brushtail possum, (l) rabbit (right side) and (m) bandicoot.

HORSE

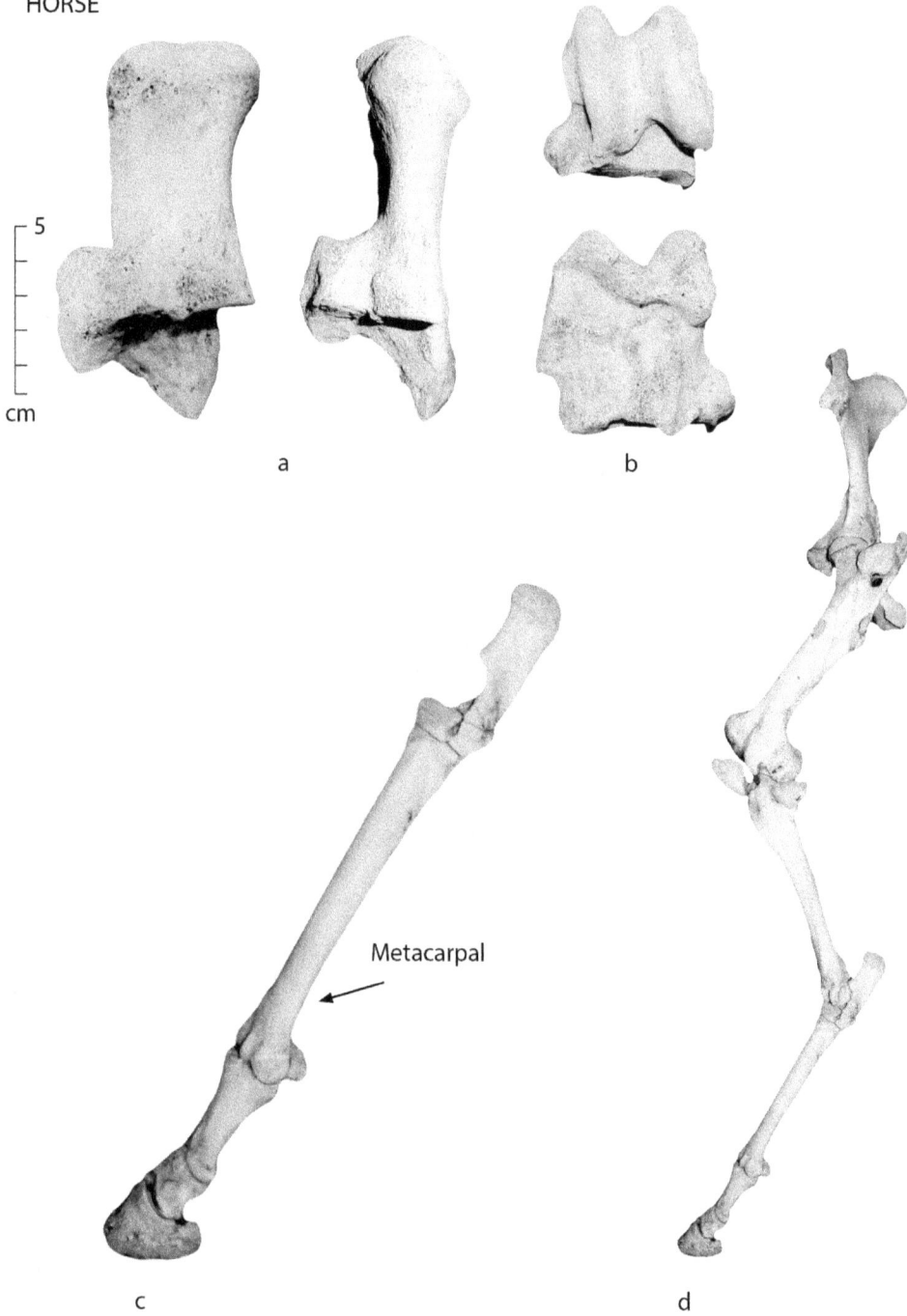

Figure 9.12: Horse (a) calcaneus, (b) astragalus, (c) articulated fore limb and (d) articulated hind limb (see also Figure 7.2). Note: (c) and (d) not to scale.

COW

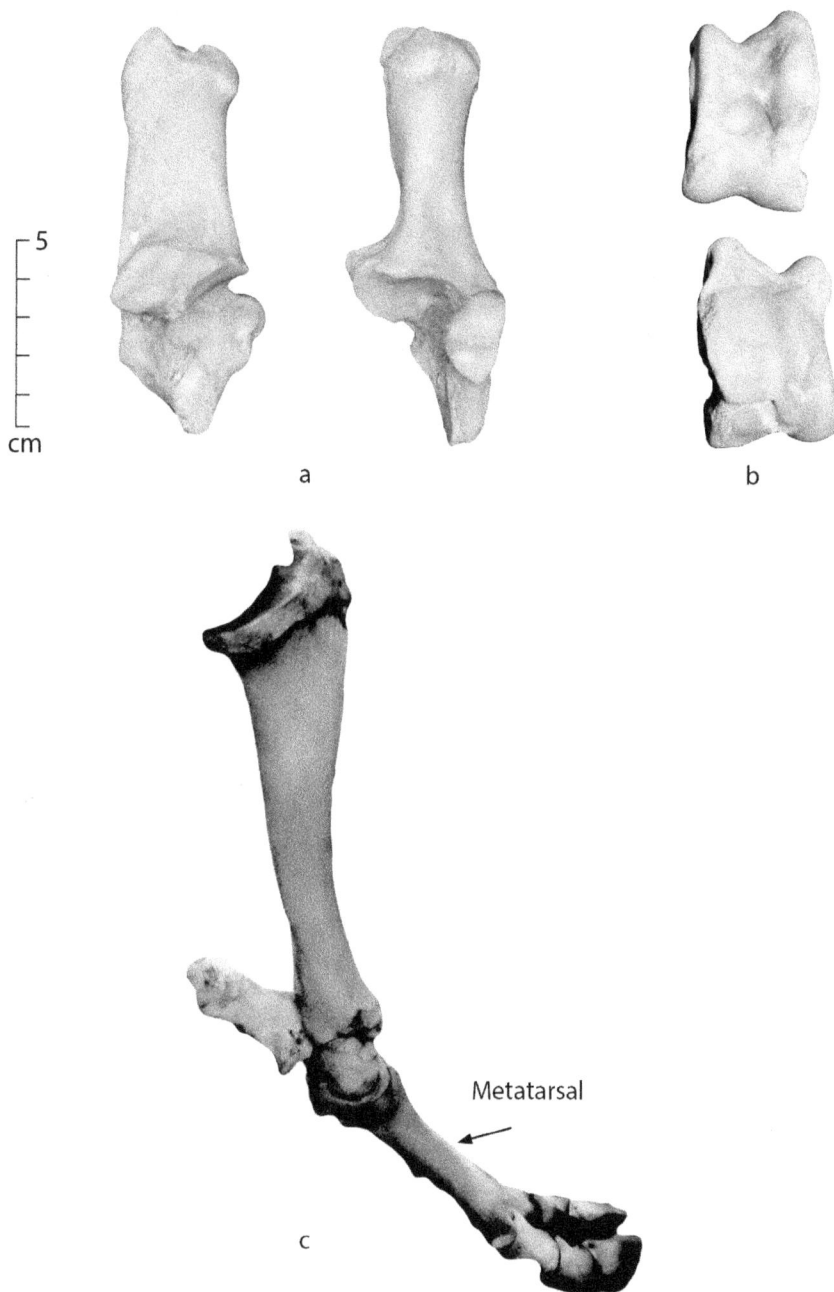

a

b

c

Metatarsal

Figure 9.13: Cow (a) calcaneus, (b) astragalus and (c) articulated hind limb.

SHEEP

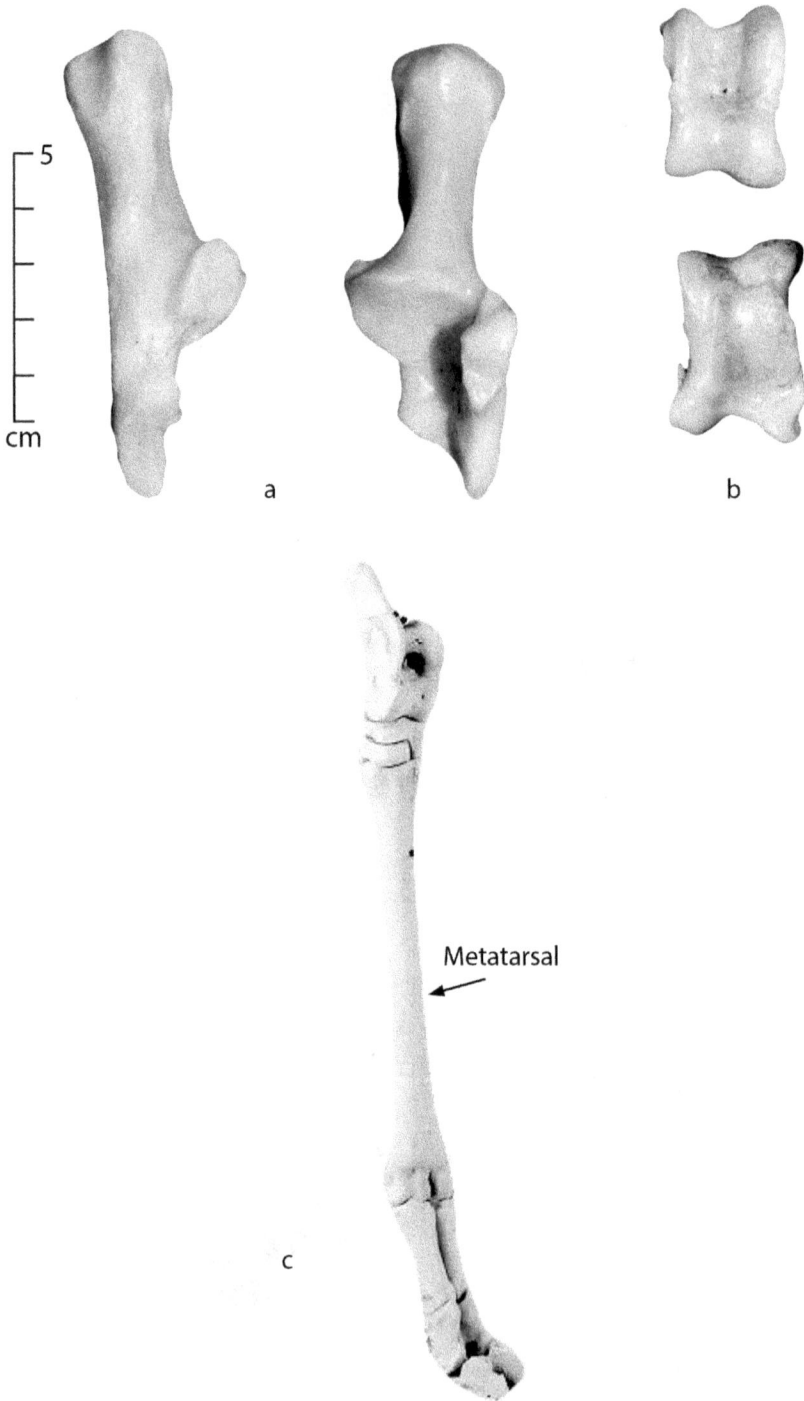

Figure 9.14: Sheep (a) calcaneus, (b) astragalus and (c) articulated hind limb.

PIG

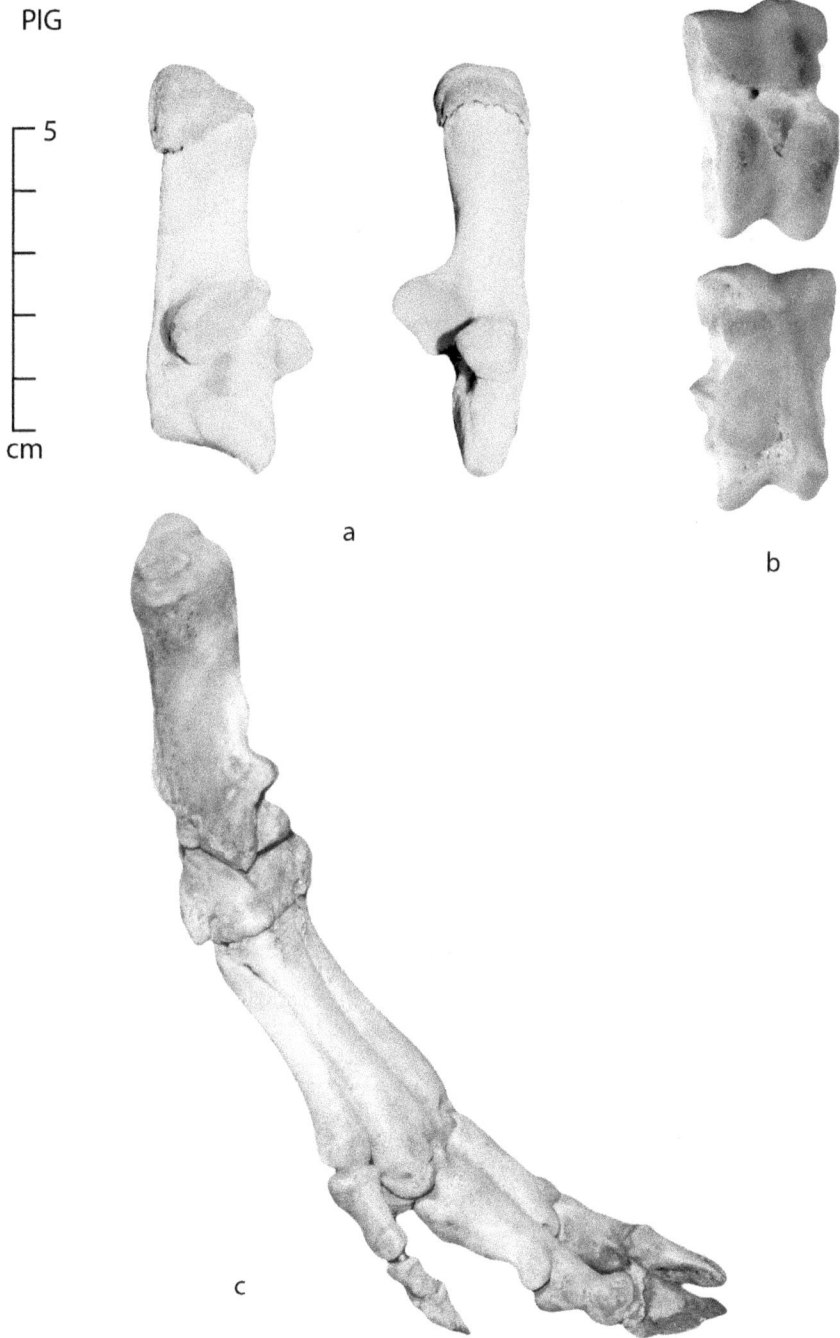

Figure 9.15: Pig (a) calcaneus, (b) astragalus and (c) articulated hind limb.

HUMAN

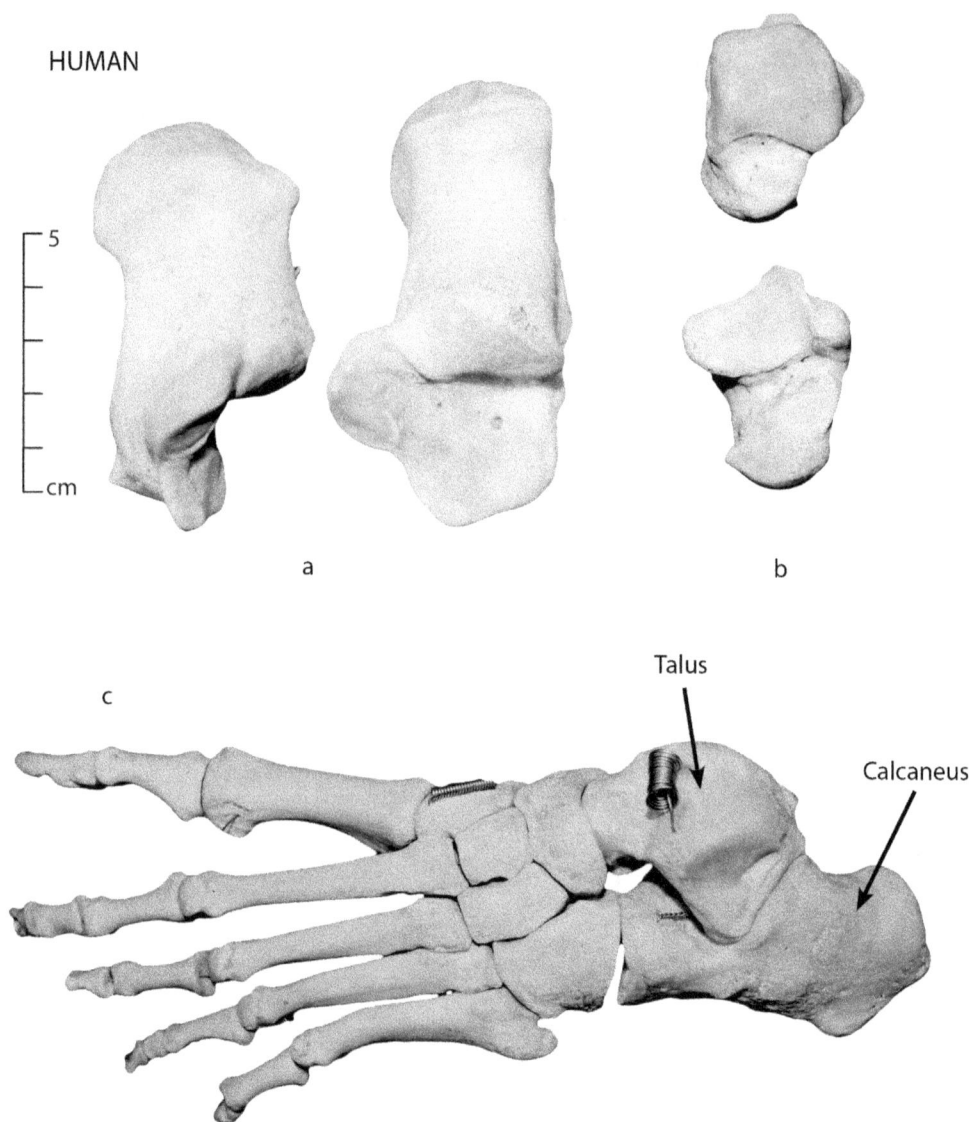

Figure 9.16: Human (a) calcaneus, (b) talus (astragalus) and (c) articulated foot.

CAT

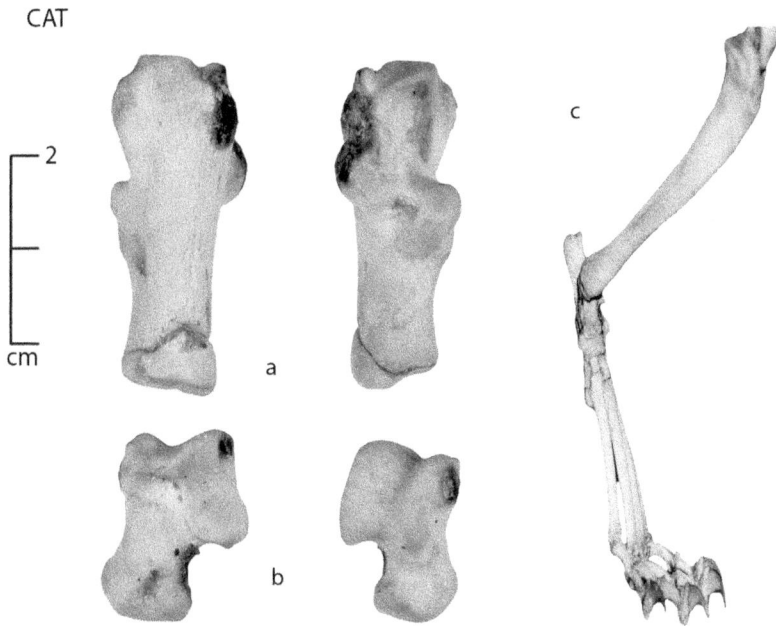

Figure 9.17: Cat (a) calcaneus, (b) astragalus and (c) articulated hind limb.

RABBIT

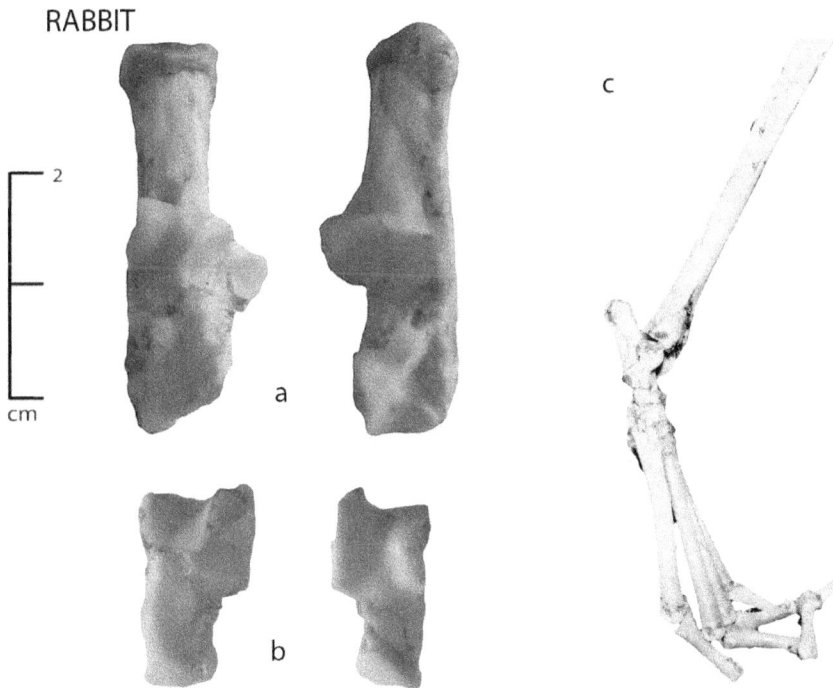

Figure 9.18: Rabbit (a) calcaneus, (b) astragalus and (c) articulated hind limb.

KANGAROO

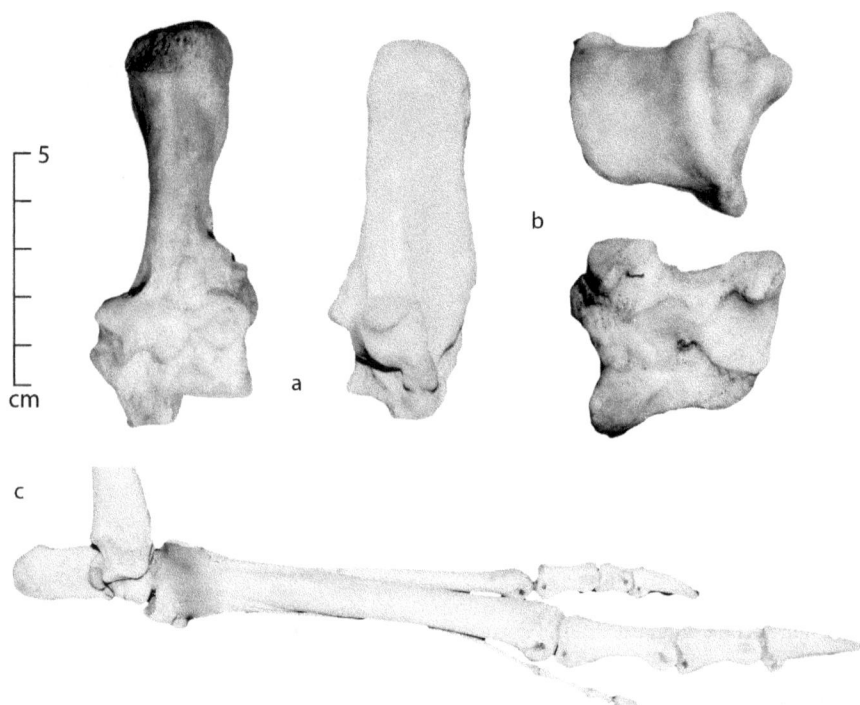

Figure 9.19: Kangaroo (a) calcaneus, (b) astragalus and (c) articulated hind foot (II metatarsal missing from view).

WALLABY

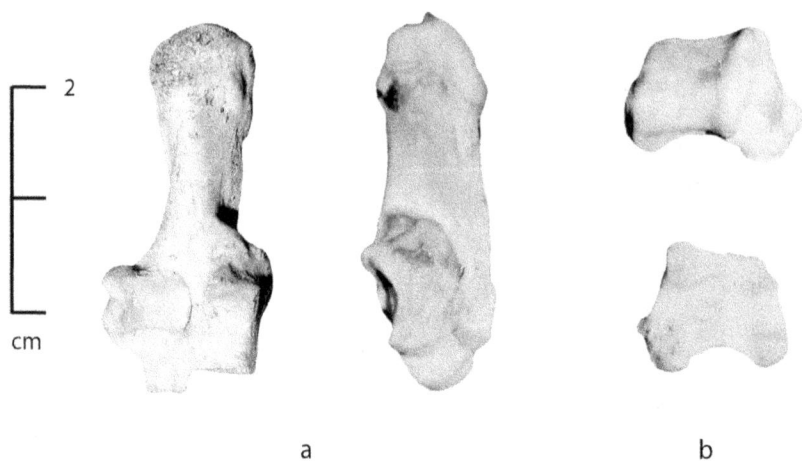

Figure 9.20: Wallaby (a) calcaneus and (b) astragalus (see Figure 9.6 for articulated view).

WOMBAT

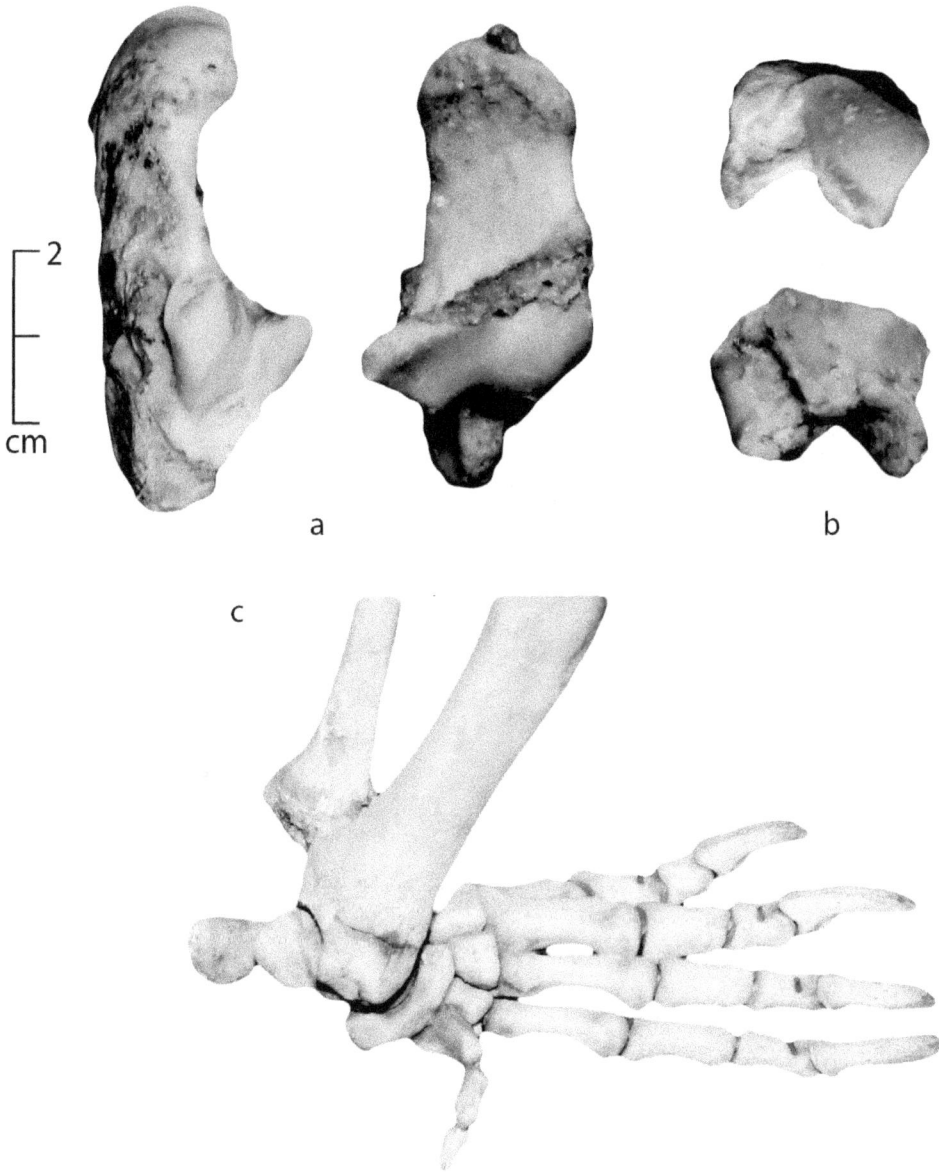

2

cm

a

b

c

Figure 9.21: Wombat (a) calcaneus, (b) astragalus and (c) articulated hind limb.

BANDICOOT

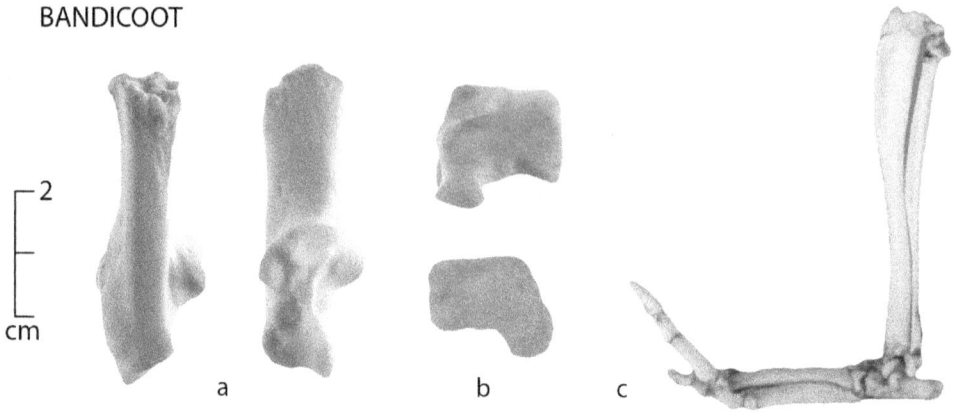

Figure 9.22: Bandicoot (a) calcaneus, (b) astragalus and (c) articulated view.

EMU

Figure 9.23: Emu articulated limb.

Theoretical and practical applications in zooarchaeology

Zooarchaeology cannot produce a catalog of ethnic index fossils – the linkage between all types of social identities and material culture items is simply too complex for such a straightforward methodology. What can be done, however, is to specify the behavioural conditions under which social interaction took place and provide an understanding of the contextual constraints that structured innovations in animal symbology and their social meanings (Hesse and Wapnish 1997:238–39).

Animal bones have the potential to illuminate many aspects of past human behaviour. Coupled with their general ubiquity at most archaeological sites, it is disheartening that their study has not been a consistent feature of archaeological investigations in Australia. Fortunately, this situation is rapidly changing, with faunal analyses playing an increasingly greater role in both Indigenous and historic contexts. We would therefore like to conclude this manual by discussing the state of zooarchaeology in Australia, and delve a bit deeper into just a few aspects of human behaviour that zooarchaeology can address. Given that this is first and foremost a manual on bone identification, we have tried to refrain from adding too much analytical information. However, we feel that it is our duty to conclude even an identification manual with a fuller discussion of the power of zooarchaeology, and to advocate its application and interpretations as the next steps in faunal analyses. We have tried to pare down a large body of work by focusing on a few specific ways in which different qualitative and quantitative methods can be used to address larger theoretical (and practical) issues. So, we would like to conclude this manual with a few words about the way in which assemblages are quantified and analysed (and have included references along the way for those interested in further reading).

The past and present state of zooarchaeology in Australia

Historically, there has been a relative lack of emphasis on zooarchaeology in Australia (see Cosgrove 2002 for an excellent summary). This situation stems from many interrelated issues; however, the dearth of both training opportunities and funding come readily to mind. At the time of publication, there were a handful of published sources of information on the identification of Australian animals (Archer 2002, Merrilees and Porter 1979,

Triggs 2004), none of which are specifically geared toward archaeologists in the field. Fortunately, the tide is turning in Australia. We believe this book in itself is 'black and white' evidence of this turn (excuse the pun). In the academic sphere, a few universities are building good comparative bone collections and are teaching students the art of faunal analyses. An increasing number of postgraduate students are analysing faunal material for higher degree theses, distinct faunal sessions regularly occur at the Australian Archaeological Association annual conferences, and faunal papers make significant contributions to the Australasian Society for Historical Archaeology's conferences. So we believe the outlook is positive. In the professional sphere, it is now commonly accepted that faunal analyses will form part of every professional archaeological consulting report – be it historical or Indigenous. The largest problem facing zooarchaeology in Australia now is the lack of trained specialists.

The theoretical power of zooarchaeology

Animal bones provide information beyond a 'simple' laundry list of species. They speak to ancient subsistence practices, and can be used to reconstruct everything from human–animal interactions (including domestication and animal husbandry), ancient environments, trade, inter- and intra-site economic relationships, to social hierarchies. For example, variation between faunal assemblages at different archaeological settlements can help reconstruct several aspects of social organisation. In historic sites, social differentiation can be addressed by using the faunal data to ascertain whether there were discernible economic differences between households. These differences can be seen in the types of fauna exploited, as well as in the anatomical elements present and their relative frequencies. Economic complexity can be addressed by reconstructing inter-site economic relationships involving the exchange, redistribution and trade of animals and animal products. A question commonly asked by zooarchaeologists is whether there is a recognisable economy built upon animals, and if so, how this economy can be identified and what it means.

A good example of the theoretical application of zooarchaeology abroad is Melinda Zeder's extensive work on animal economies and the provisioning of cities (Zeder 1991, 2003). She examined animal remains in urban and rural contexts in the Near East to ascertain whether some settlements were acting as centres of animal production while others were centres of consumption. This type of differentiation between settlements speaks to the larger issue of economic specialisation and economic complexity, wherein social and economic relationships are maintained between sites based upon trade and resource acquisition. This economic specialisation can be used as evidence of social complexity, as a common feature of all complex societies is a degree of specialisation and differentiation in production. The concept of specialisation between states involves not only economic differentiation (i.e. division of labour), but also economic individuation, in which certain persons spend a significant portion of their time on particular non-subsistence activities.

At the centre of the producer–consumer dichotomy and social complexity, is the much broader concept of human–environment interaction – an environment of which animals are a part. Flannery's Systems Theory (1968, 1971) treats humans and the environment as 'a single complex system, composed of many subsystems which mutually influenced each other' (Flannery 1971:345). The ecological perspective stresses this dynamic mutual relationship between culture and environment. This interaction has the ability to change, alter and restructure societies, ultimately influencing social complexity.

The practical power of zooarchaeology: quantification

The fundamental goal of zooarchaeology is to draw conclusions about societies using the faunal evidence for human–animal interactions. To arrive at this desired interpretative endpoint, we need to have some way of counting the number of bones in an assemblage, and then drawing a meaning from them. Several methods exist that facilitate the analysis of sample size and amalgamation in faunal assemblages. These methods include the most common quantitative units of number of identified specimens per taxon (NISP) and minimum number of individuals (MNI), to more recent analyses that calculate the minimum number of elements (MNE) present and minimum number of anatomical units (MAU). Each method of quantification has its relative merits, and the choice of which to calculate will often be governed by questions, sample size and the nature of the assemblage (see Lyman 1994, 2008 for more detail).

Number of identified specimens per taxon (NISP)

Along with MNI, NISP is the quantitative unit most frequently encountered. It is an observational unit that simply counts the number of identified bones in a faunal assemblage. So, if 30 bone fragments were identified the NISP is 30. NISP can have a meaning identified to any taxonomic level – it may be to species or even family. Thus, a NISP of 30 may mean 30 fragments from a medium-sized mammal, or it may be more specific and mean 15 identified kangaroo fragments, 10 sheep, three emu and two wombat fragments. One of the problems with NISP-based species ratios is that they fail to take into account skeletal elements that come from the same animal. Thus, a calculated wombat NISP of 100 may reflect the bones from just one individual. Calculating MNI avoids this problem. A second problem with relying solely on NISP is that the number is greatly affected by the degree of fragmentation of the assemblage.

Minimum number of individuals (MNI)

Unlike NISP, MNI is a derived unit. It is 'the minimum number of individual animals necessary to account for some analytically specified set of identified faunal specimens' (Lyman 1994:100). It is a derived measurement that may not take into account variables such as age, sex, or size. If, for example, there are three left kangaroo femurs in an assemblage and one right femur, then the MNI for kangaroos is three. That is, at least three individuals would have had to be present in the original assemblage to account for the three femurs. However, what if the right femur is from a juvenile and the left femurs are all from adults? If this is the case, at least four individuals were originally present, providing an MNI of four. To avoid this confusion, analysts state whether they are 'maximising MNIs' by accounting for variables such as size, age, and sex of skeletal elements. In addition, measurements of MNI need not be assigned to individual taxa; they may just be assigned to element. For example, an assemblage may have five right scapulae that cannot be assigned to individual species.

A simple way to calculate MNI is to determine a distinct MNI for each skeletal element – this would take into account left and right sides, and how many times that element occurred in a given individual. Thus, if there are four kangaroo left femurs and three right femurs, there is an MNI of four kangaroos based on femora. However, there may be two left kangaroo scapulae and one right, and thus the MNI for kangaroos based on scapulae is two. Once again, however, this method is blind to age, sex and other variation between individuals. One of the biggest problems with conclusions based on MNI calculations is the unpredictable response to the problem of aggregation. A solution is to present both MNI and NISP calculations, and when presenting MNI data, to do so by skeletal element.

Minimum number of elements (MNE)

While MNI and NISP measure the frequency of taxa, MNE measures the frequency of portions of skeletons of individual taxa – an analytical method tied to the more recent emphasis on taphonomy (Lyman 1994). MNE signifies the number of a particular skeletal element necessary to account for a portion of a skeletal element. Perhaps the easiest way to understand MNE is to look at two ways it can be derived. The first method involves measuring something like the complete circumference represented by a long bone shaft fragment, and then summing those proportions for each portion of a skeletal element (Lyman 1994:103). Simply calculating the portion of the bone represented by the fragment and then summing the fragments to arrive at an MNE for each skeletal portion can also derive it. So if one fragment of bone represents one half of a proximal humerus and another fragment represents one half of a distal humerus, an MNE of one humerus would be calculated. Unfortunately, there are a few different ways to calculate MNE. The best way in which to navigate this web of conflicting methodologies is to be explicit about the way in which the calculation was performed. This allows for other researchers to more accurately compare two assemblages.

One quantification method that may be particularly useful in eventual interpretation of the faunal data is the ratio between NISP and MNE. Dividing NISP by MNE can provide an idea of the degree of fragmentation in an assemblage. This can examine fragmentation of different skeletal elements, but also of different taxa. It can provide clues on the taphonomic processes that may have affected the assemblage as a whole, such as carnivore activity or extraction of marrow by humans.

Minimum number of animal units (MAU)

MAU is a standardised variation on MNI calculations and accounts for the number of specimens in a collection. Developed by Binford (1984), MAU is calculated by dividing the MNE for each anatomical unit (e.g. a proximal femur) by the frequency of its occurrence in an animal (in this case, two). This method aims to analyse survival of different skeletal parts, and reflects how many of each of the various portions of carcasses are represented.

The practical power of zooarchaeology: qualification

Once the counting is done, we can get back to the big questions by applying the data. This can be done using several main comparison methods. Here we discuss the three most common ones.

Species frequencies

Faunal assemblages may differ in the types of species present; for example, settlements raising livestock will have a different combination of species compared with settlements consuming the animal products. Examining the range of species present in a faunal assemblage will provide an insight into the overall range of animals exploited, and ultimately address variability in diet and dietary patterns.

Skeletal element frequencies (body part distribution)

Analyses of skeletal element frequencies centre on the portions of an animal that are most valuable as food (the prime meat-bearing bones). For example, pigs typically serve a sole function as meat producers. This means that, unlike sheep, goat and cattle, they offer no secondary products. However, we still may want to know whether the site in question was raising pigs or procuring meat from elsewhere. A predominance of head and foot bones (low utility elements) may indicate a place engaged in animal husbandry. If the prime meat-bearing bones, such as upper limbs (humerus and femur) are also present, the conclusion might be that the animals were being raised and consumed in the same place. If, however, there is an absence of prime meat-bearing bones, it may be that the animal was raised on site, butchered, and the higher valued portions were traded or exchanged with another site – indicating an inter-site economic relationship. It is also possible that live animals were traded or exchanged at the consumer site itself. In this case, the skeletal element frequencies would mirror a self-sustained site. This is where analysis of butchery patterns and cut marks becomes vital. If cut marks are present on some of the elements, they can be analysed as having resulted from either primary or secondary butchery (see Binford 1981). The placement and distribution of cut marks can then be viewed against skeletal element frequencies, and hypotheses drawn as to the place of butchery of the animal in question. We can also turn to the relative distribution of skeletal elements on the site itself. Perhaps one area is 'industrial' in nature, and used for butchery (yielding a lot of head and feet), while another is domestic, and therefore using the higher valued parts of the animal. This approach could also be used to address intra-settlement social differentiation, with higher utility elements appearing in wealthier contexts and vice versa.

Age and slaughter profiles

The relative ages at which individual domestic animals were slaughtered, in conjunction with the range of species present, also offers insight into inter-site economic systems. At historic sites, many animals, such as sheep, goat and cattle, are used not only for their primary products (meat), but also for secondary products, such as milk, cheese and wool. Some animal products may be collected at intervals (wool), while others may be collected only once – at slaughter. For example, younger individuals tend to have served a primary function as meat producers. If most individuals at an assemblage are younger individuals, the conclusion may be that they were exploited for their primary product – meat. If however, the assemblage is dominated by older individuals that offer secondary products, we can ask whether there is a possible trade or specialisation in secondary products. These same analyses can provide important information on hunting strategies at prehistoric sties. Hunters often aim for a 'sure' kill, and may therefore kill either old or young individuals who are too slow or naive to escape. Hunting with dogs, in groups, or with specialised technology can alter this generalisation.

Ultimately, the analysis of faunal remains is dependent on a large variety of factors. As already discussed in the introduction of this manual, taphonomy plays a large role in the preservation and eventual excavation of different skeletal elements and species. Recovery methods play an equally important role. Thus, the best way in which to approach a faunal assemblage is to combine all analyses to create a full picture of the economy in which the animals played a key role. This way, empirical studies and taphonomy play a key practical role in the more abstract theoretical applications of faunal analysis.

The analytical potential of butchery marks on bone is a useful way in which to illustrate the marriage of concrete and abstract elements of zooarchaeology. In most societies, animal production and consumption plays a pivotal role in reconstructing inter-site economic relationships. The eventual analysis of skeletal element frequencies and their variability between sites is intricately related to butchery practices and the analysis of cut marks on animal bone. The past few decades have seen a great deal of research on bone surface modification caused by both humans and carnivores. In particular, discussion and research has been directed toward discerning the differences between human-modified bone and other agents of bone surface modification, such as carnivores, trampling, root etching, etc. (Blumenshine et al. 1996, Capaldo and Blumenshine 1994, Marean and Frey 1997, Pickering 2002, White 1992). Extensive studies of hominid butchery patterns exist in the literature on early hominid behaviour, with a few Australian studies on both butchery (O'Connell and Marshall 1989) and scavenging (Brown et al. 2006; Fillios 2011; Marshall and Cosgrove 1990; Reed 2001, 2009; Solomon and David 1990).

The potential of zooarchaeology and its future in Australia

There is a fundamental relationship between humans and animals that is at the heart of reconstructing past human behaviour. We hope we have illustrated the absolute relevance of faunal remains to the study of any site – historic or Indigenous. A model of human behaviour based on rational decision-making theoretically underpins zooarchaeology and suggests that individuals act universally to increase benefits and minimise costs in any actions they undertake. Animals can be this buffer and certainly played a vital role in human actions through time.

Zooarchaeology is a natural fit with Australian archaeology as a discipline. There has been, and continues to be, a solid emphasis placed on the integration of biology and environmental science in Australian prehistory. Australian archaeologists are skilled in the use of interdisciplinary methodologies and collaborations. Unlike archaeologists in many other countries, most Australian archaeologists remain with a foot in both the professional and academic realms, and great benefits can come from specialised training. An ideal scenario is to have an archaeologist who is also trained in faunal analysis at every site. This will help to elevate and maintain a high standard of analysis (and interpretation) in both the professional and educational realms – benefiting the discipline of archaeology, and our understanding of Australia's valuable past.

Works cited

Archer, M. 2002. *Prehistoric mammals of Australia and New Guinea: one hundred million years of evolution.* Sydney: UNSW Press.

Binford, L.R. 1981. *Bones: ancient men and modern myths.* New York, NY: Academic Press.

———. 1984. *Faunal remains from Klasies River mouth.* Orlando, FL: Academic Press.

Blumenshine, R.J., C.W. Marean, and Capaldo, S.D. 1996. Blind tests of inter-analyst correspondence and accuracy in the identification of cut marks, percussion marks, and carnivore tooth marks on bone surfaces. *Journal of Archaeological Science* 23:493–507.

Brown, O., J. Field, and Letnic, M. 2006. Variation in the taphonomic effect of scavengers in semi-arid Australia linked to rainfall and the El Niño Southern Oscillation. *International Journal of Osteoarchaeology* 16(2):165–76.

Capaldo, S.D., and R.J. Blumenshine. 1994. A quantitative diagnosis of notches made by hammerstone percussion and carnivore gnawing on bovid long bones. *American Antiquity* 59:724–48.

Cosgrove, R. 2002. The role of zooarchaeology in archaeological interpretation: a view from Australia. *Archaeofauna* 11:173–204.

Fillios, M. 2011. Testing the impact of environmental zone on experimental taphonomic faunal models. *Environmental Archaeology* 16(2):113–23.

Flannery, K.V. 1968. Archaeological systems theory and early America. In *Anthropological Archaeology in the Americas.* B. J. Meggers, ed. pp. 67–87. Washington, DC: Anthropological Society of Washington.

———. 1971. The cultural evolution of civilization. *Annual Review of Ecology and Systematics* 3:339–426.

Hesse, B., and P. Wapnish. 1997. Can pig remains be used for ethnic diagnosis in the ancient Near East? In *The archaeology of Israel: constructing the past, interpreting the present.* Journal for the Study of the Old Testament Supplement Series 237. N.S. Asher and D. Small, eds. pp. 238–70. Sheffield: Sheffield Academic Press.

Hillson, S. 1992. *Mammal bones and teeth: an introductory guide to methods of identification.* London: Institute of Archaeology, University College London.

———. 2005. *Teeth.* Cambridge: Cambridge Manuals in Archaeology, Cambridge University Press.

Lyman, R.L. 1994. *Vertebrate taphonomy.* Cambridge: Cambridge University Press.

———. 2008. *Quantitative paleozoology.* Cambridge: Cambridge Manuals in Archaeology, Cambridge University Press.

Marean, C.W., and C.J. Frey. 1997. Animal bones from caves to cities: reverse utility curves as methodological artefacts. *American Antiquity* 62:698–711.

Marshall, B., and R. Cosgrove. 1990. Tasmanian devil (*Sarcophilus harrisii*) scat-bone: signature criteria and archaeological implications. *Archaeology in Oceania* 25(3):102–13.

Merrilees, D., and J. Porter. 1979. *Guide to the identification of teeth and some bones of native land animals occurring in the extreme south west of Western Australia.* Perth: Western Australian Museum.

O'Connell, J., and B. Marshall. 1989. Analysis of kangaroo body transport among the Alyawara of Central Australia. *Journal of Archaeological Science* 16:393–405.

Pickering, T. R. 2002. Reconsideration of criteria for differentiating faunal assemblages accumulated by hyenas and hominids. *International Journal of Osteoarchaeology* 12:127–41.

Reed, E.H. 2001. Disarticulation of kangaroo skeletons in semi-arid Australia. *Australian Journal of Zoology* 49:615–32.

———. 2009. Decomposition and disarticulation of kangaroo carcasses in caves at Naracoorte, South Australia. *Journal of Taphonomy* 7(4):265–84.

Solomon, S., and B. David. 1990. Middle range theory and actualistic studies: bones and dingoes in Australian archaeology. In *Problem solving in taphonomy: archaeological and palaeontological studies from Europe, Africa and Oceania.* S. Solomon, I. Davidson, and D. Watson, eds. pp 234–45. Tempus Vol. 2. Brisbane: Anthropology Museum, University of Queensland.

Triggs, B. 2004. *Tracks, scats and other traces.* Oxford: Oxford University Press.

White, T.D. 1992. *Prehistoric cannibalism at Mancos 5MTUMR-2346.* Princeton, NJ: Princeton University Press.

Zeder, M.A. 1991. *Feeding cities: specialized animal economy in the ancient Near East.* Washington, DC: Smithsonian Institution Press.

———. 2003. Food provisioning in urban societies: a view from Northern Mesopotamia. In *The social construction of ancient cities.* M.L. Smith, ed. pp. 156–83. Washington, DC: Smithsonian Books.

Further reading

Adams, B., and P. Crabtree. 2008. *Comparative skeletal anatomy: a photographic atlas for medical examiners, coroners, forensic anthropologists, and archaeologists*. New York, NY: Humana Press.

Amorosi, T. 1989. *Postcranial guide to domestic neo-natal and juvenile mammals: the identification and aging of old world species*. Oxford: BAR International Series 533.

Long, J., M. Archer, T. Flannery and S. Hand. 2002. *Prehistoric mammals of Australia and New Guinea: one hundred million years of evolution*. Sydney: UNSW Press.

Baker, B., T. Dupras, and M. Tocheri. 2005. *Osteology of infants and children*. College Station, TX: Texas A&M University Press.

Bass, W.M. 2007. *Human osteology: a laboratory and field manual*. Columbia, MO: Missouri Archaeological Society.

Behrensmeyer, A.K., and A.P. Hill, eds. 1980. *Fossils in the making: vertebrate taphonomy and paleoecology*. Chicago, IL: University of Chicago Press.

Beisaw, A.M. 2013. *Identifying and interpreting animal bones: a manual*. Texas A&M University Anthropology Series (Book 18). College Station, TX: Texas A&M University Press.

Binford, L.R. 1978. *Nunamiut ethnoarchaeology*. New York, NY: Academic Press.

———. 1981. *Bones: ancient men and modern myths*. New York, NY: Academic Press.

Brown, C.L., and C.E. Gustafson. 1979. *A key to postcranial skeletal remains of cattle/bison, elk and horse*. Reports of Investigations, No. 57. Olympia, WA: Washington State University Laboratory of Anthropology.

Cohen, A., and D. Serjeantson. 1996. *A manual for the identification of bird bones from archaeological sites*. London: Birkbeck College, University of London.

Davis, S. 1987. *The archaeology of animals*. London: Routledge.

Elbroch, M. 2006. *Animal skills: a guide to North American species*. Mechanicsburgh, PA: Stackpole Books.

France, D.L. 2011a. *Human and nonhuman bone identification: a concise field guide*. Boca Raton, FL: CRC Press.

———. 2011b. *Human and nonhuman bone identification: a color atlas*. Boca Raton, FL: Taylor and Francis.

Gilbert, B.M. 1980. *Mammalian osteo-archaeology*. Columbia, MO: Missouri Archaeological Society, University of Missouri.

———. 1990. *Mammalian osteology*. Columbia, MO: Missouri Archaeological Society, University of Missouri.

Gilbert, B.M., L. Martin, and H. Savage. 1996. *Avian osteology*. Columbia, MO: Missouri Archaeological Society, University of Missouri.

Grayson, D.K. 1984. *Quantitative zooarchaeology: topics in the analysis of archaeological faunas.* Orlando, FL: Academic Press.

Green, R.H. 1983. *An illustrated guide to the skulls of the mammals of Tasmania.* Launceston: Queen Victoria Museum and Art Gallery.

Hesse, B., and P. Wapnish. 1985. *Animal bone archaeology: from objectives to analysis.* Manuals on Archaeology 5. Washington, DC: Taraxacum, Inc.

Hudson, J., ed. 1993. *From bones to behavior: ethnoarchaeological and experimental contributions to the interpretation of faunal remains.* Center for Archaeological Investigations, Occasional Paper No. 21. Carbondale, IL: Southern Illinois University.

Iscan, M.Y., and K. Kennedy, eds. 1989. *Reconstruction of life from the skeleton.* New York: Wiley-Liss.

Jones, J.K., and R.W. Manning. 1992. *Illustrated key to skulls of genera of North American land mammals.* Lubbock, TX: Texas Tech University Press.

Klein, R.G., and K. Cruz-Uribe. 1984. *The analysis of animal bones from archaeological sites.* Chicago, IL: University of Chicago Press.

Koch, T. 1973. *Anatomy of the chicken and domestic birds.* Aimes, IA: Iowa State Press.

Lambert, P.M., ed. 2000. *Bioarchaeological studies of life in the age of agriculture: a view from the southeast.* Tuscaloosa, AL: University of Alabama Press.

Lyman, R.L. 1994. *Vertebrate taphonomy.* Cambridge: Cambridge University Press.

———. 2008. *Quantitative paleozoology.* Cambridge Manuals in Archaeology. Cambridge: Cambridge University Press.

Maltby, M. 2006. *Integrating zooarchaeology.* Proceedings of the 9th ICAZ Conference, Durham 2002. Oxford: Oxbow Books.

Mann, R., and D. Hunt. 2005. *Photographic regional atlas of bone disease: a guide to pathologic and normal variation in the human skeleton.* Springfield, IL: Charles C. Thomas Publisher.

Matisoo-Smith, L., and A. Horsburgh. 2012. *DNA for archaeologists.* Walnut Creek, CA: Left Coast Press.

Merrilees, D., and J. Porter. 1979. *Guide to the identification of teeth and some bones of native land mammals occurring in the extreme south west of Western Australia.* Perth: Western Australian Museum.

Morales, A., and K. Rosenlund. 1979. *Fish bone measurements: an attempt to standardize the measuring of fish bones from archaeological sites.* Copenhagen: Steenstrupia.

Mulville, J., and A. Outram. 2005. *The zooarchaeology of fats, oils, milk and dairying.* Proceedings of the 9th ICAZ Conference, Durham 2002. Oxford: Oxbow Books.

O'Connor, T.P. 2003. *The analysis of urban animal bone assemblages: a handbook for archaeologists.* The archaeology of York, principles and methods 19/2. Walmgate: Council for British Archaeology.

O'Day, S., W. van Neer, and A. Ervynck. 2004. *Behaviour behind bones: the zooarchaeology of ritual, religion, status and identity.* Proceedings of the 9th ICAZ Conference, Durham 2002. Oxford: Oxbow Books.

Olsen, S.J. 1968. *Fish, amphibian and reptile remains from archaeological sites.* Cambridge, MA: Peabody Museum, Harvard University.

Ortner, D.J. 2003. *Identification of pathological conditions in human skeletal remains.* London: Academic Press.

Powell, K. 2010. *Grave concerns: locating and unearthing human bodies.* Queensland: Australian Academic Press.

Reitz, E.J., and E.S. Wing. 2008. *Zooarchaeology.* Cambridge Manuals in Archaeology. Cambridge: Cambridge University Press.

Ruscillo, D. 2005. *Recent advances in ageing and sexing animal bones.* Proceedings of the 9th ICAZ Conference. Oxford: Oxbow Books.

Russell, N. 2012. *Social zooarchaeology: humans and animals in prehistory.* Cambridge: Cambridge University Press.

Schmid, E. 1972. *Atlas of animal bones for prehistorians, archaeologists and quaternary geologists.* London: Elsevier Publishing Company.

Further reading

Searfoss, G. 1995. *Skulls and bones: a guide to the skeletal structures and behavior of North American mammals*. Mechanicsburgh, PA: Stackpole Books.

Serjeantson, D. 2009. *Birds*. Cambridge Manuals in Archaeology. Cambridge: Cambridge University Press.

Sheuer, L. 2008. *Juvenile osteology: a laboratory and field manual*. London: Academic Press.

Solomon, S., I. Davidson, and D. Watson. 1990. *Problem solving in taphonomy: archaeological and palaeontological studies from Europe, Africa and Oceania*. Tempus Vol. 2. St Lucia: University of Queensland.

Stiner, M.C., ed. 1991. *Human predators and prey mortality*. Boulder, CO: Westview Press.

Triggs, B. 2004. *Tracks, scats and other traces*. Oxford: Oxford University Press.

von den Driesch, A.E. 1976. *A guide to the measurement of animal bones from archaeological sites*. Peabody Museum Bulletins (Book 1). Cambridge, MA: Peabody Museum of Archaeology and Ethnology.

Waldron, T. 2009. *Palaeopathology*. Cambridge Manuals in Archaeology. Cambridge: Cambridge University Press.

Wheeler, A., and A. Jones. 1989. *Fishes*. Cambridge Manuals in Archaeology. Cambridge: Cambridge University Press.

White, T., M. Black, and P. Folkens. 2011. *Human osteology*. London: Academic Press.

White, T., P.A. Folkens. 2005. *The human bone manual*. London: Elsevier Academic Press.

Wilson, B., C. Grigson, and S. Payne, eds. 1982. *Ageing and sexing animal bones from archaeological sites*. Oxford: BAR British Series 109.

Index

Page numbers in italics indicate a reference to the figure on that page.

innominate (of pelvis) *78*
nutrient foramen 33
mandible *8*
radius *48*, 49, *52*
scapula 19, *23*
tibia *102*
ulna 60–*61*
wombat xxv
acetabulum (of pelvis) *76*
articulated hind limb *131*
astragalus *123*, *131*
calcaneus *122*, *131*
coronoid process 62
deltoid tuberosity 32
dentition 13
femur *89*
humerus 32, 33
mandible *xxix*, 7
nutrient foramen 33

pelvis *79*
radius *51*
scapula *23*
tibia *103*
ulna *64*

Y

young animals *see* juvenile bones

Z

zooarchaeology xxviii, 133
goals of 135
in Australia 133–134, 138–139
in practice 135–138
useful applications of 134–135, 137–139